ISRAEL AND AFRICA

A Study in Technical Cooperation

THE PURPOSE of the Praeger Special Studies is to make specialized research monographs in international economics and politics available to the academic, business, and government communities. For further information, write to the Special Projects Division, Frederick A. Praeger, Publisher, 64 University Place, New York, N. Y. 10003.

PRAEGER SPECIAL STUDIES
IN INTERNATIONAL ECONOMICS

ISRAEL AND AFRICA

A STUDY IN TECHNICAL COOPERATION

MORDECHAI E. KREININ

Professor of Economics
Michigan State University

Now that I have lived to see the restoration of the Jews, I should like to pave the way for the restoration of the Negroes. . . . That is why I am working to open up Africa.

THEODOR HERZL
Altneuland, 1902
Book 5, Chap. 5.

FREDERICK A. PRAEGER, *Publisher*
New York • London

FREDERICK A PRAEGER, Publisher
64 University Place, New York 3, N.Y., U.S.A.
77-79 Charlotte Street, London W-1, England

Published in the United States of America in 1964
by Frederick A. Praeger, Inc., Publisher

(c) 1964 by Frederick A. Praeger, Inc.
Library of Congress Catalog Card Number: LC 64 – 11671

Manufactured in the United States of America

TO MY WIFE, MARLENE

ACKNOWLEDGEMENTS

This study was made possible by a generous grant from the Office of International Programs at Michigan State University, out of money appropriated by the Ford Foundation. Dean Glen Taggart of International Programs, and his associates, Dr. Ralph Smuckler and Dr. Eugene Jacobson, have continuously provided moral support and intellectual stimulation. Their help is gratefully acknowledged. Hilda Jaffe of Michigan State University supplied invaluable editorial assistance.

Thanks are due Messers. Ehud Avriel, Aaron Remez, Hannan Yavor and Gershon Fradkin of the Israeli government for their cooperation in the study. And last but not least, the author would like to express his sincere appreciation to the hundreds of individuals from Israel, Africa, Asia, and Latin America, who generously gave of their time, and willingly responded to his questions during lengthy personal interviews. These are the people who in different capacities make up the technical assistance program. They provided the material for this study and were a major source of stimulation to the author.

Officials of Israel and Afro-Asian countries, who cooperated generously in the process of gathering information, are in no way responsible for the content of this volume. The views expressed are those of the author alone. They do not reflect the thinking of the governments or individuals involved in the technical assistance program.

CONTENTS

PART *I*

PART *I* WHY TURN TO ISRAEL?

"From a scribbled word in a black notebook the Israeli Government has built an aid-to-Africa program that has broken down some political barriers and made the Israelis possibly the most welcome strangers in Africa," wrote The New York Times, on October 16, 1960. More recently, Newsweek Magazine depicted the "bond between tiny Israel and the vast reaches of Black Africa" as "one of the strangest unofficial alliances in the world."* Indeed, no one following the Israeli press in the past two years could fail to be impressed by the continuous influx of dignitaries from African and Asian countries. More than half a dozen delegations, led by heads of state, visited Israel during 1961-1962, as did a much larger number of study missions at the ministerial levels. They included the presidents of the Malagasy Republic, Upper Volta, Dahomey, Gabon, the Central African Republic, Liberia, and the Ivory Coast, and the prime ministers of Burma and Nepal (in Asia), Eastern and Western Nigeria and Uganda (in Africa), and Trinidad (in the Caribbean). In return, President Ben-Zvi of Israel visited several African countries in the summer of 1962.

While the Afro-Asian delegations represent a variety of cultural and geographical backgrounds, they all have one interest in common — a desire for technical cooperation with Israel. To that end, each mission examines and relates to its needs what Israel has to offer in the social and economic spheres. What usually emerges from the preliminary deliberations is a bilateral agreement on the general area of technical assistance; this is later translated into workable projects at lower levels of government.

Thus Israel, the beneficiary of a large USOM aid program until mid-1962, has herself become a supplier of technical assistance. In 1961, thirteen hundred trainees from sixty African, Asian, Latin American and Mediterranean countries came to her shores to attend courses and seminars in a wide variety of fields, while hundreds of Israelis were providing service and advice in thirty countries. This development was given as a major reason

---

* "A Surplus of Brains," Newsweek, August 20, 1962, p. 44.

for terminating American technical aid to Israel. In the ceremony marking that termination in 1961, Bruce McDaniel, the first USOM director in Tel-Aviv, said: "When I came to Israel just over a decade ago to inaugurate the USOM program, I was optimistic, but I never dreamt that within a decade Israel would be engaged in technical assistance programs in other lands."

Israel's small size and meager resources, and her own recent development make an investigation into the reasons for this phenomenon important. Why do underdeveloped countries seek technical aid from Israel when they could obtain it on much better terms from the industrial nations of the West or from behind the Iron Curtain?

CHAPTER 1 POLITICAL AND SOCIAL REASONS

POLITICAL NEUTRALITY

The long period of colonial oppression has made African leaders extremely sensitive to the issue of political domination. Even countries who won their independence virtually without a struggle are apprehensive about foreign interference in their affairs. The strength of their feelings was attested by a resolution adopted at the twenty-nation Lagos conference of February, 1962, to take concrete and immediate measures to boycott, economically and diplomatically, all foreign and colonial powers which do not cooperate in giving dependent territories their independence at the earliest possible date.[1]

Whether realistically or not, such nations are fearful that political strings may be attached to any aid they receive. They have experienced Western colonialism, and know that in some cases the struggle for freedom has not been easy. They are also aware of the more powerful pressures that can come from the Eastern bloc. Indeed, one multilateral aid agency noted that all countries of Africa insist on a demonstration that any technical assistance is non-political.[2]

By reason of her small size Israel poses no such threat. "You can barely manage to dominate yourself," one African leader is reported to have told an Israeli official.[3] Israel is thus considered a relatively neutral source of assistance whose advice is geared solely to the needs of the recipient — even when these needs are in conflict with the interests of the previous colonial

---

1. The States represented at the conference were: Cameroun, Central African Republic, Chad, Congo-Brazzaville, Congo-Leopoldville, Dahomey, Ethiopia, Gabon, Ivory Coast, Somalia, Liberia, Sierra Leone, Senegal, Malagasy, Mauretania, Nigeria, Niger, Togo, Upper Volta and Tanganyika.

2. Foundation for Mutual Assistance in Africa South of the Sahara (FAMA), Third Annual Report, Lagos, 1961, p. 33.

3. Unless otherwise specified, quotations refer to verbal statements in interviews or to unpublished working papers.

power. "The great advantage of Israel," stated a high ranking FAO[4] official, "is that she is acceptable politically to both blocs of the African nations." African leaders often express themselves in the same vein. "Accepting aid from Israel, we have no fear of getting involved in a power struggle," stated a Mali politician,[5] while the president of the Central African Republic is reported to have told Israeli officials: "We need ideological and not geological solutions. You bring solutions that we can get only from the Soviet — but without the big shoe." At times the political reason for seeking an Israeli technician is very direct, as is illustrated by an article in the Nigerian Outlook (Enugu) commending the services of an Israeli town planner in the Eastern region:

> . . .Mr. Elon came to us through the auspices of the Government of Israel at a time when we most wanted town planners to undertake the planning of Port Harcourt. Considerable trouble had been taken to arrange for three French architects and town planners through an international body to undertake the work, but the political atmosphere surrounding the atomic tests in the Sahara by the French Government made it impossible for us to bring out the French town planners. . . . It was at this juncture that the Government of Israel came to our aid by arranging for Mr. Elon to be seconded to us from the Haifa College of Technology where he is Senior Lecturer in Town Planning. . . .

While the United Nations agencies are also non-political, assistance from them often involves long delays. Experts requested for specific assignments are sought in all member nations, and the final screening and selection is made by the appropriate U.N. agency and the recipient country — a process which may take from six to twelve months. By contrast Israel is quick to reply to requests for technical aid, and promptness is often important. Israeli embassies in Africa are authorized to make decisions on the merits of an appeal, and can get a technician on the spot in a matter of a few weeks. Even when the applications are forwarded to Israel, there is a minimum of red tape. In several cases experts were dispatched without a word in writing.

Two historical factors add strength to the political bond between Israel and Africa. Both the Jews and the Negroes have had a tragic past. "We all traveled a long path of discrimination, sorrow, and pain — some for color, some for religion," said Israel's foreign minister to a visiting African delegation. "Henceforth," replied President Dacko of the Central African Republic, "neither you nor we will know what it is to be lonely again."[6] On another

---

4. Food and Agricultural Organization of the United Nations.

5. Report in The New York Times, October 16, 1960.

6. As an interesting side-light, Premier Ben-Gurion is reported to have

occasion Premier Akintola of Nigeria's western region remarked: "Because they are comparatively weak and victims of oppression, Israelis appear to be exceedingly sympathetic to developing nations."

In the more recent past, Israel's successful struggle for independence from British rule has been reassuring to many Africans. Israeli leaders' acceptance of British imprisonment is generally admired by their African counterparts, some of whom have been subjected to similar treatment. Leaders of the liberation movement in certain African countries "have seldom shown reluctance to go to prison. In Africa, as in Asia, the fraternity of the prison graduate is a noble one and greatly respected by the common people." [7] Indeed, the citizens of Kenya and Mauritius have vivid recollections of the exile of Israel's underground fighters to their lands by the British authorities, while few Cypriotes have forgotten the concentration camps erected on their island for Jewish refugees who had tried to reach the shores of Palestine.

In sum, as President Dacko said when addressing a reception audience during his 1962 visit to Israel, "You have not tried to create us in your image. Instead, Israel has contented itself with showing the new African nations its achievements, in helping them overcome their weaknesses, and in assisting them in learning. In so doing you have conquered Black Africa."

SOCIAL AND ECONOMIC SYSTEM

Israel's absence of colonial ambition is an "enabling condition." However, without a content of social values and technical skills, it would not be sufficient to attract the interest of African governments. Perhaps the first phenomenon which catches the eye of visiting delegations to Israel is the non-dogmatic socialism evolved by the Jewish community in Palestine and continued in Israel. Once exposed to the idea, said a noted African anthropologist, most African countries are attracted to socialism. Not only does it appeal to their social values but, lacking a middle class and having few potential entrepreneurs, they feel that only the government can mobilize resources for rapid development. At the same time, they recognize the need to encourage any private (domestic or foreign) initiative that might emerge. "Capitalism is too complicated a system for a new independent nation. Hence the need for socialism," wrote President Nkruma of Ghana.[8] And President

---

told an East African visitor of the old plan which would have settled the Jews in Uganda instead of Palestine, to which the visitor replied: "It is a good thing that the plan was never implemented; otherwise, the Jews would have been kicked out now."

7. George Kimble, Tropical Africa, Vol. II (New York: The Twentieth Century Fund, 1960), p. 289.

8. Quoted from Arnold Rivkin, Africa and the West (New York: F. A. Praeger, 1962), pp. 6, 16-17.

Senghor of Senegal stated recently: "We aim to hold firmly to a middle of the road socialism which is liberal and undoctrinaire – one which socializes all that should be socialized beginning with the rural economy, but no more than that."[9]

This is precisely what they find in Israel. The government as well as the labor movement is controlled by the same socialist labor party. Both are intensely engaged in development through cooperative and publicly-owned enterprises. Yet neither body hesitates to form partnerships with private interests, nor to encourage private investments.[10] The growing influx of private foreign capital attests to the viability of the economy and to the favorable investment climate prevailing in it. In the words of Dr. Hayut, deputy director of the political department of the Federation of Trade Unions (Histadrut):

> The source of the Histadrut's influence in Asia and Africa, is its overwhelming contribution to the development of the country. In many Asian and African countries, as in Israel, the labor movement preceded political independence, and the trade unions as well as the socialist movement took active part in the battle for independence. Now these movements are striving for a pioneering role in developing their economies and democratic institutions.[11]

Dedicated to the precepts of a welfare state, Israel's socialist movement doggedly guards the principles of democracy and has learned to work in coalition with parties to the left and right of center. Israel has succeeded in achieving within a democratic framework a continuous military preparedness, mobilization of natural and spiritual resources for economic development, and inculcation of a sense of national purpose in her citizenry. It was the combination of a welfare state, strong and closely associated labor and co-operative movements, democracy, and non-doctrinaire socialism which gave to Burma and Ghana the initial impetus to seek cooperation with Israel (see Chapter 2).

In Israel the visiting delegations find an economy which was transformed from an underdeveloped to a developed state in less than a generation; and this indeed is the overriding goal of the new African states. Africa is a "continent in a hurry," completely absorbed in one main objective: jet-propelled growth. Its leaders are seldom satisfied with the answer that "Rome was not built in a day" which they get from the West, and are often reluctant to

---

9. Ibid.

10. It is noteworthy that the Israeli government is attempting to sell some of her profitable industrial holdings to private investors. See The New York Times, November 4, 1962, p. 1 of the Financial Section.

11. Moed (Hebrew), pp. 139-146.

turn East for assistance. By contrast, "the dynamism of Israel's development effort, the spirit that pervades it, and its visible achievement in difficult circumstances have undoubtedly excited the interest of many underdeveloped countries, providing an attractive model with which to identify themselves."[12] United Nations' officials continuously emphasize Israel's contribution in giving African leaders hope as well as a target to aim at. As a visitor from Uganda phrased it, "We request of you, our elder brothers and sisters, hope, direction, and the benefit of know-how." Israeli officials like to depict their model as a third force between East and West, and at least one competent observer of the African scene lends his support to that view:

> The forced pace of Russian and Chinese development is likely to be attractive for new political leaders in underdeveloped countries laboring under a compulsion to show tangible results within a single generation; for those impatient with democratic processes for obtaining a consensus on development policies; for those unsure of their position and fearful of the political pressures likely to accompany economic growth; for those attracted by the argument that poor nations cannot afford the luxury of relatively unplanned growth in the private economic sector; and for those whose anti-colonialism leads them to regard all private enterprise with suspicion and to consider private ownership of the means of production a dangerous relic of the colonial past.
>
> The Israeli model may well prove to be a sort of economic 'third force' — an alternative differing from the western pattern, but certainly far more compatible with free-world interest than any Communist model.[13]

Furthermore, much of Israel's growth has been accomplished by relatively primitive people, immigrants from Afro-Asian countries reared in a patriarchical tradition. Israel gained valuable experience in educating individuals of diverse backgrounds who were from all cultural levels. She has developed methods for imparting a homogeneous language, for quickly training people of all ages in a variety of necessary skills, and for organizing workers of different national origins into useful production patterns. African countries which face the problem of introducing modern techniques into a traditional society have a deep interest in this experience. Indeed, one sight which always makes a profound impression on visiting delegations is that of primitive people employing complicated machinery. Unlike Africa, Israel had a hugh inflow of foreign capital, a large supply of technically skilled manpower, an already established social framework and tradition of agricultural work, and the tools of self-government. Despite the vast differences between

---

12. A. Rivkin, op. cit., p. 71.

13. Ibid., p. 84.

the two, however, there are those who believe that important guidelines can be drawn from Israel's experience.[14]

Not the least important of Israel's lessons is that her phenomenal progress was achieved through hard work. She has evolved a social value-system which attaches prestige to manual occupations (particularly on the farm) and to the technical professions. In Africa, by contrast, the greatest prestige attaches to government positions at almost all ranks, inducing young men to seek training in the liberal arts in order to qualify for that status. Any trade or profession requiring work with the hands is regarded with disfavor and avoided whenever possible. Since development cannot be accomplished simply by "well lubricated" government ministries, a change in national attitude toward vocational pursuits, technology, and farm work is a most import educational objective for the African nations.

African visitors and trainees in Israel can see men of letters performing manual work and taking pride in it, and observe cabinet ministers washing dishes in a <u>Kibbutz</u> while home for the weekend. Although it is declining, Israel's spirit of pioneering and innovation is still evident, as is illustrated by a recent decision of comfortable city youth to set up a new cooperative city in the midst of the Negev desert. In the words of a Nigerian official, "African students in Israel are impressed by the zeal of the people and their determination to make something out of nothing. The attitude toward work is a good lesson." A Kenyan agricultural official wrote (in reply to an inquiry), "The great enthusiasm and unselfish sacrifice for an ideal, together with the vast store of professional and technical skills which are being devoted to the rapid solution of problems, can provide guidance and inspiration to the African people," and a FAMA officer said: "Israelis are used to working under arid and arduous conditions and their drive is remarkable. We hope Africans will acquire such a drive." That this spirit is often carried over into the technical assistance field is evident from the following statement by a visiting African minister:

> The philosophy which places a high value on physical work, central to this country, is characteristic of the Israelis in technical cooperation programmes. An Israeli agricultural expert gives much of his instruction right in the field, either in shirt sleeves or overalls, and he quite naturally works alongside the trainees. There is nothing of the elevated office executive about him. He also has no sense of racial superiority and is often ready to mix with the people.

---

14. See Dr. R. Weitz, "Israel in an Awakening World," <u>Molad</u> (Hebrew), June-July, 1960.

APPLICABILITY OF ISRAEL'S EXPERIENCE

Even in the more narrow technical sense (as distinguished from broad social organization) Israeli know-how is considered more useful for new nations than knowledge obtainable in Europe or North America. Far from being a drawback, the recency of Israel's development experience gives Israeli advisors an edge over their counterparts from other countries. Many of Israel's new agricultural crops and industrial products are the results of recent experiments. The transition from the experimental to the production stage can still be readily observed in many sectors of the economy, as is the social transformation to a modern society. African and Asian trainees see how solutions to pressing problems are sought, tried out, and applied; they are not merely told of accomplishments ex post facto. Likewise, at times Israelis come to developing countries when they have just put the finishing touches on a new technique, and when processes are still fluid they can be better adapted to different situations.

Furthermore, it was not so long ago that Israel herself was the recipient of technical assistance. Such fields as agricultural extension, poultry rearing, vocational education, irrigation, and tourism were developed with generous aid from the USOM and the United Nations. Now that the Israelis, in their turn, are ready to "pass along their experience to some of the new African countries," they find of great value the insights they gained as they watched foreign experts learning to adapt their know-how to Israel's different social organization and philosophy.[15] Said one Israeli nurse who had served in Burma: "When foreign advisers came to Israel and told us that something was not right, we used to get offended. Consequently, my approach in Burma was to teach by doing rather than by ordering, and to keep showing how things are done in Israel without insisting on quick changes." The errors and difficulties Israel encountered in her development process are no less instructive than the successes, as is demonstrated by an example drawn from the field of planning legislation. An Israeli town planner who had surveyed a west African country criticized proposals a well-known British expert had advanced because they were modelled on the experience of Great Britain:

> We in Israel made a very serious mistake when we did not change
> our planning legislation (introduced by the Mandatory Government),

---

15. W. L. Karrer, "Water for Survival," The Jerusalem Post (supplement, marking the termination of USOM aid to Israel [Mission Accomplished], July 4, 1962, p. 11). In the case of carp breeding, Israelis are now teaching the Yugoslavs advanced and more intensive versions of methods they had learned from the Yugoslavs themselves in 1938. (The Jerusalem Post, August 17, 1962.)

which was also on the model of Great Britain. Our experience has revealed serious defects in that system. I refer in particular here to the proposal to assign local planning powers to competent local authorities or to local planning committees. In a country in which there is a shortage of qualified town planners, such decentralization is very dangerous. In addition, young local governments are influenced very much by private interest groups which makes the shortage of technical personnel more serious.

The scale of Israel's enterprises is generally considered more suitable for African needs than the large plants common in the more industrialized countries. "It seems logical that, since we are small, we can learn more from a small, efficient country than from a big, efficient country," said a visiting Senegalese official. At the same time, history has forced the Israelis to seek and find quick solutions, to improvise, and to overcome obstacles without the help of elaborate tools. Thus, an American agricultural expert in Peru once diverted a trainee from the United States to Israel because, he said, the "scale in Israel is more appropriate. In the United States trainees get used to elaborate laboratories, and can't work without modern instruments upon their return home. In Israel there is more necessity for improvisation." In the same vein the Liberian ambassador to Israel noted that "people trained in advanced Western countries, with modern equipment and many resources, find themselves frustrated in the Liberian reality. By contrast, Israel lacks many tools and has consequently learned to improvise. A person who knows how to adjust to a situation where instruments are lacking is better."

Finally, there are certain climatic and agro-technical similarities between Israel and several African countries (and with regard to East Africa, there is also geographical proximity and availability of a sea route from Tanganyika to southern Israel). Israel is semi-arid in the north and arid in the south, as are several African countries north of the rain forest belt. The semi-arid zone stretches across the continent between 8° and 12° north of the Equator as well as certain other areas. Thus, a Kenyan agricultural officer wrote, "The general ecological conditions in Israel are to a large extent comparable to those obtaining in Kenya." And Ghana's ambassador to Israel noted:

> Because Israel has some geographical aspects that are common to Ghana and to most African states (e.g., climate, vegetation, and rainfall, as one travels inland towards the centre of Africa), the Israeli technicians are more accustomed to working under almost similar conditions, and their productivity in the African states may be greater than can be expected of technicians from the temperate zones.

AVAILABILITY OF KNOW-HOW

All of these factors would be of little value if Israel did not have technical skills to export. The fact is, however, that in many fields ranging from agriculture to medicine Israel has at least some surplus of competent manpower. "Not only is she rich in technical knowledge," said the premier of Western Nigeria, "but, because of the diverse origin of the technicians, her practical knowledge is more varied and representative than you can get elsewhere." In technical expertise Israel is unique among the small nations. In an article entitled, "We Are Not a Beggar Nation," the West African Pilot (October 13, 1962) criticized offers of assistance made to Nigeria by many underdeveloped countries, but classified Israel with the industrialized nations in terms of her ability to extend technical aid:

> It is common these days for representatives of small, poor, countries . . . . to tell the Press how eager their countries are to help develop Nigeria by offering us the services of some of their teachers, technicians and at times capital, which they do not have. Often they speak of offering scholarships . . . . Nigeria is richer than all these countries put together. If we want to accept aid, any kind of aid, it must be from countries like USA, USSR, UK, Western Germany, Canada. No country in Africa and in the orient, except Israel, can afford to be of any help to us, and none in the Middle-East.

In sum, stated a United Nations representative in Nepal, "the study of Israel's unique efforts and achievements in the field of economic development, with agriculture under ecologically unfavourable conditions as its very backbone, provides the curious visitor with more useful hints for the solution of problems in under-developed economies than any other country known to me." And a high-ranking official of the European Economic Community is reported to have said: "Israel has become a unique storehouse of ideas and achievements, on which other young nations must draw."[16]

WHY HELP AFRICA?

What are Israel's motives for rendering technical assistance to the newly emerging nations? First, there is the satisfaction of being able to help others. During her first decade of independence Israel was the recipient of both economic and technical aid, and that she can now impart her knowledge and experience to others is in itself rewarding. In the words of Israel's minister of agriculture, "In our relations with other countries we always found ourselves asking for something: loans from the industrial nations,

---

16. The Jerusalem Post, October 17, 1961.

military assistance from France, a mutual security pact and friendship treaties with Western countries, and release of Jews from Russia. We have not yet been asked to give anything in return. True, we once gave the Bible to the world—but that was a long time ago. With Africa we have an opportunity to restore some balance to our international relations."

Second, there are obvious advantages in gaining friends in the increasingly important Afro-Asian bloc, and thus breaking through the economic and political isolation of the Middle East. If Israel can establish a reputation founded on constructive economic and technical cooperation, she will add a new and favorable dimension to her image. Also, in the long run it is hoped that technical aid will pave the way for an expansion of export markets for her products.

A third reason, which applies to only a few skills, is that technical cooperation with other nations can provide employment for a small but significant manpower surplus.

While many observers tend to place a continuous emphasis on the second reason, The Guardian, as a recent statement shows, feels the first motive should be given a wider importance: "Israel's policy towards Black Africa should perhaps be seen in wider terms, and should be recognized to be not just part of its defense line against the Arab world, but also of a genuine desire to be of help. Africans respond because they recognize this."[17]

---

17. Quoted from The Jerusalem Post Weekly, August 17, 1962.

CHAPTER 2 HISTORY AND SCOPE
OF ISRAEL'S PROGRAM

HISTORY

Political ties and technical cooperation between Israel and the Afro-Asian world were preceded by ideological contacts established through the socialist and labor movements. They can be traced back to the 1950 International Trade Unions Congress in Belgrade. At the invitation of R. Barkatt of the Israeli delegation, three Burmese delegates stopped in Israel on their way home from the Congress as the guests of the Federation of Trade Unions (Histadrut). Impressed by the social ferment and economic progress they found there, they spoke frankly of their earlier hesitation to come. Arab propaganda had led them to consider Israel a colonial and socially backward nation. Contrary to their expectations, the visit convinced them that Israel was the only truly socialist country in Asia and that much could be learned from her experience. The next step was taken two years later at the Asian Socialist Conference in Rangoon. Israel's delegation was headed by the foreign minister M. Sharett, in his capacity as a leading member of the Socialist Labor Party. His discussions with the Burmese government resulted in an exchange of ambassadors between the two countries. In addition, the Israeli delegation established initial contact with representatives from several Asian and African nations, and one of its members was elected to the anti-colonial committee of the Congress.

Relations with Burma had to be built on a different foundation from those developed with Western nations. Routine diplomatic efforts concerning the Arab-Israeli conflict were unlikely to strike a responsive note in Rangoon. A totally different approach was called for if ties between the two countries were to be cemented. To paraphrase a high-ranking Israeli official:

What did the Burmese know about Israel? Their experience with Britain had not been favorable. They were well aware of the 'divide and rule' policy frequently practiced by the British in their colonies, and believed that the Jews had been brought into Palestine in pursuit of the same objective. The British rather than the

Germans were the object of their animosity, and Lord Balfour was
to them a colonial reactionary. They knew nothing of Zionist
ideals, and had never heard of a nation claiming her land after two
thousand years. Jewish contributions to civilization, as well as
the persecution of Jews in Europe and elsewhere, were not topics
foremost in their minds. Identification with the poverty-stricken
Arabs came more natural to them than identification with Israel.
And to top it all, the million Moslems in Burma and the Moslem
nations surrounding it furnished a fertile ground for seeds of hostility to Israel.

David Hacohen, the first Israeli ambassador to Burma, was not chosen
for the assignment because of any innate qualities of tact or diplomatic
finesse he might have possessed. Rather, it was his extensive background
in building the industrial empire of the Histadrut that determined his
selection. It was decided to cultivate relations with Burma on the basis
of possible Israeli contributions to Burmese economic development. Since
Burma and Israel attained their independence from Britain in the same year,
the new ambassador was able to draw useful parallels between the two
countries in discussing their development programs with Burmese officials:
"We in Israel have a tire factory without a single rubber tree—why shouldn't
you have one?" "We were advised against establishing a merchant marine —
today our fleet is the largest in the Middle East." Having just experienced
political independence, he could effectively point out that using the former
colonial power as a scapegoat on which to blame poor domestic performance
merely diverts energy from the development tasks that lie ahead. He emphasized that the process of trail and error is inevitable, that mistakes are
unavoidable, and that excessive fear of failure must be overcome if the
economy is to progress.

Technical cooperation between the two countries was at first confined
to the military field, with Israel training Burmese technicians in her military
industries and supplying maintenance crews for Burmese planes. But since
1954 Israel has dispatched to Burma a variety of agricultural, medical,
and industrial experts, many of whom have worked in the Defense Service
Industries (the economic branch of Burma's armed forces). A joint Burmese-
Israeli construction company was set up subsequently, and Israel's Shipping
Lines (Zim) was invited to take over management of Burma's Five Star
Line. Likewise, a succession of agricultural projects led to Israel's in-
volvement in the army resettlement program in 1959-1960.

From Burma Israel's reputation spread throughout the Far East, and
relations were established with Ceylon, Thailand, and the Philippines.
Although India does not recognize Israel, there is extensive cooperation
with private Indian groups. Likewise, several Israeli advisors function in
Asian countries under United Nations' auspices.

Relations with one West African country commenced practically with the creation of Israel. Liberia voted in the United Nations for the partition of Palestine, and was the third nation to recognize Israel. Since the early fifties there has been an honorary Israeli consul in Monrovia although diplomatic missions were not exchanged until 1957, and though a private Israeli construction firm began operating there in 1956, the governmental assistance projects in such fields as agriculture and medicine only began in 1958.

It was the effect of Israel's cooperation with Ghana, however, that radiated all over the African continent. And the seeds for that tie were sown in meetings between Ghanaian and Israeli leaders in international socialist conferences, and at the International Confederation of Free Trade Unions (ICFTU). Subsequently, when Ghana's Minister of Labor (Mr. Botsio) met the Israeli representative to the 1956 inauguration ceremony of the Liberian President, he asked that a consulate be set up in Accra. Thus H. Yavor became the first Israeli consul in an African country (Ghana) one year prior to its independence; he was replaced a year later by Ambassador Ehud Avriel.

In Ghana, as in Burma, emphasis was placed on technical and economic cooperation. In the small hotel room which housed the consulate, plans were laid for the Black Star Shipping Line and the Ghana National Construction Company to be set up after independence as partnerships between Ghana and two Israeli firms. Subsequently, plans were developed for Ghana's flying school, assistance to the Kumasi College of Technology, and cooperation in the fields of agriculture and youth organization. In that fashion two former segments of the British Empire, unconnected by historic ties, traditions or habits, were brought together solely on the basis of newly developing mutual interests.

Contact with other African countries spread from there. R. Kawawa, the vice-premier of Tanganyika, was introduced to Israel's foreign minister by President Nkruma at a Pan-African socialist meeting. At about the same time, Joseph Nyrere, brother of the first prime minister of Tanganyika, participated in a Socialist Youth League conference in Israel which led to his subsequent interest in Israel's youth organizations. Likewise, the Western Nigerian ministerial delegation was induced in 1957 to include Israel on its itinerary while studying foreign cooperative movements.

By that time Israel was facing an increasing flow of visitors from many lands who were intent on observing her trade union and cooperative movements. To accomodate that interest, the Histadrut organized the first Afro-Asian Seminar in Cooperation in 1958, whose success resulted in the expansion of Israel's foreign training activities in both trade unionism and cooperation. Similar requests from several nations led the Israeli government to inaugurate such programs in a variety of other fields. Technical assistance ceased to be an idea expounded by a few "crazy individuals" and became an integral part of Israel's foreign policy.

In Israel's relations with Latin America, political ties preceded technical cooperation. Several Latin American countries supported the creation of Israel in 1947 and have constantly raised their voices in the United Nations for a peacefully negotiated solution to the Middle East conflict. To this favorable pattern of relations a new dimension was added in 1962 – that of technical cooperation.

It was Latin American visitors to Israel who first discovered specific trends and achievements which offered possible solutions to some dominant problems in Latin America. Subsequently Latin American trainees participated in various courses in Israel, primarily in the field of agriculture. Under an agreement with Brazil (signed in Racife on March 12, 1962) Israel will supply a staff of technicians to organize a search for underground water resources and will provide training in irrigation methods. Another group of technicians will help organize farming cooperatives on the San Francisco River. The Israeli program will be conducted for the Brazilian Federal Northeast Development Agency, through which United States Alliance for Progress funds are being channelled. It is expected that in 1962-1963, 260 Latin American trainees will come to Israel to attend courses in agriculture, cooperation, and youth organization.

SCOPE OF THE PROGRAM

Technical assistance concerns the transfer across national boundaries of a most important factor of production: know-how. While there is no universally accepted criterion by which to measure success in this field, few students of the subject would disagree with the following statement: A successful technical assistance project is one which introduces a new product or brings about improved methods of producing existing products, coupled with an attitudinal and/or social change—and is one in which these changes survive the withdrawal of the foreign technicians. It was the unique social organizations evolved in Israel through decades of development—agricultural cooperatives, structure of the labor movement, and youth organizations—which first attracted the attention of Afro-Asian leaders. Their interest in the modern techniques employed in Israel came later, but in most cases it was submerged in admiration for the social framework within which the techniques were practiced. In the words of one Ghanaian cooperator:

> It seems as if the Asian and African states were not so much interested in adapting modern Israeli techniques per se, as in studying concepts and patterns of life evolved under the specific con-

ditions of a developing country which are relevant to their own societies.

This is one reason why the technical assistance program at first emphasized short courses and seminars in Israel. New techniques can be demonstrated anywhere, but exposure to social patterns can be accomplished only where such patterns exist. Another reason was pragmatic. Israelis had little knowledge of African ecological conditions, and a training program in Israel could be better controlled to assure success than activities in an unfamiliar country.

These are compelling reasons. But a program confined to such course-work is subject to important limitations. Many of the courses cannot impart knowledge in sufficient depth to achieve concrete results, and the students are not always adequately prepared to absorb material on a high enough level. Even when this is not the case, it may be too much to expect that the average trainee will be able, independently, to transplant knowledge he has gained outside his own country. Consequently, as Israel gains more experience, many of the training and service activities should be shifted to Africa. On the other hand, it would still be desirable to supplement projects undertaken abroad by the training of competent senior personnel in Israel.

In many cases the best approach to successful technical cooperation is the "integrated project": An expert or a team of experts goes abroad and embarks on a project which must always include the training of indigenous personnel. Some of the outstanding trainees are then sent to study in Israel, and when they come back they work with the Israeli team until the project can be safely turned over to them. However, starting with a program which emphasizes course-work in Israel, a more practical approach in the short run would be the dispatch of an Israeli instructor with each returning contingent of trainees. His support and advice would be invaluable in helping his ex-students translate their Israel-acquired knowledge to the African reality. In any event, the training activities in Israel should ideally be an integral part of the technical services and advice rendered abroad. In some fields Israel's program is moving in that direction but, of necessity, the changes are relatively slow.

During the three years ending in August of 1962, about 3,000 individuals from Afro-Asian countries completed training in special courses organized for them in Israel and taught in English and French. The number of Israeli technicians sent overseas by the government was about one tenth of that but, in addition, some 500 Israeli foremen and engineers worked abroad under the auspices of Israeli companies which had established partnerships with African and Asian governments. The various segments of Israel's foreign assistance program are outlined below.

Training in Israel

1. Short conferences of the survey type, usually designed for upper-echelon civil servants and professionals. They included seminars on rural planning and the role of women in a developing society, the latter leading to a series of specialized courses in community development.

2. Intensive courses in specialized subjects, lasting from three to ten months. Designed primarily for intermediate-level personnel, they constituted the bulk of the training program, and included: agriculture, youth organization, community development, cooperation, trade unionism, public and police administration, and vocational training.

3. Sub-academic courses lasting between one and three years, and including accelerated training of physical education teachers and nurses.

4. Individual training by means of practical work or observation tours ranging in duration from a month to a year.

5. Special academic courses, offered in English, in agricultural engineering and medicine.

6. Training of a few individual students in Israel's institutions of higher learning. Intensive training in Hebrew, offered by special institutes designed to teach the language to new immigrants (Ulpan), is a prerequisite for enrollment. In some cases graduates of the short courses stay on for further academic work.

Israeli Assistance Abroad

1. Survey and fact finding missions lasting from one to four months. These include general surveys of a branch of the economy, investigation of particular problems, or missions exploring the possibility of Israeli contributions to the country's development. Their value lies in familiarizing the Israelis with African problems and conditions as much as the recommendations they supply to the host government.

2. Experts working in Africa and Asia in advisory and planning capacities or carrying out specific assignments (one to four years of service).

3. Advisors under the auspices of United Nations agencies. Strictly speaking, these are not part of Israel's program.

Joint Commercial Ventures

Enterprises in various African and Asian countries, jointly owned by Israeli companies and a local government body, with the latter owning the controlling share. The key administrative and technical personnel is usually supplied by Israel, but the ultimate aim is the gradual transfer of management to local hands. Their main sphere of activity is in what may be called the development of infra-structural facilities.

ORGANIZATION AND FINANCE

The nerve-center of Israel's technical aid program is the Department of

International Cooperation in the Ministry of Foreign Affairs. Headed by A. Remez,[1] it holds final responsibility for all government activities in this area, but has little jurisdiction over the joint c o m m e r c i a l enterprises. Professional supervision and execution of training and other projects are usually "sub-contracted" to professional bodies. Thus, agricultural instruction is administered by a Foreign Training Department in Israel's Extension Service; courses in cooperation and trade unionism are sponsored by the Federation of Trade Unions (Histadrut); vocational education is organized and offered by various trade schools; and candidates for overseas assignments are selected by competent professional authorities.

Partly because of deliberate choice, but also as a result of its relatively small size, the program is not built on carefully planned foundations. Rather, projects are started as the need for them arises or as they are requested by another government. One way in which many of them were initiated was through discussions with visiting ministerial delegations. After observing Israel's economic achievements, the visitors delineate in broad terms the fields in which Israel's experience promises to be of help to them. Their visit may then be followed by an Israeli survey mission to determine precisely what might be done, and detailed negotiations are then carried out at the ambassadorial level. Alternatively, the foreign government may approach the Israeli ambassador directly and request the loan of a technician for a specific job. Most of the early courses in Israel were organized in response to foreign requests. Subsequently, however, when foreign needs were known, the course programs were planned for a year's period and publicized in advance by the Israeli embassies to elicit response and recruit trainees.

Being relatively poorer in finances than in brain power, Israel cannot afford to finance all the advice and training it supplies. The cost of the program has not been made public, but according to one source the government's annual expenditure increased from $3 million in 1959 to $5.3 million in 1962. Expected cost in 1963 was estimated at $7 million.[2] Although no hard and fast rules are adhered to, the usual arrangement is for Israel to defray all local expenses of the visiting trainees,[3] and for the organization sponsoring the students to pay for their transportation. The same procedure applies to the visits of foreign missions or delegations, seminars, study tours, and university scholarships. Most Israeli survey missions abroad are paid for by Israel. But when Israeli experts work overseas, which is the most common form of government-sponsored advice, the host government is

---

1. Former commander of the Israeli Air Force.

2. The New York Times, June 9, 1963.

3. A six-month course may cost Israel between $25,000 and $35,000.

usually responsible for both transportation and salary. On occasion, financing has been secured from a third country through an outright grant to the aid-receiving African nation.

Financially, therefore, Israel's aid offers fewer attractions than assistance rendered by other countries or by the United Nations. In fact, one might even ask just how the advice of an Israeli expert abroad can be considered technical assistance? The Liberian government has to pay for the services of an Israeli doctor just as it would have to pay the salary and expenses of a doctor it hired in Germany. Yet there are differences between the two cases. Israelis are recruited through their government (and not, say, by a newspaper advertisement) which assures the host country of their competence. But, more important, at least some of the experts operate within well defined self-liquidating projects which include advice, execution, and training. These projects are designed to bring about a change in methods of production coupled with a social or attitudinal change, and eventually to transfer the management to local hands. Thus, the Israeli doctors who set up and operate an eye clinic in Monrovia will leave behind a viable, first-rate medical installation. The beneficial effect of their services will long outlast their presence in Liberia. Such projects are technical aid in the real sense of the term, regardless of who pays for them.

PART *II*

PART *II* ASSISTANCE IN RURAL DEVELOPMENT

It is widely recognized that rural development must play an important role in the economic progress of underdeveloped areas. Even when industrialization is chosen as the overriding goal, the agricultural sector cannot be neglected. In most African countries agriculture employs up to 80 per cent of the working population, and it is quite unlikely that large segments of this group could be shifted to other sectors over a short period, no matter how rapid the pace of industrialization. Moreover, agricultural progress is often a necessary prerequisite to economic growth. Two economists have recently stressed its potential role in helping to increase the food supply and improve local diets (thereby increasing productivity), in providing foreign exchange through farm exports, contributing to savings and thus enhancing capital formation, and in increasing rural effective demand as a stimulus to industrialization.*

In view of the importance of rural development, it is gratifying to note that Israel—a relative newcomer to the field of technical aid—concentrates about half of her assistance in this area. This is no accident. Israel's own first decade of independence was marked by a rapid expansion of the rural economy in the face of unusual social and economic difficulties. In several farm commodities she was transformed from a role of net importer to a position of self sufficiency or net exporter. Even in such industrial crops as cotton and sugar beets which were introduced as late as the 1950's, domestic production already satisfies a large share of local needs. Israel's agricultural expansion is now approaching the bounds imposed by the most important limitation—the availability of water. It is this experience which qualifies her agricultural experts to help the newly emerging nations. The next five chapters are concerned with assistance in various phases of rural development.

---

*See B. Johnson and J. Mellor, "Agriculture in Development," American Economic Review, September 1961, pp. 566–594.

<table>
<tr><td>CHAPTER</td><td>3</td><td>AGRICULTURAL
COOPERATIVES</td></tr>
</table>

MERITS OF COOPERATIVE FARMING

Application of more modern methods, such as the use of fertilizers or scientific crop rotation, can go a long way toward increasing productivity on the farm. But most farmers in underdeveloped countries are not receptive to new techniques because of the overriding power of tradition and custom, and because novelty seems risky. Their conservatism leaves them with little confidence in their advisors and the methods they propound. Therefore the introduction of change in the methods of cultivation requires not only the application of modern extension practices, but also an environment in which individual farmers can see the possibility of personal gain from technological improvement. Tenure conditions must be such as to give the farmer security on the land, assure him a full reward for his efforts, and permit him to exercise managerial functions. On the other hand, land units should be large enough to facilitate some introduction of mechanization on the farm. While the large and efficiently run plantation farm answers the need for a farm unit of economical size, it does not allow for land ownership by the farmer, and does not meet the other conditions listed above.[1]

Another solution to the organizational needs of the rural economy is offered by cooperative farming. While this term encompasses many kinds of cooperatives, the most suitable type would allow a combination of large-scale production with individual ownership. It would also restrict the sale and inheritance of land in the interest of preventing fragmentation, ownership concentration, and speculation.

For the African countries, the advantages of cooperative farming have been summarized as follows:

---

1. For further discussion see W. Arthur Lewis, "Thoughts on Land Settlement," Journal of Agricultural Economics, X, No. 1 (June, 1954); and V. D. Wickizer, "The Plantation System in the Development of Tropical Economics," Journal of Farm Economics, Vol. L (February, 1958).

The government official sees it as a way of capitalizing on the African's instinct for teamwork, which none who have watched him in action as a hunter, tree feller, bush burner, road builder, or dancer can deny. He also sees it as a way of lifting the African's lowly economic status, essential to the development of a stable middle class. The cooperator sees it as a way of escaping from the clutches of the moneylender, the middleman, and the petty trader, and of getting more for less. The educator sees it as a mold capable of carrying, besides the raw material of economic advancement, the essences of order, efficiency and self-help.[2]

In terms of social stability, "cooperation might help fill the vacuum left after the disintegration of tribal society"[3] and economically, "it can do for agriculture what the corporation did for industry." Cooperatives can serve as a short road to capital accumulation by tapping the main unused resource in undeveloped economies – underemployed labor. The investment of such capital in rural processing industries may in turn prevent land fragmentation by absorbing the excess labor from large families.

The Honorable S. K. Day, India's Minister of Community Development, views a strong cooperative sector as a school for building local leadership and a means for decentralizing economic power. Consisting of small self-governing business units, but with an overall federated structure, he feels this sector can amass considerable power:

An unbridled private sector leads to concentration of power in a few hands and may become a menace to political and economic freedom. An ever-expanding public sector may also lead to regimentation and to the emergence of totalitarian trends. A large cooperative sector becomes therefore necessary as a balancing force between the private and the public sector.[4]

Finally, the United States Agency for International Development regards cooperatives as a means for channeling economic assistance which would benefit the people quickly, and also emphasizes their role as democratic institutions capable of ongoing progress.[5]

It is in the context of these advantages that Israel's wide network of cooperative enterprises has drawn the attention of African observers as a general source of inspiration and an organization worthy of emulation. Most of Israel's agriculture is organized along cooperative lines. Since cooperatives and agricultural development went hand in hand in Israel, visitors and

---

2. Kimble, Tropical Africa Vol II (New York: The Twentieth Century Fund, 1960) pp. 212–213.

3. Statement by Professor Halperin of the Hebrew University, Jerusalem.

4. From remarks made at Michigan State University in the spring of 1961.

5. See Economic World, Washington, D. C., July, 1961.

trainees can see the cooperative idea applied to the process of economic development.

AGRICULTURAL COOPERATION IN ISRAEL

The cooperative movement in Israel permeates much of its economy. The entire bus transport system is organized along cooperative lines, as are many industrial plants and a large number of service institutions, but in no sector is cooperation more paramount than in agriculture.

There are three kinds of agricultural cooperatives in Israel, the Kibbutz ("collective"), the Moshav Shitufi ("collective village"), and the Moshav ("cooperative village"). The Kibbutz, with memberships ranging from sixty persons to over a thousand, is a true collective and functions as a single democratic unit. All major decisions are made in general meetings and executed by elected officials. Each member performs assigned tasks but receives no monetary remuneration, since all his needs are provided by the Kibbutz in accordance with the principle, "from each according to his ability to each according to his need". The community dining hall, the children's creche, and communal cultural facilities are major features of Kibbutz life, and symbolize the collective principle which unites its members.

As an economic unit the Moshav Shitufi (of which there are only twenty in Israel) is not too dissimilar to the Kibbutz, but shows its difference in its guiding principle, "from each according to his ability, to each equally." Its lands are collectively cultivated, the dairy is collectively owned, and the work is organized by one elected works manager. However, profits are distributed equally, in money, among the members, who live as individual families in separate households. This necessitates the maintenance of services, such as a village store, not required in the Kibbutz.

Most of Israel's recent settlements are of the Moshav type. The Moshav, with up to 150 farm family-units, is a community supported by a strong "multipurpose" cooperative organization. Each family is an economic and social unit, living in its own house and working its own fields; hiring of outside labor is prohibited except under unusual circumstances. Each farmer is, so far as the internal management of his farm is concerned, an independent entrepreneur, but in case of need members are expected to help each other. Self labor and mutual aid are basic principles of the Moshav. All external dealings, however, are conducted through the single village cooperative society to which all the settlers belong. The cooperative handles the purchase of equipment, machinery, seeds, and other supplies, and the marketing of farm products. Credit to the individual is channeled through the same society, with the returns on his marketed products held as collateral. On a national level, the multi-purpose society is federated into a separate organization for each of its functions. All settlements are served by nation-wide cooperative marketing and supply associations (called Tnuva and Hamashbir respectively). Other cooperative economic activities are the use of farm machinery, use of the communal pasture and, at times, cultivation of certain tree plantations.

In the non-economic sphere, all educational, social, cultural, recreational, and health services are provided cooperatively. Village management is based upon democratic principles. General policy is determined at periodic meetings of all adult members, and day-to-day activities are entrusted to elected officers and committees.

In this manner, the Moshav combines individual initiative and responsibility with a cooperative approach to the problems of farm purchasing, marketing, and credit. While each family retains its individuality, the cooperative facilitates a more efficient farming and community service system. The "multi-purpose society" is known also in other countries, but in few of them does it embrace as many activities as it does in Israel.

Each Moshav is carefully planned by the national Central Planning Authority either for mixed farming or for industrial crops. In recent years, partly because of the surplus of eggs, milk, and vegetables, most new villages have been of the latter type. The land is nationally owned; the farmer gets it on long-term lease, automatically extendable for the farmer or his heirs. But the contract prevents the sale or fragmentation of the farm unit and secures adherence to the Central Authority's plan for the village. The plan for each farm unit provides for proper crop rotation, an even division of family labor throughout the year, a sufficient water supply for irrigation, and other such technical requirements. It is based on 450 to 500 work days per year, and is calculated to assure a net income of over $2,000 at the final stage of development. Capital investments average $16,000 per unit, most of which is obtained as a loan, with repayment starting five years after settlement. Plots are usually planned as part of a greater land block for each crop grown, so as to facilitate the use of large-scale mechanized techniques. The village scheme thus sustains individual tenure rights while making possible voluntary cooperative efforts in plowing, planting, spraying, and the like.[6]

6. For a detailed discussion of the Moshav, see   E. Yalan, Planning of Agricultural Settlements in Israel, Jerusalem, 1960;   and Principles of the Moshav: the composite Rural Structure, Jerusalem, 1960.

SCHEMATIC SUMMARY OF THE THREE TYPES OF SETTLEMENTS

Type of Activity	Kibbutz	Moshav Shitufi	Moshav
Working of land,etc.	collective	collective	family
Purchase of household and personal supplies	mainly collective	individual	individual
Purchase of agricultural equipment, seeds, etc.	collective	collective	cooperative
Marketing of produce	collective	collective	cooperative
Housing	adults, individual; children, collective	family	family
Care of Children	collective	family	family

Flexibility of Approach

An important feature of Israel's cooperative movement is that there is no rigid or single approach to problems of cooperation. No one form is considered superior to another, and time-honored practices are often modified to suit the background of new settlers.

One example is the temporary "loosening of the cooperative structure" designed to facilitate the adjustment of some immigrants from traditional society to cooperative living. Before the French occupation of North Africa, the Jewish population of that area formed small communities composed of large patriarchal families of three or four generations. When these Jews immigrated to Israel many such communities arrived together.[7] But the Settlement Authority disregarded former group composition, and many new Moshavim consisted of unrelated families. However, the traditional kinship structure soon reasserted itself and the composition of most settlements

---

7. The account is based on Y. Talmon-Garber, The Family in Israel (mimeographed).

has changed rapidly. Settlers sought out their relatives and encouraged them to settle in the same village. Others left the village and joined their relatives in some other settlement. After a considerable reshuffle and change of population the villages have emerged with two to three big kinship groups and a number of smaller ones in each settlement.

Not only was the kinship structure reconstituted, but it also began to assume new functions of political significance. Moshav politics revolve about the control (by majority vote) of community-wide institutions, primarily that of the central committee. Since such control carries prestige as well as financial advantages, the kin groups become rival factions struggling for power. Political alliances are formed and reformed, always with the bigger kinship groups at the center, and ties between kin are strengthened in the process.

The strengthening and reconstitution of the kinship unit has helped the immigrants to adapt to the new setting. The kinship group is by tradition a strong cooperative unit. Now it mediates between the nuclear families and the community, and in this way links the old traditional order to the new one.

Yet the growing dominance of the kinship group is a danger to the village community, since strong loyalty to the group often destroys the loyalty to the village as a whole. Village officers and committee members may function as representatives of their kinship unit and have little concern for the interests of the whole village. In such cases they may discriminate against members who are not their relatives and see to it that their kinship unit and its allies get as large a share of the available facilities and rewards as possible. Such nepotism breeds inefficiency and suspicion, and often results in bitter feuds. When the hostile factions reach a deadlock, the management of cooperative institutions on the village level may be immobilized for months.

The Settlement Agency now accepts the kinship unit as vitally important to the orderly absorption of traditional immigrants, but it tries to restrict their influence on the cooperative institutions. In some villages office holders are replaced by hired experts. In addition to being better trained, they are not involved in village feuds, and are more objective and efficient. Management is thus partly dissociated from the relations between the kinship units, and cooperative institutions can continue to function even where there is severe tension. A certain loosening of the cooperative structure tends to have a beneficial effect. Dependence of the settlers on the central institutions of the village enhances the importance of political control of the central committee. Restriction of cooperation to a more limited sphere narrows the area of tension and diminishes the intensity of conflict.

Another illustration of deviation from established procedures is in the area of marketing. Lacking confidence in the cooperative, new immigrants often refuse to supply their agricultural produce to the central society (Tnuva) for marketing on a commission basis. Consequently, Tnuva has created a special subsidiary for making outright purchases. Later, when the immigrants have started to believe in the efficacy of the organization and have acquired faith in it, they are gradually persuaded to adopt the usual system wherein the cooperative acts as their agent for the sale.

It is generally believed that cooperative societies should be initiated by the people themselves. Initiative from above goes against the principle of cooperation.[8] This is particularly true of cooperative farming, which requires a higher level of personal involvement than, say, a consumer cooperative. But in underdeveloped areas where people may lack the knowledge and experience for effective cooperative organization, initiative must often come from above. Provided a society established by the government or an apex organization helps meet a vital need, members can later be induced to take over the management. Israel has acquired considerable experience in such procedures in Jewish and Arab settlements alike.

TRAINING IN COOPERATION

An unusual feature of Israel's cooperative movement is its affiliation with the General Federation of Trade Unions (Histadrut), and it was the Histadrut which initiated the first three-month (November 15, 1958 – February 15, 1959) Seminar in Cooperation for sixty participants from Asia and Africa. (It is also for this reason that some of the subsequent courses contained material on both trade unionism and cooperation.) This international seminar inaugurated Israel's formal instructional program, although many individual visits had preceded the seminar. Thus, S. A. Frenando from Ceylon visited Israel in 1953 to observe agricultural cooperatives in connection with a resettlement plan contemplated by his government, and there were similar visits by cooperators from India, Malaya, Nepal, Singapore, and the Philippines. The Seminar, in its turn, was the forerunner of additional courses in the field and, finally, of the Afro-Asian Institute For Labor Studies and Cooperation.

Realizing that "there can be no mechanical transplantation from one country to another,"[9] the avowed purpose of the Seminar was to "place Israel's experience (in cooperative activities) at the disposal of people wishing to utilize it." The program consisted of an initial six weeks of class-

---

8. For further discussion of this point see Professor Infeld, "Cooperative Farming in Low Income Countries," Archives, 1960, No. 7, pp. 76–86; and Kimble, Tropical Africa, Vol. II, p. 209.

9. From an introductory statement by R. Barkatt, then head of the Histadrut's international department.

room lectures and discussions which was followed by three weeks of active participation in the three types of cooperative villages, and concluded with two weeks of special study in any type of cooperative which had particular interest for the individual student. There were some twenty-five lecturers and a number of guest speakers; discussion sessions were broadened by contributions from six of the trainees, who discussed the cooperative movements in their own countries.

The lectures were designed to provide an overall (though necessarily cursory) view of the entire field of cooperative activity, and included the following topics:

I. The International Cooperative Movement
II. The Cooperative Movement in Asia and Africa
III. The Cooperative Movement in Israel
    a. The economic structure of Israel and problems of development.
    b. History and structure of the cooperative movement.
    c. Cooperative agriculture; cooperative farming and settlement, marketing and supply, crop and cattle insurance, irrigation societies, inter-village assistance and cooperation, municipal services.
    d. Consumer cooperation, wholesale societies, consumer stores.
    e. Industrial societies and transport cooperatives.
    f. Credit, insurance and banking societies.
    g. Housing cooperative.
    h. Provident funds.
    i. Cooperative law in Israel.
IV. Organization and Management of Cooperatives
    a. The nature of cooperative organization.
    b. The administrative process; planning, coordination, control mobilization of resources; personnel management, etc.
    c. Cooperative administration as compared with other types of administration.
    d. Evaluation and application to problems of low-income countries.

Most of the participants were enthusiastic about the Seminar, feeling that this experience with Israel's cooperative movement would help them greatly in their work in their own countries. This sentiment is attested by the following fairly representative statement:

> On the whole, it was a huge experiment in international living and studying together; it provided a forum for the mutual exchange of ideas among the different participating countries, and at the same time enabled all visitors to learn about the host country and take from it as much as they considered beneficial to their own work.

But like any initial experiment, the Seminar had problems, most of which can be summed up under the heading of diversity. The sixty participants came from seventeen different countries, both English-speaking and French-speaking,[10] and thus the Seminar had to be conducted in both languages. While this variety of participating nationalities made for a valuable international experience, it also meant that there was no common level of cultural background among the participants: their educational and occupational attainments were extremely diverse. Side by side in the classroom were college graduates and high school drop-outs, veterans of cooperative movements and novices who had never seen one in action; government officials shared the same lectures and discussions as trade unionists, teachers, farm representatives, and cooperators.

The participants' diversity of interest was reflected in the number and variety of fields they chose to specialize in during the final period of the Seminar — cooperative villages, credit societies, agricultural (including citrus) marketing combines, the central wholesale society, retail consumers' stores, cooperative housing, passenger and goods transport, printing, crop and livestock insurance, and various agricultural services which included joint use of machinery and artificial insemination. To quote one participant:

> The varying educational background and occupations of the participants at this seminar must have presented the greatest difficulty in planning the different courses designed to meet the requirements of the individual. No specific line appears to have been drawn regarding academic qualifications and/or experience, and while the cooperative movement in Israel is unique in its wide ramifications, it seems planning would have been far less arduous and perhaps far less expensive if the Seminar had drawn its participants from within a defined level of education and experience. It would have been preferable to have only 20 participants with a homogeneous background.

The lecturers and guest speakers were chosen, of course, as experts in the various areas of cooperative activity in Israel. An undesirable but practically inevitable corollary was their almost universal ignorance of conditions outside of Israel — a deficiency that was only partially rectified in subsequent Seminars. Thus the students were given no help in relating the Israeli experience to African conditions. While most of the participants found the Seminar, for survey purposes, much too long, the great number of topics covered in the curriculm deprived the Seminar of a focus, and inadequate coordination resulted in considerable overlapping and, at times, conflicts. As a result, participants who had had no previous experience with

---

10. Burma 1; Ceylon 1; Dahomey 5; Ethiopia 2; Ghana 10; India 11; Ivory Coast 3; Japan 4; Kenya 1; Liberia 2; Nigeria 10; Northern Rhodesia 1; S. Rhodesia 1; Senegal 3; Fr. Sudan 3; Tchad 1; Thailand 1 (a total of 45 English-speaking and 15 French-speaking students).

cooperatives gained little from what was for them too diffuse and superficial a survey, and those whose future plans did not include actual engagement in cooperative work found the Seminar's general value dissipated in a multiplicity of details. Trainees and lecturers alike joined in recommending for future Seminars a greater concentration on specific subjects centered around two or three major themes, and felt that having fewer teachers would result in a more unified coverage of the subject matter.[11]

Despite its drawbacks, however, the participants' tremendous eagerness to learn and the Israelis' willingness to show and teach made the Seminar a considerable success. One of its important results was to whet the appetites of the participating countries for additional training and greater exposure to Israel's cooperative movement. In response to their requests Israel organized further international Seminars and courses designed for specific national groups. While certain elements of diversity continued to plague the international gatherings (though to a lesser extent than in the first Seminar), the groups who came for the special courses were of a more uniform composition.

Examples of the "homogeneous" courses can be drawn from both Africa and Asia. Following a three-week study tour by four Guinean Labor leaders, a delegation of ten cooperators from Guinea spent seven months in Israel (February - September, 1960), studying the trade unions and cooperative movement. They paid particular attention to agricultural cooperation, and part of their training involved work in the villages and study of their organizational structure. In terms of their background and their ability to comprehend the possible application of the material to their own countries, the members of this group were highly qualified, and upon their return home, they all entered various phases of cooperation. The group was sponsored by the Guinean Ministère de l'Economie Rurale et de la coopération.

In the summer of 1959, ten students (five of them Africans) from a French school for cooperation, headed by Professor DeRousche, came to Israel for a month as part of their study. Each of them investigated a problem for a research paper. A few months later, a high-level study mission of the Indian Ministry of Community Development and Cooperation spent five weeks in Israel studying cooperatives, having just completed a similar visit in Yugoslavia.[12] Their tour was financed by the Ford Foundation.

In the spring of 1960, a group of twenty-eight members of the Boodhan

---

11. For the views of one lecturer, see Professor Infeld, "The Meaning of the Afro-Asian Seminar in Cooperation in Israel," Archives 1959, No. 5, pp. 171–179.

12. See the Report of the Study Team on the Working of the Cooperative Movement in Yugoslavia and Israel (New Delhi: Government of India, Ministry of Community Development and Cooperation, 1960).

(Land Gift) movement in India came to Israel for a six-month course in cooperation. The boodhan is an organized movement for exerting moral pressure on large land-owners to give up their holdings for redistribution among the landless; it has so far achieved the pooling of five million acres in 500 villages. With a goal of changing "the present order of competitive society into a cooperative order of non-violent and non-exploiting society," it derives considerable inspiration from the principles of non-exploitation, self-labor, and equality of Israel's agricultural cooperation. The Boodhan's leader visited Israel in 1958, since when he has requested the loan of Israeli agricultural and cooperative advisors, and has sent to Israel a number of teams for study tours and courses of which the 1960 group is the largest (it followed a three-month visit by a small delegation). The program for this group was patterned, for the first three months, after the first Seminar in Cooperation. The last three months was devoted to individual specialization in various types of agricultural cooperative societies. Two cooperators from Kenya were attached to the group during most of its stay.

Other examples of one-country delegations are a twenty-man study mission from the African territory of Ruanda-Urundi (now constituting the countries Rwanda and Burundi), and a nine-man mission from Cyprus. Their training was preparatory to setting up agricultural cooperatives in their own countries.

Among international gatherings have been two courses in cooperation for French-speaking Africans, offered in the summers of 1960 and 1961. Sponsored by the Histadrut and the Foreign Ministry, each had about fifty students drawn from over twelve countries. While the courses were monolingual, there were some problems of diversity, as may be surmised from the large number of lecturers (over thirty) and from the age, educational, and occupational characteristics of the participants in the 1960 course tabulated below:

Education		Age Group	Number	Occupation	
Grade school	8	17 - 30	32	Gov't. officials	43
High school	31	31 - 40	14	Trade unionists	4
College	15	Over 40	8	Teachers	6
				Students	1
Total	54		54		54

The program for the courses combined theoretical studies (topics similar to those in the first Seminar) with a period of work and observation in the cooperative settlements. Although the students recognized the importance of the field work for gaining first-hand experience and insight, some of them balked at having to engage in manual labor. But their main complaint concerned the inability of the Israeli villagers to provide adequate explanations of the structure and administration of their villages.

Another international course in agricultural cooperation was organized by Israel's Ministry of Agriculture for twenty-three English-speaking students from East Africa. Their background and interests were both uniform and adequate. In fact, the Israeli official in charge of the program took an active part in selecting them. The four-month course consisted of theoretical studies and practical work in the villages. Like their French-speaking counterparts, some of the trainees complained about the lack of specific treatment in the coursework, the nonavailability of proper instruction on the farm, the multiplicity of lecturers, and the teachers' meager knowledge of African conditions. Yet their overriding reaction was that of satisfaction. Without a doubt this was one of the most successful courses in the field.

Since 1960 the newly established Afro-Asian Institute for Cooperation and Trade Unionism has taken over the training in cooperation. For the most part its functions are carried out in four-month courses in which both cooperation and trade unionism are taught, although trainees are given some opportunity to specialize in specific subjects. The discussion of the Afro-Asian Institute will be deferred to Chapter 9.
(For discussion of Israel's assistance in non-agricultural cooperation, see Appendix II.)

Applicability of Israel's Cooperative Methods to African Conditions:

A common feature of most courses in cooperation as well as in agriculture is the work period on the cooperative farms. One objective of this phase is to acquaint trainees with the structure of Israel's cooperative settlements and their contribution to the country's development. It is then up to the trainees to determine how far it seems possible to adapt any features of the cooperatives to their own countries. If such adaptation is possible, Israel's technical assistance can transcend purely technical matters, and reach into the realm of social change. Views of African trainees, along with those of other observers, will now be drawn upon in an attempt to assess the degree of possible adaptation.

It does not appear that the Kibbutz or Moshav Shitufi are capable of wide-spread emulation. "Kibbutz can succeed only under Jewish idealism" stated the Tanganyika Standard (June 23, 1961). Along the same lines, W. Arthur Lewis writes:

Most observers seem to agree that the success of these collectives has depended so far upon the special emotions associated

with immigrant Jewish agriculture in Israel, and upon the part
played by collective organization in the military defense of isolated settlements. Sooner or later the special strains and emotions
involved in creating a Jewish National Home will wear off, and if
the collectives then retain their primitive communism, and succeed
economically, they will be doing so contrary to all previous human
experience.[13]

Indeed, recent immigrants to Israel from Asia and Africa were not able to
accept the collective way of life, and very few of the settlements established
since 1948 have been Kibbutzim. Over 75 per cent of them are Moshavim.

Nevertheless, it cannot be argued that the collective idea holds no
attraction for the Afro-Asian world. There are some known cases where its
people have organized collectives without any outside influence or advice.
In Dahomey an Israeli expert reports seeing a village organized much like
a Moshav Shitufi. And in Nigeria there is a fishing village which operates
on the Kibbutz principle (fishing is an activity which lends itself to cooperation.)

It began in the late 1940s as an attempt by a small group of Yor-
uba-speaking fishermen, influenced by Bible reading and under
the guidance of three outstanding local men, to break away from
the old tribal system of living and strive for a fuller life and better
conditions. The site chosen for the attempt was an unpromising
stretch of foreshore about a hundred miles east of Lagos. Today
the Apostle Community, as it is called, of Aiyetoro ("The World
Is at Peace") is a progressive, well-run, thriving town of some
3,000 people. Yet it is still deeply committed to cooperation — or,
as the leaders of the community prefer to think of it, apostolic
Christianity. All profits derived from fishing are placed in a community chest and used for the benefit of the group as a whole. No
money is credited to individuals. Instead they get free rent and
excellent housing, clothes in great variety, free food in abundance
and, recently, even free electric light. They have discovered that
when people are willing to put community above compound, and
industry before idleness, the cooperative principle can be made
to work.[14]

Given certain conditions and attitudes, it is quite conceivable that a
few collectives can be established in Afro-Asian countries. But the main
value of the Kibbutz is not so much as an object for direct emulation, as for
the general inspiration it provides. The Boodhan movement, for example,
derives considerable inspiration from the Kibbutz, although it does not

_____

13. The Theory of Economic Growth, London: George Allen and Unwin
Ltd., 1955, p. 65.

14. G. Kimble, Tropical Africa, Vol. I, 1960, p. 275.

regard collectives to be practicable for India. To African trainees the Kib-butz can and does teach one important lesson: the dignity of labor. They see in it an organization where all pursuits have equal prestige, where work is performed efficiently without the usual market incentives,[15] and where men of letters engage in manual agricultural labor and take pride in it. More-over, they can observe Kibbutz members who have risen to positions of power and prestige in government service engaging without shame in ordi-nary manual occupations when they come home for weekends or vacations. African visitors note with admiration that Israel's prime minister is associ-ated with a Kibbutz in the Negev desert, and that the daughter of the foreign minister is an active member of another Negev Kibbutz. Much of the value of active work on the settlements by African cooperative and agricultural train-ees lies in their acquiring a different attitude toward work. If upon their re-turn home even a few of them did not shun the manual occupations, a very useful purpose would have been served.

Finally, the Kibbutz is a most advanced mixed farming enterprise, and offers great possibilities as a means of instruction in almost every sector of mechanized farming (see below, Chapter 5).

Yet, even though the pooling of land can provide a solution to the immense problem of land fragmentation in Africa, most observers believe that collective farm organization is unlikely to gain wide acceptance. One Israeli cooperator who returned from a survey in Nigeria observed that "only under rare conditions of close extended-family ties, and absence of close bond to the land, can a Moshav Shitufi be established." African farmers appear to prefer ownership of land in independent operating units. In the words of the registrar of cooperatives in Nigeria's eastern region, "we have reason to believe that Africans will not go along with any measure of collective land ownership."

In the opinion of one competent FAO economist, the great difficulties in developing large-scale production in Africa along the lines of the collective farm, lie in the field of farmer incentives:

> Farmers will inevitably develop an attitude toward the land, the crops and the livestock, typical of a hired worker who has only a rather remote personal interest in the ultimate outcome of the pro-duction process and the overall efficiency of the enterprise. He receives his income in the form of wages and, in some cases, of dividends on a stock share he owns in the land, which he cannot identify with his own individual efforts and care. The biological nature of the production process in agriculture requires a rather intimate relation between the farmer and his crops and livestock in order to adjust his work closely to the rhythms of climate and

15. One African remarked that if a Kibbutz were established in Africa, its members would spend all day sleeping.

growth processes in plants and animals . . . . A well-organized
and adequate-sized family farm enterprise is technically and economically more efficient in the use of productive resources than
even well-managed large-scale enterprises mainly depending upon
hired workers.[16]

On the other hand, the same observer believes that the Israeli Moshav
(like the Gezira Scheme[17] in the Sudan) is capable of wide application in
Africa. The Moshav combines individual ownership and management, provides
safeguards against fragmentation of land, and permits economies of scale in
activities which lend themselves to cooperative execution. Thus it has
great promise as an institutional framework capable of bringing about rural
progress. Similarly, most Afro-Asian trainees and visitors to Israel share the
view that the Moshav can be adapted to their countries with considerable
benefit — especially in new settlement areas. The following statement by an
Ethiopian student is quite typical: "The Moshav with its individualistic
nature suits the temperament and personality of the Ethiopian farmer. Since
he can achieve the objectives of large-scale production and services and
mutual aid without risking his privacy, I feel the small-holders' settlement
as found in Israel is near to our way of life and can be adapted without too
much difficulty."

Most African countries had at least some experience with "single-
purpose cooperative societies" engaged either in credit extension or in the
marketing of a single product. The one distinct advantage of such societies
over the multi-purpose variety is simplicity. They do not require a complex
accounting system to allocate costs properly to the different activities of
the society. Easier to manage, they avoid the bewildering problems that
often cause dissension in multi-purpose cooperatives.[18] But African cooperators are attracted to the Moshav in large part because of numerous
advantages they see in the multi-purpose society. Such a cooperative tends
to have a larger turnover and lower overhead expenses, and can better afford
to engage specialized staff. It has one administrative center, one account

---

16. R. Schickele, "Settlement Problems and Policies," Netherlands
Journal of Agricultural Science, November, 1957, pp. 244–250.

17. In the Gezira Scheme, farm families produce cotton under large-
scale farming conditions and under central management and supervision.
But they produce forage crops, maize, vegetables, and animal products under
family-type farming conditions. Individual holdings range between thirty and
forty acres, of which about one third is planted to cotton. However, the emphasis in the program is on cotton and not on the development of the family-
farm part of the scheme.

18. In the eastern region of Nigeria, for example, such complications
resulted in a break-up of the Cocoa and Palm Produce Marketing Union.

per member, and one worker for the accounts. Transport cost is one area in which savings can be affected. Trucks employed in shipping agricultural produce can return to the village with supplies when the marketing and supply functions are combined in one cooperative. Also, the individual farmer delivers his crops to one packing center rather than to a different location for each product.

Availability of credit through the society can add markedly to its stability. Disloyalty to the marketing society often results from the need for cash which draws farmers to private dealers. Therefore, states an FAO expert reporting on Sierra Leone, "the further development of cooperative organizations will greatly depend on the extent of credit made available to members against security of the crop."[19] Being well informed of the farmer's overall financial position, the multi-purpose society can provide credit on a basis suited to the farm economy. The farmer's anticipated returns on his crop are more important in assessing his repayment capacity, than the amount of land he can put up as collateral. Also, credit extension can be more closely related to the production programs of the state.

The multi-purpose society, dealing with the peasant's economy as an entity, induces a higher degree of personal involvement in the farmer. By contrast,

> When an individual's interests as a consumer, a borrower of money, a seller of paddy, a seller of milk, a seller of coir, products, etc., would necessitate his being a member of a large number of societies, some located outside his village, he becomes no more than a "sleeping partner" of each of them. His interest in the societies gradually declines, his vigilance slackens and corruption among office-holders and employees goes unchallenged.[20]

But the attainment of multi-purpose societies calls for capital, part of which must come from the government, as well as disciplined and somewhat sophisticated farmers. They must have confidence in, and loyalty to, the society, and in African countries they often do not. Not the least important is the supply of well-trained cooperative managers. The failure of a bus cooperative in an African country because drivers were trusted to collect fares without the sale of tickets illustrates this need. The shortage of trained personnel[21] is worsened in underdeveloped countries because their

19. E. H. Jacobi, Report on a Visit to Sierra Leone (mimeographed) (Rome: April, 1960).

20. From a statement by Mr. Sirwardene, Assistant Commissioner of Cooperative Development in Ceylon.

21. Because one multi-purpose society performs the same amount of service that would require several of the single-purpose variety, it actually

cooperative movements are mainly agricultural and the intelligentsia tends to desert agriculture for better-paid or less physically strenuous city jobs.

It is these prerequistes which limit the ability of African cooperators to draw on Israel's experience. Although the level of sophistication of some Israeli settlers is often similar to that of the African villager, other conditions are totally different. Israel has an abundance of trained personnel as well as of foreign capital, and her new settlers immediately receive the support of strong central cooperative organizations. Above all, Israel started with a clean slate. Her problem was establishing new settlements, not trying to introduce cooperatives into existing villages, and therefore the settlement authority could aim from the start at multi-purpose societies.

When it came to the introduction of cooperatives into existing Arab villages, Israel's goals were much more modest. Early attempts in this direction failed altogether, in part because of the individualistic attitude of the Arab peasant and his lack of confidence in the principles of co-operation. Subsequent efforts, which centered on the development of single-purpose societies and capitalized on urgent needs, met with a larger measure of success. Over half of the societies so developed were irrigation and water-supply cooperatives which offered obvious advantages to the farmer—water makes it possible to grow several crops on his land and to work the land intensively all the year round, thereby increasing yearly production and annual income. It makes possible the introduction of sanitary installations in the home and, last but not least, it frees the Arab woman of the heavy burden of carrying full buckets of water over considerable distances. For these reasons irrigation schemes through cooperative action almost always met with a welcome and unanimously favorable reaction from the villagers. But water has also acted as a basis for mutual cooperation and understanding in other fields, with the water cooperatives slowly developing into the central institution of the village. Only in the summer of 1962 did Israel's settlement authority approve an application of a Druze group to lease land near Mount Carmel for the purpose of setting up the first non-Jewish Moshav in the country a development which was hailed as "a significant landmark in Israel's social and agricultural history." [22]

In certain Asian countries such as Ceylon and India, a fairly wide network of single-purpose cooperatives already exists and efforts are being made to convert them to multi-purpose societies. Although such tasks are usually performed by the villagers themselves, the inspiration often comes from Israel. A case in point was the experimental introduction of cooper-

---

economizes on managerial talent. But the calibre required to run it is considerably higher.

22. Jewish Observer and Middle East Review, July 27, 1962, p. 17.

atives in a few Indian villages.[23] While the villagers were considering means to improve their production methods, a social worker returned from Israel after a short period of study. Having been impressed by the success of the cooperative efforts there, he urged that cooperative farm organization be considered by the village people. It was ultimately agreed that "cooperative farming....may be tried on an experimental basis for the improvement of agriculture in the area".[24] The first farming society was formed in 1959, subsequent to which four others were organized. Farmers pooled their land, cattle, machinery, implements, and masonry wells, and elected an executive committee to manage the affairs of the society with major decisions reserved for the entire membership. All members received a fixed, uniform monthly pay, and surpluses are divided according to the lands pooled. The new organization has resulted in the following benefits for its members: improved methods of cultivation through better utilization of land and manpower, extension and diversification of cropping, manuring and use of fertilizers facilitated by bulk buying, increased bargaining power with suppliers and a resultant improvement in quality of the goods supplied, improved implements and a better irrigation system, introduction of village industries, elimination of the middleman, and a substantial increase in leisure time. The Report concludes, "Since cooperative farming has resulted in the modernization of agriculture, it is providing a special appeal to a few educated young farmers to continue in agriculture because it is no longer necessary for them to perform unpleasant chores like ploughing. Instead they can take to such duties as tractor driving and operating pumper plant and other machinery".[25]

Likewise, the Ceylonese trainees in Israel have come to regard the Moshav pattern as their final goal for their country. Once such village societies are sufficiently widespread, they will federate nationally on a functional basis in a cooperative wholesale society, purchasing society, and a cooperative bank.

Asian observers have also expressed admiration for Israel's pragmatic approach to the problems of cooperation, and urged its adoption by their respective countries. So, for example, states the Report of the Indian Government Mission (see above, Section C), to Israel:

Practices should be suitably adapted and, if necessary, even modified, so that in the initial stages new members of co-operative

23. The experiment was reported in a pamphlet entitled: Cooperative Farming Saghan Chetra Dhanaura District Moradabad, published by the co-operative Department U. P. Lucknow.

24. Ibid., pp. 2—3.

25. Ibid., p. 10.

societies can be acclimatized to co-operative principles and practices. . . It would be an advantage if, at the village level, cooperative societies of varying size, types, forms, and with varying
functions, are promoted according to local preferences and condition. (pp. 95, 111)

With particular regard to the organization of cooperatives, the Mission's
Report says:

We are aware that ordinarily the co-operative movement is intended
to be built up from below. In other words, first of all, sound and
autonomous primary societies must be built up and thereafter further superstructure has to be created. The experience of Israel
shows that this process can be reversed and yet equally satisfactory results can be achieved with greater speed. In fact, Israel is
now proposing to even change the cooperative law so as to stat-
utorily recognize the role and functions of central societies. We
would suggest that in India also action on these lines may be
initiated. If necessary in the initial stages, with adequate Government participation in the share capital, strong central cooperative
societies should be built up, and in turn these societies should
be assigned the task of promoting the movement at lower stages.
(p. 113)

On the other hand, most African countries do not appear ripe for the
introduction of multi-purpose societies in existing villages. The appetite
created among African trainees in Israel for the establishment of Moshavim
will have to be satisfied for the time being in new settlement areas. Indeed,
graduates of Israel's courses in cooperation from Tanganyika, Mali, Rwanda,
Burundi and perhaps Cyprus, are contemplating the establishment of new
Moshav-type settlements in their countries. Israel has already dispatched
experts to Nigeria, Burma, and Brazil to advise on the setting up of Moshavim.
In most cases the settlers are of above-average intelligence and education,
which gives at least a minimum assurance of success. In western Nigeria,
for example, the new settlements will be used to attract school leavers to
the farm. If successful, the Moshavim can later be used for demonstration
purposes in converting single-to multi-purpose societies in old villages.
Some of these projects will be discussed in the next chapter which is concerned with Farm Settlement.

In existing villages the most feasible approach will be to encourage the
formation of single-purpose societies. Only gradually can these be amalgamated into multi-purpose cooperatives. While such societies should usually
be started in the conventional fields of marketing or credit, they can often
be introduced along with a new branch of agriculture. Thus an Israeli survey expert in the Congo suggested that newly developed citrus plantations
be cooperatively owned and cultivated, and another such expert urged the

introduction of cattle herds in Mali along cooperative lines.

To facilitate such a program, where farmer sophistication is lacking, there is a need for a thick network of cooperative personnel. For that reason, an Israeli advisor in eastern Nigeria properly recommended (and the government accepted) the establishment of a cooperative college in the region. It is best for personnel to receive basic training in the environment in which they will later function. Since the eastern region has voiced an interest in the establishment of Moshav-type settlements, Israel can be of help in setting up the proposed training facilities. Once they exist, training in Israel should be confined to senior-level personnel, and focused primarily on specialized subjects.

But as long as basic training is offered in Israel, it is essential that the returning trainees be channeled into cooperative work, and be given continued support from the "alma mater." An encouraging sign that this may be in the offing was the dispatch of one Israeli cooperator to the Ivory Coast under FAO auspices. After having taught at the summer 1961 course for French-speaking Africans, he supervised the subsequent specialization of ten students from the Ivory Coast in a few cooperative institutions. In the spring of 1962, he was scheduled to accompany them to Abijan where they would attempt to introduce cooperatives in villages near that capital. On the eve of his departure, the expert said that, not knowing conditions in Africa, he would have to feel his way before deciding on an exact course of action.

With the increasing demand for cooperators from Israel, it is hoped that such arrangements, capitalizing on the training received in Israel, can be expanded.

CHAPTER 4 LAND
SETTLEMENT

African trainees in Israel, from Tanganyika to Mali, have tried to put the Moshav idea into practice by establishing such settlements in their own countries. However, it is not the Moshav itself which fires the imagination of most visitors to Israel, but the whole complex of social, and economic regional planning of which the Moshav is the smallest unit. A region so planned is known as a composite village structure. Almost every visiting minister of agriculture or economic planning comes away from Israel saying, "I would like to have a Lachish Region in my own country." Israeli experts, in turn, have proposed regional settlement schemes in several countries, and in some instances the plans have been put into effect.

REGIONAL SETTLEMENT IN ISRAEL

The composite village structure is a pattern of settlement wherein five or six Moshavim are grouped around a rural center, and a number of such collections of villages and rural centers around a central regional town. Lachish is an area of 25,000 acres in southern Israel settled in this fashion over a five-year period beginning in 1952. The settlers were new immigrants from the four corners of the earth. Inexperienced in agricultural work, they started as employees of the settlement authority, but as they gained knowledge and confidence the land was parceled out to them. Now they produce mainly industrial crops, such as cotton, ground nuts, and sugar beets, which are processed in the regional town.

Both economic and social considerations led to the adoption of this form of settlement. On the economic side lay the need to fill an uninhabited area with immigrants in need of settlement; to create economically viable units with agriculture and industry integrated into a whole plan; to provide an organizational framework suited to the application of modern technology; and to produce and process industrial crops efficiently for export as well as local consumption. No less pressing were the social reasons: new immigrants, many very primitive and all unaccustomed to farm work, had to be introduced to modern agricultural techniques; newcomers from a variety of geographical and social backgrounds had to be integrated into the life of the nation, but gradually, to prevent excessive social friction; social amenities and welfare services had to be provided on an economically efficient scale in order to minimize the immense attraction of city life; and professional and technical personnel had to be attracted from the main centers of population to the newly settled region. Finally, the population of a vacant area in a country surrounded by hostile neighbors was important to national security.

The Village

How were these requirements met? Each Moshav in the region is occupied by one ethnic group only, which prevents daily contacts between people of different cultural backgrounds. Basic services are provided in each village. They include a synagogue run according to the settlers' tradition, a cooperative store supplying daily household needs, a clinic staffed by a qualified nurse which is open two or three times a week, and a kindergarten and two-grade primary school which also provide the children's noon meal. Instructors in agriculture and home economics are also resident in the village. Land is parceled in such a way as to give access to a road and the irrigation network, and to facilitate the cooperative use of farm machinery.

The District and Its Rural Center

Located so as to be equidistant from each Moshav in the district (about a mile or a mile and a half from each), the rural center serves the community's needs at the higher level. Its social services include the district health center; staffed by a doctor and a nurse, it provides both therapeutic and preventive medical care. The doctor also supervises the individual village clinics. To fulfill the state requirements for compulsory education there is an elementary school for 500 pupils in the six to fourteen age-bracket. The Ministry of Education provides one teacher for every twenty-five pupils. While this would not permit an individual village of 80 families to maintain a full range of classes without charging fees, the 400 families of the district can, by pooling resources, have an adquately staffed and well-equipped school in the rural center. The school is also used for adult education in Hebrew, village administration, and agricultural subjects. The rural center also has a youth club which organizes educational and cultural activities for the fifteen to seventeen year-olds.

In the rural center also are located certain economic services for the district. A tractor station fills the heavy mechanization requirements of the surrounding villages. It is formed as a subsidiary of the settlement authority, but is designed ultimately to be taken over by the settlers on a cooperative basis. For the present, the settler pays a fixed rate (subject to regular review) for each operation the station performs. The concentration of tractors and such machines at a central location not only reduces depreciation and running costs, but makes possible an easier utilization of technical information by the settlers. Second, the rural center contains the district market center, where vegetables are graded and later sold by the central purchasing company. Finally, there is the district shop (which sometimes adjoins a café); it sells a wide range of goods including light agricultural implements, seeds, clothing, and textiles.

The district is run by a council made up of representatives from the villages. It has at its disposal a professional team, headed by a community worker, which consists of a physician, nurse, social worker, director of cultural activities, secretary of the rural center, and a representative of the school staff.

The Regional Town

The regional town is the administrative, commercial, industrial, and cultural center of the entire area. It contains the planning authority for the region, extension workers with highly specialized knowledge, and a comprehensive professional team to supervise the rural centers. Plants for processing the industrial crops of the region are located in it (accessible by road and rail to all parts of the country) as are all the commercial services, and a small hospital. Its cultural facilities include a cinema, a cultural hall, an open-air amphitheatre, a library, a museum, a secondary school, an agricultural and technical high school, and sports grounds.

What has been gained by multi-stage regional development? Socially, immigrants from different cultures are kept apart in their daily life, but come in frequent mutual contact when they avail themselves of the services of the rural center and the regional town. Moreover, the children from the various villages mix at the rural center's school, thereby achieving cultural fusion in the second generation. The system has made it possible to transfer professional staff from the big cities to the rural centers and the regional town, closer to the farmers who use their services. Because many of them are required in the centers, they do not suffer from intellectual and professional isolation. The existence of the centers also lessens the settlers' sense of isolation and the attraction of the big population centers is thereby diminished.

Social and economic services furnished on a large-scale basis make better services available at a lower cost than would be possible for a single village. The crops grown are processed locally and leave the region as finished products. Light industry can also locate at the rural centers, providing employment for surplus farm population. Should trends necessitate the enlargement of the size of farms and the displacement of some operators, the latter can continue to live in the village and work in the center.

As evidences of success, one may note the cost reduction effected by the composite village structure, and its relative stability. The proportion of Lachish settlers who have left agriculture in recent years is only half the national average. This pattern of settlement is now being adopted in other parts of Israel. In another type of composite settlement (the Taanakh region), the individual village consists of several neighborhoods, each with 60 farmsteads, and a few service families. Different ethnic groups live in separate neighborhoods, but they all enjoy the more advanced services at a common center. Several such multi-nuclear villages surround, and are served by, the regional town. It is worthy of note that the Kibbutz unit does not lend itself to a composite structure. Being more self-sufficient than the Moshav, it can attain its own economies of scale, and tends to establish its own processing industries. Its cultural standard is usually higher than that of a small regional town. For these reasons, the collectives obtain their needs directly from the big cities, and cannot provide the necessary rural hinterland for a regional town.

DEMONSTRATION TO AFRICANS

Most African trainees in agriculture and cooperation become familiar with regional planning in Israel through several days of observation and lectures on that topic in their courses. Occasionally, some of the course graduates wish to go deeper into the subject and remain in the country for an additional period of specialized work. This was true of five Ethiopian students of agriculture and three trainees in rural cooperation from Kenya and Tanganyika — both in 1961. The latter group trained at the Agricultural Planning Bureau in Haifa, where an excellent program was drawn up for them on a short notice. The program included farm and village planning, soil survey, and land parcellation. Following a set of lectures and tours concerned with these topics, the students planned a Moshav-type settlement based on data from East Africa. They were full of praise for the training program, the way it was executed, and its value to their jobs at home which involve work on land consolidation.

At about the same time, a ten-day study plan was arranged for a group of OEEC planners who were engaged in a land settlement project in Sardinia.

Finally, in response to a growing demand, Israel organized a six-week seminar devoted exclusively to rural planning in the fall of 1961.[1] Thirty-

---

1. Rural planning constituted a major subject in a seminar on housing organized a year and a half earlier for thirty-eight participants (mainly architects and engineers) from sixteen countries. The seminar's main theme was

eight participants from nineteen Asian, African and Latin American countries studied the physical, economic, and social planning of the Moshav and Kibbutz, as well as regional and country-wide planning. These subjects were covered in thirty days of lectures and seventeen days of observation tours. The seminar was well planned. It was housed in a resort hotel especially leased for that purpose, with arrangements for simultaneous translation between English, French, and Spanish. At the end of the seminar an International Association for Rural Planning was formed by the participants for the purpose of exchanging ideas and experiences.

Although the success of the seminar in getting its message across is beyond question, it suffered from two major shortcomings. First, the large number of lecturers (almost thirty) resulted in considerable overlapping on the one hand and too much fragmentation of subjects on the other. "Instead of twelve lectures on the Moshav, six would have sufficed," said one student. Secondly, the interests of the participants were too diverse. While all were university graduates, many had no prior exposure to settlement work. Not only did the school teachers among the participants slow down progress by asking elementary questions, but the seminar's value for their future work was rather limited. Moreover, insufficient effort was made to bring to the seminar, agronomists and planners who work with Israelis on settlement projects in Asia and Africa. Burma, for example, was not represented at all. The exception demonstrates the rule: two Nigerian trainees who at home are involved in a settlement project headed by an Israeli expert (under FAO auspices), derived considerable benefit from the seminar. Likewise, a British participant who for a long time had been engaged in land settlement in Tanganyika[2] stated: "Seeing the Moshav and regional planning completely opened my eyes. Both the cooperative aspects and the physical set-up offer solutions to many of our own problems."[3]

---

national housing policies and housing schemes as a means of achieving other policy goals. At least half of the curriculum was related to the planning of rural settlements.

2. His project involves resettling farmers from an overpopulated region with fragmented land in another area. Land was leased by the government on an inter-tribal arrangement: the Masai tribe leased it to the Wa Arusha tribe, in return for which the Masai tribe was given water supply in another area. The new settlement is based on extensive grazing, with each farmer receiving 25 acres.

3. Another high level conference was convened in the fall of 1963, when 77 delegates from 29 countries came to Israel to discuss and study comprehensive agricultural planning in developing economies. The conference may lead to the establishment in Israel of a center for higher studies in development planning to serve all the under-developed countries. The New York Times, August 30, 1963, p. C 4.

ISRAELI ASSISTANCE IN FARM SETTLEMENTS

Impressed by the concept of the composite village structure, certain less developed countries have requested Israeli assistance in land settlement. As a result, Israel has committed herself to developing such a project in Burma and to assisting in one in Western Nigeria. A settlement project in Eastern Nigeria is also patterned after Israel's composite village structure and Israeli expertise may be utilized in its execution. In addition, Israeli experts made agricultural surveys in Nepal and Tanganyika and recommended land settlement schemes, and an Israeli team may "plan the rehabilitation of the earthquake-stricken area in Persia." [4]

Burma

The most advanced settlement project in which Israel is involved is the settlement of Burmese ex-servicemen in the Shan State, near the Chinese border. Over 30,000 acres in the sparsely populated Namsang region are being settled with fifteen new Moshavim, each numbering seventy families. The village of Namsang will be developed into a regional town of 8,000 people, while another village is to become a sub-center. Groundnuts, soybeans and wheat are the main cash crops grown on the fifteen-acre plots, Each village will have a cooperative shop, a community meeting hall, a library, a dispensary, a kindergarten, and a sports field. The regional town will contain large stores, tractor sheds, offices, a hospital, a school, processing and other industries, and residential dwellings.

Israeli involvement in the region dates back to the mid-1950's. Experts on farm machinery, agricultural planning, and field crops had served in a consulting capacity under the sponsorship of the Burmese army.(The army in Burma carries on many industrial and agricultural enterprises, and much of Israel's technical assistance to that country is rendered through the armed forces.) Early in 1959 the Israeli government committed itself, on a political level (without prior technical investigation), to aid in resettling Burmese soldiers and to create an economically viable region in northern Shan state. Only in the fall of that year did an Israeli planner arrive in the area to investigate the feasibility of the project. He could, however, draw on the accumulated information of fellow-countrymen who had previously served there. After selecting his staff in Israel he returned to Namsang in March, 1960, accompanied by an agricultural planner, a physical planner, and a farm machinery adviser. The team served for one year, and two of its members remained for a subsequent year. During that period six villages were either set up or initiated, and almost the entire area was staked out for future settlements.

---

4. The Jerusalem Post Weekly, December 28, 1962.

Western Nigeria

In Nigeria's western region, the settlement project was initiated by Chief Akin Deko, the former Minister of Agriculture.[5] In 1959, instead of going to the Sudan to examine the Gezira scheme for possible adoption in Nigeria, he decided to go to Israel after having by chance read a book on land settlement there. His impression of the Moshav and the composite rural structure induced him to consider a similar scheme for implementation in the western region. Because of political pressures, however, the government decided instead to establish twenty-five individual Moshavim scattered throughout the country, at least one in each district. The project is entrusted to an FAO team headed by an Israeli planner. The head of the team had been in Nigeria before to make a preliminary land-use survey in the western region, and subsequently accompanied Chief Deko on his visit to Israel. While the members of the team are well qualified technicians, not all of them believe in the usefulness of cooperative settlements.[6]

At the initial stage thirteen dispersed settlements are being built. From 1963 to 1969 the plan calls for the establishment of ten new settlements every other year, with fifty farm units in each. In the alternate years 500 settlers will be placed in existing settlements, thus absorbing the annual output of trainees from the Farm Institutes set up to train the prospective settlers (see Section 3 below). Many of the settlers are "school leavers," namely, "standard six" school graduates, who would otherwise be attracted to the big cities. They are selected from within a thirty-mile radius of the site of their settlement. Communal land for the project was acquired by the government from the tribal chiefs, and a variety of social amenities will be provided in the villages on a cooperative basis. Total investment per unit was originally contemplated at $11,000 — but was later scaled down to half that sum, as is evident from the example reproduced in Figure 4.1

(The settlement described in the table is to consist of two villages, occupying 3,680 acres: a main village with 200 settlers containing all services, and a small village with 50 settlers and no services.)

---

5. Now FAO representative to Africa.

6. In addition to its head the team consists of a farm management economist (Indian), an education and extension expert (Scotish), a livestock expert (Australian) an agricultural engineer (British), and a veterinarian (British). It is regrettable that the Israeli planner had no hand in selecting his team.

Figure 4.1. Plan For IFO Settlement in Nigeria's Western Region

(Prepared by the FAO Team, Ibadan, February 1962)

	In Village	Per Settler
Land Distribution (in acres)		
Cocoa	1,250	5
Grapefruit	500	2
Oil Palm	750	3
Village site and arable land	750	3
Roads and wasteland	430	—
Total	3,680	13
Laying hens	24,000	96
Investments Required*		
Buildings		
Settlers residence	87,500	350
Village stores and		
Community Hall	10,000	40
Poultry	31,750	127
Mechanical Equipment	24,100	97
Plantations	306,307	1,225
Total	£459,657	£1,839
Government Contribution (Grant)		
Clearing of Village Site	£ 37,500	£ 150
Roads	5,000	20
Water Supply	10,000	42
Total	£ 53,000	£ 212

*Estimates given in Nigerian pounds. £1 = $2.80.

Most of the investment is in the form of a loan repayable over a twenty-year period, with payments commencing about ten years after settlement. In that fashion it is hoped eventually to build a $50 million revolving loan fund to support continuous settlement.

Farm units are well planned in advance of settlement. The FAO team prepares agricultural and farm management plans based on crop studies for individual homesteads and villages. At the initial stage over 1,000 work-days are required each year per farm unit, of which 3/4 is to be supplied by hired hands. But for a fully developed farm, the requirement would drop to 450 work-days, and the use of hired labor would be discontinued. Each farm is expected to yield a net income of from $800 to $1,000.[7] The planned crop combinations are shown in Figure 4.2.

Figure 4.2. Preliminary Suggestions For Farm Sizes Under Different Crop-Combinations

(Western Region – Nigeria)

1. Rubber Oilpalm

    10 acres oilpalm
    6 acres rubber
    1 acre homeplot
    96 laying hens

2. Cocoa Oilpalm

    10 acres cocoa
    10 acres oilpalm
    2½ acres homeplot and
      arable land
    96 laying hens

3. Cocoa Grapefruit

    10 acres cocoa
    3 acres grapefruit
    2 acres arable land
    96 laying hens

4. Cocoa, Oilpalm, Grapefruit

    10 acres cocoa
    2½ acres oilpalm
    2 acres grapefruit
    2½ acres homeplot and
      arable land
    96 laying hens

Eastern Nigeria

In the eastern region of Nigeria the settlement project grew out of the government's interest in the western region's scheme, coupled with an agricultural survey conducted by an Israeli team. The brief survey en-compassed the whole field of agriculture, so that most phases received only a superficial treatment. Problems such as agricultural education,[8] land tenure, land utilization, fragmentation of holdings, methods of cultivation,

---

7. For discussion of the settlement scheme, see Future Policy of the Ministry of Agriculture and Natural Resources, Ibadan: Government of West-ern Nigeria, 1959; Farm Settlement, Ibadan, June, 1960; and Farm Institutes, Ibadan, June, 1960.

8. Although the surveyors regard the field of agricultural education as

dissemination of research results, organization of the agricultural ministry, credit shortage, absence of plannings, and specific crops,[9] were not delved into deeply. Instead, the report addressed itself to one main topic: the recommended settlement of 2,700 farm units in three six-village blocks throughout the region.[10] (In a subsequent personal interview, the authors indicated that what they meant was the establishment of government plantations which could later be transformed into settlements by dividing the land among the workers.) Although the report was subject to severe criticism, primarily for failing to take into account Nigerian conditions,[11] the government adopted its basic concept of settlement, utilizing the composite village structure.[12]

According to the plan, each settlement would consist of six Moshavim of 120 units each, surrounding a common nucleus. The nucleus would contain a school, a community hall, a health center, a post office, a tractor station, cooperative shops, markets, chick brooder houses, fish ponds, and processing mills for the produce (e.g., a "Stork mill" for processing palm fruit, a rubber sheeting and crepe factory, and rice mills). It would serve as a social center for over 700 families living on an 8 to 12 thousand acre area, who would thus be provided with all the necessary amenities.

Settlers are to be experienced farmers, perhaps assisted by "school leavers." They will all be members of a multi-purpose cooperative as in the Israeli Moshav. In order to prevent land fragmentation, change in tenancy can take place only by inheritance of the entire holding by one child of the land-holder, by eviction (if the settler does not comply with the regulations), or by the settler's voluntary decision to leave the farm. Labor is to be provided by the settler's family. But in the stages of initial preparation and

---

extremely important, all they recommended was the establishment of a commission to study the problem.

9. Israelis in general are not familiar with tropical crops, such as cocoa and palm oil.

10. See, Gavrielie and Kedem, Preliminary Survey of Agriculture in Eastern Nigeria, Jerusalem, 1960.

11. Other points of criticism were not fulfilling the terms of reference (that is, not making a general agricultural survey), giving only a tenuous rationale for the settlement project, and failing to make any serious attempt to estimate settlement cost.

12. For discussion, see Eastern Nigeria Farm Settlement Scheme, Agricultural Bulletin, 2, Enugu; "Farm Settlement Schemes in Nigeria," Nigeria Trade Journal, January/March, 1962, Lagos; M. O. Ijere, "Challenge of Economic Progress," Nigerian Outlook (Enugu), February 12, 1962.

bush clearing it is hoped to enlist the free help of relatives from the surrounding area, thereby mobilizing the most abundant resource in Africa, unskilled farm labor.[13] The proposed crop combination of the six settlements is given in Figure 4.3, along with estimated cost. In the long run, it is hoped to establish a revolving loan fund of £ 12 million, which would make possible continuous settlement.

Figure 4.3.   Composite Sub-District Planning

Eastern Region — Nigeria

Farm Type *	Unit Size	Invest.** Per Unit	No. of Farm Units Per Village	No. of Villages	Total * Invest.	Estimated Net Annual Income
(1) Oil-Palm-Rubber (+ 50 laying hens)	11 acres	£1,830	100	6	£1.1m	£369
(2) Cocoa-Oil-Palm (+ 50 laying hens)	15 acres	£1,990	100	6	£1.2m	£452
(3) Oil-Palm-Citrus (+ 50 laying hens)	17 acres	£2,335	100	6	£1.4m	£279

*Plan includes two settlements of types 1 and 2 and one of type 3. The sixth settlement will probably be based on oil palm and rice, at an estimated cost of £1.1m.

**Estimates given in Nigerian pounds. £1 = $2.80.

Surveys

In Nepal, where the government was already planning settlement projects, an Israeli survey team proposed the adoption of a regional settlement scheme with five Moshavim grouped around a rural service and processing center.[14] However, because of possible difficulties with the introduction of cooperative farming, the team suggested alternative interim plans involving either state farms or large plantations with the ultimate aim of apportioning the area among the workers after they have been properly introduced to modern farming. Similarly, in Tanganyika, a regional settlement project was

13. See. R. Nurkse, Problems of Capital Formation in Underdeveloped Countries (Oxford: Basil Blackwell, 1953).

14. See Kantor, Kedem, and Eden Proposed Israeli Cooperation in Agriculture and Water Development in the Kingdom of Nepal (Jerusalem: March, 1961).

proposed by an Israeli expert for the Kilombaro valley, after a two months' survey.[15]

In the arid region of northeastern Brazil, Israel expects to help set up a _Moshav_, with the possibility of expanding it to a composite structure based on intensive agriculture and irrigation.[16]   And a USOM agricultural officer writes from Bankok:

> With the strong interest in regional development on the part of the Thai government, it is expected that indications of official interest in Israel's regional planning (e.g., the Lachish area) will lead to more extensive Thai requests for technical assistance in this area.

Elements of regional planning can also be used to improve the lot of the population in existing settlements. For example, an Israeli town planner proposed the development of regional towns for services and processing industries in the agricultural hinterland in Sierra Leone. His survey report (dated 1961) states:

> Observe for example the problem of under-employment in the big cities, created mainly by migration from rural areas where under-employment is even more severe. Developing industries in the big city tend to intensify urban over-crowding as well as aggravate rural stagnation as the city becomes even a greater magnet and migration increases. But if agricultural development accompanies industrialization and conditions of rural life are improved, and if suitable industries are directed to regional urban centers, then a better balance can be achieved in the distribution of population, industry and employment.

As an illustration, he pointed to a newly developed town in the southeastern part of the country. In that forest region a furniture factory employing 250 workers was opened which produces for domestic consumption as well as for export. The town that sprang up there already has a high school, and can easily be converted into a regional center. The survey expert suggested the development of several more towns serving similar functions. One of them would be in the cattle raising district of northern Sierra Leone. Currently cattle must be brought south to Freetown for slaughtering, and have lost a quarter of their weight by the end of the nine-day hike; such weight-loss could be prevented by having a regional processing center in the north. In addition, the placement of educational facilities in such a center would make it unnecessary for students to go to Freetown for a high

---

15. See, B. Kaplan, New Settlement and Agricultural Development in Tanganyika, August, 1961. The Tanganyika National Union (TANU), a youth organization, has already started a _Moshav_ of its own in that area.

16. Reported in The New York Times, March 3, 1962.

school education. Another service town was proposed for the center of the country, with processing facilities for the iron ore mined there. Tanganyika provides an example of a reverse process, the creation of rural settlements around an existing urban center. The government is planning to use unemployed youth in Dar-es-Salaam to clear the area around the city, in return for relief payments. With simple tools, a few hundred families can eventually be settled in villages around the city at a very low cost.

Similarly, one school teacher from Sierra Leone, while on training in Israel, suggested the establishment of rural service centers in the midst of several villages which would provide health, cultural, and social facilities. Prominent among those would be a school with an agricultural orientation which could produce future cooperative farmers for the area.

It is noteworthy that such plans are likely to enjoy political support. The aforementioned Israeli planner was originally brought to Sierra Leone merely to prepare a master plan for Freetown. However, since the tribal chiefs were opposed to such a scheme as long as it was restricted to the capital city, his terms of reference were broadened to include the regional centers.

An undertaking of the sort proposed here is best performed within the framework of a comprehensive national plan. Such a plan, states the Sierra Leone Report must be constructed

> by a team of economists, sociologists, physical planners, educa-
> tors and politicians, and can best be constructed by a United Na-
> tions agency. There are deficiencies, shortcomings and ills in
> so many fields, and they must be treated all together. Treating
> one of them may only aggravate, and bring about increased diffi-
> culties in other fields.

Planning Institute

In an attempt to learn more about the potentials of rural planning, the National and Hebrew University Institute of Agriculture in Israel has formed a team for the comparative study of regional settlement that consists of a rural sociologist, an agricultural economist, a settlement specialist, an architect, and a specialist in agricultural organizations [17] The team is expected to make comparative studies of regional developments all over the world. Its intention is to arrive at general principles of land settlement techniques and regional development.

Another subject with which the team might beneficially concern itself is the need for, and the rationale of, land settlement. With over seventy years of settlement experience in her own country, Israel is uniquely qualified to provide advice in this field, but there is always a danger that

---

17. It would be helpful to add an African anthropologist to the team.

Israelis would draw too close a parallel between conditions in Israel and those in other countries, and be overly inclined to propose settlement projects. The work of the team may help clarify Israel's thinking on this matter. We turn now to a discussion of this and other issues raised by the settlement projects in Burma and Nigeria.

PURPOSES OF SETTLEMENT

Farm settlement is an expensive proposition. No matter how much economy is introduced, it is difficult to cut costs below £ 1,000 (= $2,800) per farm unit of around ten acres. And most projects cost substantially more. In Nigeria's eastern region, the settlement project received an allocation of £ 6 million out of the six-year development budget of £ 76 million, while in the western region a somewhat larger sum was allocated out of a £ 90 million budget. In both cases, over 8 percent of the total development budget is to be spent on settling a few thousand families. (a much higher percentage if resettlement is taken as a proportion of the allocation to agriculture). The question may well be asked whether such an expenditure is warranted and what purpose it would serve.

Special Cases

In some cases settlement is justified on other than purely economic grounds. In Burma, it resulted from a need to discharge a large number of regular army personnel. The military authorities did not wish to relinquish responsibility for the servicemen after their discharge, partly for fear they might join rebel groups. At the same time, they wanted to fill with "loyal" troops a sparsely populated area in the Shan State which is somewhat hostile to the central government. Hence followed the decision to make farmers out of veterans of fifteen years' military service. The decision was based on security grounds, and the Namsang project is financed out of the defense budget. Indeed, it was Israel's experience with the soldier-farmer combination (see Chapter 7) as well as the composite village structure, that induced the Burmese to seek Israeli assistance.

Special reasons may arise under other circumstances. In Ghana, for example, the Volta river project is expected to flood 110 villages, making it necessary to resettle the displaced farmers elsewhere. Mali needs to settle workers who returned from Senegal after the separation between the two states.

In such cases, land settlement is a by-product of other political or economic measures. Its own merits require no justification on general economic grounds. Once the decision is taken to embark on a settlement project, it might as well be executed with the best social and economic tools available, and Israel's composite village structure is certainly one of them.

Rural Progress

Barring such unusual circumstances, the justification must be couched in terms of the project's expected contribution to national economic progress, relative to the contribution of alternative investments. The support for African resettlement comes first from farm experts who believe that, regardless of efforts, very little can be done for the African farmer within the present village framework. Existing conditions in the villages simply give very little reason for hope. The following description of these conditions pertains to Nigeria, but applies equally well to most other parts of Africa:

> Very few large-scale farms are to be found. Those that exist are operated mainly for the production of export crops by overseas firms or public corporations. Most of the farmers in the region are peasants who give priority to the production of food crops mainly for the needs of the family on holdings that are small, fragmented and scattered. For the majority of farmers cash crop production is still subsidiary to the production of the basic food needs of the family and these cash crops are also produced on small fragmented holdings originally cleared for food production and subsequently planted with cash crops. Their implements are of primitive design and construction; they practice shifting cultivation, and their business is unorganized and under-capitalized. Consequently production per head and per acre is low. Although some animals are kept, they are not integrated into the farming organization and their manure is not used for increasing fertility; nor are cattle used for draught purposes.

> While good facilities exist for the marketing of the major export crops, the storage, distribution and marketing of food crops leave much to be desired and discourage many farmers from producing in excess of their immediate needs. The inadequacy of these facilities also results in high costs of distribution and low returns to the farmer as well as large seasonal fluctuations in the prices of basic foods. This agricultural pattern is uneconomic and normally provides only a low standard of living.[18]

A change in this picture appears impossible. Illiteracy makes it difficult to teach new techniques, poverty prevents investments in new facilities, and a land tenure system which does not establish legal land boundaries and security of tenure deprives the farmer of an asset against which to raise loans and gives him no incentive to invest in long-term improvements. Add to this a variety of social and economic prejudices,[19]

---

18. Farm Settlement, op. cit., pp. 1 − 2.

19. In Tanganyika, for example, the prestige of cattle growers is determined by the number of heads. Therefore people graze for sheer number and not for quality.

and there emerges a picture of farming as an occupation associated with illiteracy, low income, heavy manual labor, and lack of social amenities. The vicious circle can be broken only by starting anew. Improved skills and habits can be learned and new organization provided only under controlled and carefully supervised settlement conditions. In addition, there is urgent need to bring more arable land under cultivation, and to relieve population pressures in certain areas.

Not only is this a powerful argument, but examples can be cited to show that important objectives can be attained through settlement. In the Sudanese Republic of West Africa, the French Office du Niger settled (until 1958), 30,000 people on 100,000 acres of land at a cost of 100 million dollars. Using "European-improved African methods" of production, but supported by large-scale mechanized techniques employed by the central office, the settlers have been able to earn $200 per person annually. In Tanganyika 30,000 people moved from overpopulated to underpopulated areas with government support and guidance. In the Congo the Belgians instituted a successful resettlement scheme coupled with community development programs. As a result, not only have settlers netted $400 a year (compared to $10 earned before in subsistence agriculture, and $200 on plantations), but their whole outlook has been transformed. The backward, lethargic, and undernourished inhabitants, producing nothing but their own necessities and living under conditions that had not changed for generations, are now industrious people, proud of their achievement. They have effected an economic and social revolution.[20]

But these success stories can be countered with equally impressive failures. Kimble, after discussing several unsuccessful projects in Ghana, Nigeria, and Tanganyika, offers the following as common reasons for failures: the lack of information on which to base settlement plans; the need for rural pioneering work before a scheme can be instituted, the reluctance of Africans to migrate and sever ties with their extended family, and (often) the insufficiency of material improvement as an inducement for Africans to undertake the hardship called for in the scheme.[21] Successful projects have been those in which careful groundwork was laid before settlement, and in which the "human material" was appropriate. To cope with the incentives problem, one observer suggested that the best people for settlement were those who had been exposed to higher living standards in the past. In the Tanganyika survey mentioned above, the Kilombaro valley was selected because the coffee growers in the area had been well off during the war when prices

---

20. For a detailed discussion, see Kimble, Tropical Africa, Vol. I, Chapter 5 and Vol. II, pp. 193—194.

21. Ibid., Chapter 5.

were high. Since then they had to lower their standard of living because of
a drop in the world's price for their main cash crop. Likewise, the Gurkha
soldiers in Nepal are considered by an FAO official excellent candidates
for settlement because "they are all literate, disciplined, and have been
around. They also want to be settled and will be receptive to new methods."

But even when the conditions for success do exist, the question of cost
looms important. The successful plan of the Office du Niger cost up to
$10,000 per ten-acre farm unit, and could not have been executed without a
large infusion of foreign capital. Projects costing millions of pounds cannot
be evaluated on their own merits. They must be fitted into a national development plan, and their merits weighed against other alternatives. All too
often this is not done. The Israeli experts who proposed settlement in
Eastern Nigeria, for example, did not even bother to interview officials at
the Ministry of Economic Planning. And this kind of oversight is more a
rule than an exception. (Partly this is because settlement projects are proposed, and their contributions assessed, by agricultural experts rather than
economists.) As a general proposition, resettlement cannot be considered
a solution to African rural problems (although it can be used to effect a
rapid expansion in the production of cash crops), and can hardly constitute
a "new deal for the African farmer." It would be simply prohibitive to resettle even a small portion of the farmers in Africa.

School Leaver's Problem

High costs have resulted in some retreat from another lofty purpose,
the settlement of school leavers. The advent of compulsory education in
Western Nigeria has increased the number of "standard six" school graduates from 70,000 in 1954 to 180,000 in 1960. Having been exposed to a few
years of schooling, the youngster becomes disenchanted with the drudgery,
rigor, and monotony of rural life, with the village devoid of all amenities,
and with the annual income of $50 which traditional farming offers him. His
fellow villagers would consider him a failure if he returned to the farm.
Barely literate, technically untrained, he drifts to the city in search of
amusements and a white-collar job:

> An office employee even of the lowest grade (the primary school
> leaver) earns at least £ 6 (=$16.80) a month and sees no prospect
> of earning even half as much if he takes to farming. Often he is
> scared by the continued use of old fashioned farm tools and by the
> drudgery typical of traditional farming methods. His assessment of
> farming prospects derives, of course, from what he sees either of
> his farmer parents or relatives, or of the farming peasantry in gen-
> eral in his village community. This young man's conception of a
> farmer's life is that of an occupation that is arduous, menial, and
> at the same time unremunerative. Quite apart from the effects of
> this concept that farming does not pay, difficulties created by our

land tenure system and by the almost complete absence of any credit facilities, constitute additional grave obstacles in the way of the young school leaver entering upon a commercial farming venture.[22]

Because government offices cannot absorb all the school leavers, and industrialization is not proceeding fast enough to offer sufficient blue-collar jobs, the school leavers join the ranks of the unemployed and some-times the delinquent. By 1967 there may be 500,000 unemployed school-leavers in the eastern region, and 700,000 in the west.[23] Since the problem is quite common on the African continent, severe social and economic pressures are created in most urban areas. In underdeveloped countries, investments in literary education may quite often produce harmful rather than beneficial results.

In Western Nigeria it was the original intent of Chief Deko to arrest the flow of young people to the towns by settling them in newly formed Moshavim, where amenities would be provided, modern methods employed, and income would be several times as high as in subsistence agriculture. Only the offer of lucrative farming will induce them to stay in the rural areas. Chief Deko was impressed by Israel's success in introducing primitive people to modern farming and in attracting professional and technical personnel to the rural districts. He was therefore intent on adapting the system which produced these results. But where will the resources be obtained to settle hundreds of thousands of school leavers over a reasonable period of time?

Opponents of the settlement concept suggest that, instead of concen-trating large sums of money on a few selected thousands, financial resources should be spread more evenly among the rural population. Thickening the extension network, for example, is an alternative expounded by many officials and foreign advisors in Africa. That approach could be supplemented by more intensive but reasonably cheap projects, such as the palm groves rehabilitation scheme in Eastern Nigeria. It calls for a £1.9 million in-vestment to replace wild palm with new seedlings, with approximate tripling of yields. Coupled with it is a subsidy to farmers who agree to consolidate their land holdings. About 20,000 people would be affected by this plan, at a cost of below £200 to £300 ($560-$840) per farm unit. Another such possibility is the nucleus plantation idea, which calls for the development of a publicly or privately owned plantation, to be used for educating "satellite farmers" and supplying them with seedlings.

Demonstration

When cost considerations are given their full weight, there is little

---

22. Future Policy of the Ministry of Agriculture and Natural Resources, op. cit., p. 9.

23. "Nigeria Works It Out," The Economist, London, July 7, 1962, p. 44.

doubt that rural progress will for the most part have to proceed within existing villages. What then is the function of new settlements? In addition to efficient production of farm crops, their modified purpose, as offered by their proponents in Nigeria and Tanganyika, becomes experimentation and demonstration. In the words of one settlement expert, "In new areas, somewhat removed from traditional patterns, people are more willing to adapt themselves to new methods of production." The planner can try out new crops, and examine the settlers' reactions to social organization and improved techniques. If successful, these can be later introduced elsewhere. The second objective is to demonstrate that farming can be a lucrative, efficient, and attractive occupation, and that village life does not have to be devoid of social amenities. The settlements can thereby be regarded as "models for others to copy" and serve as "another extension method with a view to accelerating agricultural development." [24] The following quotations will serve to illustrate the values attached to this objective:

> Demonstrations on Government farms rarely appeal to the farmer; the results being often attributed to some special factor provided by Government which is beyond the reach of the ordinary farmer. Under the proposed scheme the farmer himself will, under direction, be applying new techniques to his own plot of land. All aspects of the experiment will, as it were, be known and open to him. He will thus be trying out and verifying for himself the effects of the new techniques. He will no longer attribute the success to hidden factors or to causes beyond his means. As a result, gossip, interest and enthusiasm regarding these new techniques that have yielded so much success will spread from the cooperative farm settlements to neighboring private farms. This aspect of the cooperative farming scheme will in itself be a revolution in agricultural methods.[25]

> Previously in Western Nigeria, the demonstrations by the Agricultural Extension Services section of the Ministry of Agriculture had little effect on the illiterate farmers who thought there was some magic about the Government farms which they could never capture. Now, with the settlers drawn from neighboring villages keeping in constant touch with their parents' villages, it is easy to show that no magic is involved, but science.[26]

There is strong support for this point of view in many quarters. One FAO official said; "I used to believe in a gradual uplifting of existing

---

24. Future Policy of the Ministry of Agriculture and Natural Resources, Ibadan, Western Nigeria, p. 5

25. Ibid.

26. Nigeria Trade Journal, January/ March, 1962.

agriculture. Now I have shifted to Akin Deko's approach of a complete
break from subsistence agriculture for some farmers." In the same vein the
eastern Nigerian Minister of Agriculture feels that this is the only way to
change farmers' attitudes, the social system and rules of land tenure, thereby
attaining a more rational production system. The first demonstrative impact
would be on the surrounding villages whose population has been thinned
out by the resettlement of some of their farmers. From there it would spread
to other areas. The Minister also feels that only a breakout from the subsistence system would make possible repayment of the investment loan.
This achieved, a revolving fund can be created over a period of several
years which would continue to serve the settlement purpose.

Most Nigerian extension officers support the resettlement scheme as an
excellent teaching device. Extension has not been successful so far, partly
because agricultural officers engage in services (such as supplying
seedlings) rather than in education, but mainly because farmers are not
receptive to the methods proposed. "No alternative other than settlement
has been proposed so far," said one of these officers. "The settlement
program got the villagers excited. They all want new Moshavim nearby, and
the scheme served well to pull farmers out of their traditional apathy. Its
demonstration effect will make farmers receptive to expert advice." In reply
to the American advisers who claim that extension was not given a proper
chance and that the settlement project will deprive extension of finances,
they point out that exactly the opposite has been true. Prior to the advent of
new settlements the government was getting weary of agricultural progress,
and shifted emphasis to industrial development. The settlement project has
brought a change in that attitude by providing a political showpiece in
agriculture. It has given the politician something tangible to show, not
unlike an industrial complex, when election time approached. The imper-
ceptible annual increase in agricultural production in existing villages has
little appeal to the voter. By contrast, a modern settlement complex, based
on the composite structure, is a visible achievement that can be used to get
votes. Consequently it has made more rather than less money available to
agriculture, and to the extension service in the process.

But not everyone believes in the demonstration effect. "What farmer
will attempt to emulate the settler whose farm was built with £ 3,000 (=$8,400)
of government capital?" asks one economist. Along the same lines, the
FAO African Survey wrote:

> In Nigeria the desire for a rural transformation has led to ambi-
> tious settlement schemes, in which the farmers receive education,
> training and material help (in the shape of regular wages for work
> performed in the initial period) to enable them to raise their output
> (partly mechanized) toward a goal of £ 500 p.a., against a national
> average of less than £ 50 per farming unit. The cost of these

schemes, £ 3,000((nearly $9,000) per family unit, could no doubt
be reduced. But even at a fraction of the cost such schemes would
be self-defeating in a country where the population is growing at
the rate of some 800,000 – 1,000,000 per annum, and with a per
caput national income of at most £ 30 per annum. The demonstration effect is also very limited, since no ordinary farmer would
have the capital to emulate the example of the settlers. The experiment is therefore liable to create a new small privileged class,
the reverse of what was intended, though it is early to reach a
final conclusion.[27]

Chief Deko himself disputes this contention and feels that the high
costs are justifiable. He views "the Farm Settlement challenge as the
spearhead of a possible agrarian revolution, which, like any other revolution,
might warrant a drastic departure from existing order." When asked to
economize on housing costs he replied that "if, in order to encourage a
housing settler in our Housing Settlement in towns, Government could
support loans of up to £ 4,000 ($11,200) to an individual who promises the
nation no real economic return for the loan, it will be difficult to justify
Government turning its back on a Farm Settler who demands no greater
financial assistance for a project whose economic potentiality for the nation
is tremendous."

Although these points have merit,[28] and while economics must sometimes be tempered with vision, it is certainly reasonable to assume that the
demonstration effect would be more striking the lower the cost and the less
drastic the departure from existing practices. Indeed, the FAO planners in
the western region have been able to lower costs from the original estimates,
in part by reducing housing costs from £ 550 to £ 350. In Figure 4.1 costs
per unit are shown to be below £ 2,000 – and further slashes may still be
possible.

Most Nigerians who are concerned with the farm economy believe that
there will be a strong demonstration effect on established farmers as well
as on school leavers, and that the settlement project is an excellent extension device. While agreement on this point is not unanimous, it is sufficiently widespread to warrant the attempt.

Viewed in this light, the settlements should be located in the heart of
a populated area. That indeed is what the Nigerian plans call for. They
also stipulate that settlers should be from villages in the immediate vicinity.
In the western region, the idea is to purchase communal land from the
peripheries of a few neighboring villages, and establish the new settlement

_____

27. FAO African Survey, Rome, 1960, p. 94.

28. They may of course simply reflect misallocation of resources in
the urban sector.

in their midst. From here demonstration can radiate to the "satellite" villages. In the eastern region each settlement requires more land, as it consists of a block of villages. Because free land in populated areas is scarce, the number of such blocks may be reduced from the six contemplated at present. That would be all to the good. For demonstration purposes there is no need for more than two or three settlements scattered throughout the region (the same applies to the number of settlements in the western region). On the other hand, it would be desirable for the nuclear village to contain a school with demonstration plots which could be used for instructing not only the settlers, but also selected farmers from the surrounding old villages. The latter can be brought in for short courses in specific subjects (e.g., the use of fertilizers), taught in the light of the settlers' experience. At the same time the visitors can be introduced to the social organization of the Moshav. Upon their return home, these farmers should be visited by extension officers and their farms made a "living example" for the village. The settlement project will have achieved its purpose only if it is used to inculcate new methods and social organization into the general rural population.

TRAINING OF SETTLERS

In Burma (as may be the case in Nepal) the settlers were ex-servicemen who knew nothing about agriculture. In Western Nigeria most settlers were young school leavers whose exposure to agriculture was confined to what they had seen in their parents' villages — which is exactly what they would like to escape. In the eastern region settlers were to be drawn from the ranks of experienced farmers assisted by school leavers, and even they were unfamiliar with modern farming methods. In all three instances, few of the settlers knew much about the Moshav organization or the composite structure which they were expected to form. They all had to be trained if the experiment was to succeed.

Burma

Burma elected to send the first groups of servicemen who volunteered for settlement, along with their families, for one year's work and training on an Israeli Moshav. Two consecutive contingents of men, women, and children, numbering 53 and 103 respectively, underwent such training and gained first-hand experience in modern agriculture and cooperative organization. While the private soldiers worked in various branches of agriculture, officers were assigned to specialized six-month courses in the following fields: planning of settlement, management of farms, bookkeeping, cooperative purchases and sales, organization of work, agricultural norms and statistics, and preparation of budgets. The children went to school, and learned

Hebrew in the process. Women utilized their time in learning home economics, first aid, hygiene, kindergarten education, poultry, gardening, and cultural and welfare activity.

Training for these and other settlers continued on the settlement site in the form of intensive extension work guided by Burmese specialists and the Israeli advisory team. It consisted of weekly visits by officers to farmers, evening lessons, study days before the sowing season, visits to the best plots in the village with the owners explaining management practices, and inducements in the form of prizes for high crop yields.

Another device used for both experimentation and extension has been central experiment plots. These consisted of 72 acres in which thirteen different crops were grown, employing the same techniques as those used by the settlers. Although a wealth of agricultural data had been accumulated by the Israeli advisers who had worked in the area prior to the settlement project, additional experimentation was deemed necessary. The central plots were used for experimenting with new crops, checking the amount of labor needed for each crop, trying different methods of tillage, employing various tools and dates of sowing, applying fertilizers and insecticides, and the like. But unlike the procedure at an ordinary experiment station, these were carried out under actual, not laboratory, conditions. Continuous visits to the plots, and seasonal short courses around them, served to illustrate to the farmers what they could achieve with their own tools.

Subsequent experience has shown that while the intensive instruction on the spot paid off, the training of the Burmese soldiers in Israel was a failure. The performance of those trained in Israel, measured by work methods as well as yields, was no better than that of other settlers. The concensus is that it would have been better to send to Israel only qualified key personnel for specialized training.

Western Nigeria

In Western Nigeria, the training takes place in five Farm Institutes set up especially for that purpose. They cost one million pounds to build and operate for the first five years. Each occupies 600 to 1,000 acres and can accommodate 200 students. The two-year curriculum includes lectures and demonstrations in general agricultural science, the study of animal husbandry and of crops grown in the district, farm management and general subjects. Modelled as cooperative farm settlements, the Insititutes also inculcate the principles of cooperative organization and attempt to build a community spirit among the students.

After their Institute training, settlers spend their first two years on the settlement site, living, working, and training communally. They are paid a subsistence wage. During the following three to five years, they are gradually allocated their land holdings, and are allowed to bring their wives to the farms. They still continue to draw monthly allowances. Only in the subsequent stage, when the farms come into full production, do settlers become independent and begin repaying their loan to the government. A thick network of extension staff is used through the intermediate stages. Each group of fifty settlers is served by one agricultural superintendent, three agricultural assistants, and thirteen field overseers. By contrast, the permanent staff in each village will consist of one agricultural assistant and two field overseers.

An Israeli farm planner who was invited to survey the scheme[29] after it had already been launched, proposed the training of a large number of settlers in Israel, patterned after the Burmese experience. His recommendation was strongly opposed by most Nigerian officials. The two agronomists from the region who attended the course in rural planning in Israel noted:

> The settlements in Israel are very well developed indeed. What a visiting group of settlers from our region will see (and we know them so well) are the beautiful buildings with water, closet, re-frigerator, gas stoves and the multifarious amenities enjoyed by these settlers. When they come back home, the Ministry of Agri-culture will certainly face series of petitions and agitations from those boys (we had some in the past). If the settlements have been enjoying some level of success on their holdings and can see a clear picture of what the future holds for rewarding their efforts, one may consider the possibility of sending some representatives from each settlement to see agriculture in Israel. At present, there can be no benefit to settlers or Government if the boys are sent to Israel.

In the same vein, Chief Deko insisted: "You would send your best settlers and upon return they would cease to serve as an example because the others would say 'give us the same opportunity and we will do the same'."

Add to this the expense involved, and the failure of the Burmese experiment, and the case against training farmers abroad becomes very strong indeed. On the other hand, the Nigerian Ministry of Agriculture decided to send several agronomists to Israel for a four-month training course in agricultural techniques and cooperative organization. At the same time, a few Israelis may be brought to Western Nigeria to live and work closely with the settlers on both cooperative and farm organization.

Eastern Nigeria

In the eastern region, where the settlers are mainly experienced farmers, training will be offered right on the site. After the initial bush clearing, to be done partly by machines, the farms will be allocated to the settlers. Because the land is procured and the settlers recruited from the surrounding

---

29. See Kedem, Some Problems of Cooperative Settlements in Western Nigeria, January, 1960.

villages, it is expected that free labor from the settlers' families will be available during the clearing stage. Once settled, the training will be done mainly through a thick extension network, and the agricultural school at Umudike has embarked on a crash expansion program to supply the necessary staff. Each settlement of six villages is to be served by the following staff: one agricultural officer who will serve as estate manager, an agricultural superintendent as assistant estate manager, one agricultural engineer, one mechanical demonstrator, one poultry officer, six agricultural superintendents, twelve agricultural assistants, and twenty-four field overseers. An extended training of cooperative secretaries is also contemplated. Thus the emphasis in the eastern region is on quick introduction of the settlers to their holdings in order to reduce costs and cut down the transition period. One feature of the Burmese program that could be borrowed by the eastern region is the use of experimental plots at the settlement nucleus. These could be used first to instruct the settlers, and then for demonstration purposes to farmers from the surrounding villages.

SOCIAL AND ECONOMIC ADJUSTMENTS

A common feature of all three settlement projects is their adoption of the Moshav system. The problems of adjustment to a new social organization will have to be solved on an ad hoc basis. Observe, for example, the role of women who, in traditional African society, are entrusted with the marketing function. Even women who are not petty traders like the idea of an independent income. In a Moshav the woman is expected to assist her husband on the farm and the marketing is performed by a multi-purpose cooperative, which leaves no place for the independent tradesman. Wives of the settlers will have to be reoriented toward the performance of new roles, but the planners must make the adjustment as easy as possible. This is one reason why the head of the FAO team in the western region, despite his own collective background, resisted the government plan for cooperatively owned poultry (and perhaps other livestock). Under his scheme the wife would take charge of the family poultry farm and derive from it independent income. This flexible pragmatic approach is indeed reminiscent of the treatment of new immigrants in Israel. A similar decision was made in the case of cocoa processing:

> Weighing the various advantages and disadvantages of the two systems of fermenting and drying on a central and cooperative basis and on an individual basis, the balance of advantages is in favor of individual fermenting and drying. The latter provides scope for employment of family labor especially of women and children as the tasks involved do not call for hard labor. It also avoids any trouble over weight or quality of produce which may

prove difficult to manage in a Central System.[30]

Another problem of adjustment is the level of the settlers' income that should be aimed at. It is generally agreed that settlers should make a complete break from subsistence agriculture, that farming should be made sufficiently lucrative to repay the government loan and still provide for reasonably comfortable living. But several reasons militate against making the income "too high." First, it should not be sufficient to permit extensive use of hired labor. "Every effort should be made to prevent the emergence of two classes: the high-income farmer and large underpaid labor force."[31] Second, cash income must be kept low enough to prevent relatives from moving in with the settlers (in accordance with African tradition) and thereby nullifying the gain in the farmers' standard of living. One competent observer of the African scene suggested that family ties are not breaking fast enough, and that the proximity of the settlements to the villages from which the settlers came makes it predictable that relatives will join the settlements. To counteract this, part of the settler's income would have to be distributed in the form of improved social services — namely, in kind rather than in cash. At the same time, small-scale industries may have to be built on the site, to employ those relatives who do move in.

A related issue concerns the use of farm machinery. In all cases machinery is used for the initial clearing of the land, But many experts argue in favor of "improved traditional methods" of tillage in subsequent stages. The shortage of maintenance crews and the intensified demonstration effect are the reasons commonly advanced. In Burma the use of a locally-made plow with bullocks is advocated. (This practice met with resistance from the settlers, who felt that the Israelis were unwilling to pass on to them all the knowledge at their disposal.) Similar methods can be employed in areas of Africa that are not infected by the Tsetse fly. In general a balance must be struck between the need to break out of subsistence agriculture on the one hand, and the desirability of not making the break too drastic on the other.

Finally, a common subject of concern in settlement projects is the settlers' dependence on the government. Immigrants to Israel are usually brought in by the central authorities, and are dependent on the government even before they are settled. In Burma, where the army settles ex-servicemen, the situation is not very different. But in the Nigerian and most other cases, settlement projects involve the transfer of established farmers to new areas. Once transferred they are prone to blame most of their mishaps (including bad weather) on the government, and expect it to bail them out. This is

---

30. FAO team (Ibadan), Crop Studies, — Cocoa, p. 4.

31. Kedem, op. cit.

one reason why governments supervise such projects closely. But, even so, the settlement authority must not inculcate a feeling of dependence into the farmers. The head of the FAO team in Ibadan states:

> Every provision should be made to prevent the scheme from becoming an enterprise run by government for a few selected and lucky farmers. These settlements must be erected and developed by the settlers with all the hardships and difficulties to be encountered. Government should only advise, direct and help out but never do the job itself. Only then will this settlement be successful as a proving grounds and living demonstration for the farmers in the region.

Upon arrival at the scene, the head of the FAO team in the western region found the settlement plans in a fairly complete form. His attempts to introduce changes were sometimes frustrated and always difficult. "It would have been easier to start from scratch," he stated. Among the features he considered objectionable were the Farm Institutes, the long transitional period until holdings are allocated to settlers, the large number of settlements, and the rejection of the composite structure concept. He lauded the eastern region's project for not restricting the settlement to school leavers, for the immediate allocation of farm holdings, for the construction of homes by the settlers themselves, and for other "do it yourself" measures which minimize dependence on the government. "The early allocation of land," he claimed "would establish a firmer relation between the settler and his farm."

Another element in the western region scheme which concerned him was the payment of daily wages to the prospective settlers regardless of performance. Contrary to the views held by some Nigerian and FAO officials, he felt that the system did not contain sufficient incentives to work hard. By contrast, "a piecework pay scheme would encourage more and better work, show the settlers that work is rewarded, reduce expenses, and make possible the exclusion from the scheme of those unwilling to work." It required considerable efforts on his part to change the system.

PROSPECTS

It is too early to assess the success of the ventures discussed here, and it is certainly early to say much about their demonstrative effect. Yet some indication of future performance can be offered.

In Burma the settlers are still in uniform, and the project is managed by the army command. Its outcome appears to depend on a few central issues. The first is the extent of future government support. Because of changes in the army recruitment policies, there has been a reduction in the pressure to settle ex-servicemen. And since settlement serves no important economic or social purpose, support for it may decline in the future. In its favor are the security objectives involved in populating the Namsang region, the impressive beginning made in the past two years, and the prestige value attached to the project.   The authorities can ill afford to let the project taper off now. Full backing would mean, in addition to financial and moral support, the relegation of more independent decision-making authority to the local commander than is usually allowed under army procedures.

Second, proper counterparts must be found to replace the Israeli planners and technicians. In addition to being technically competent, such men must be willing to take initiative and assume responsibility without fear of making mistakes. Possibly additional training in Israel for key personnel would help. The third problem is that of transport facilities to connect the region with the main markets in the country. Completion of processing mills in the Namsang town with the products leaving the area in semi-processed form, would help considerably in that respect.

Finally, and most important, looms the problem of inducing the settlers to work hard and remain in the area. There is some indication that many of them volunteered for settlement only to obtain early release from military service, and that they would leave the area once they gained their objective. Only the provision of lucrative farming and social amenities in the region could prevent such a regrettable outcome. With the solid foundation laid by the Israeli team in the initial stage, the project's success appears to depend on the willingness of the Burmese authorities to push vigorously ahead. Once fifteen flourishing Moshavim and a prosperous town are in existence, the settlers' identification with the project and their incentive to keep advancing it will undoubtedly grow.

In both regions of Nigeria the inauguration of the settlement program was marked by public enthusiasm. By 1961, 100,000 acres had been acquired in the western region, and there was no shortage of applicants. Chief Deko stated:

> Perhaps the most significant achievement of the settlement idea is the general awakening in the agricultural life of the nation which it has indisputably provoked. Farming is fast assuming a new status in all the Regions. Already the eastern region wants to imitate, and the project has had repercussions all over West Africa.

As indicated in a previous section, the eastern region's scheme seems to have been better planned in several respects. The adoption of a composite structure rather than scattered settlements makes possible production on a larger scale, and facilitates the provision of amenities, instruction, and demonstration at the rural center. Even electricity and movies can be more readily provided in the nucleus. Reliance on experienced farmers and the

---

32. The scheme has become something of a showpiece for several Southeast Asian countries.

shortening of the transitional period are useful in preventing excessive dependence on government support. The planners in the east have the advantage of being able to learn from the mistakes of their western counter-parts, and it is to the credit of both that there is a constant exchange of views.

But final success in both regions will depend not only on continuous government backing and proper incentives among the settlers; it will also revolve around the integration of the projects into the national economy. If substantial increases in tree crops are to be forthcoming, their possible effect on market prices must be determined in advance; this is true also of the integration of the new cooperatives into the national marketing system. If the plan is to be demonstrational, it must be linked to the national extension service. Furthermore, the extension agent should know how to advise farmers who, after studying in the nuclear center, are sufficiently impressed to want to emulate the new system, and at least in the surrounding villages communal land should be demarcated in advance and its possible uses discussed with the farmers.

While resettlement cannot be considered a panacea for all of Africa's rural problems, it can serve certain useful purposes. In some areas it may help solve specific problems, but in most countries its main value lies in experimental application of new methods and demonstration. If necessary conditions for success exist, Israel's experience with cooperative agriculture and regional planning, coupled with her flexible approach to social problems, can serve as a very useful guide.

Recognizing, however, that large-scale settlement is beyond the means of most African countries, Israel's policy in this area of technical cooperation has shifted toward smaller projects. Settlement on a small demonstrative scale is part of an agricultural training school to be set up in the Upper Volta and of Israel's work with youth organizations in several countries. These projects will be dealt with in Chapters 5 and 7 respectively.

CHAPTER 5 AGRICULTURAL
TRAINING

TRAINING IN ISRAEL

If rural development in Africa is to proceed mainly through the gradual modernization of indigenous agriculture, then the training of officers on the intermediate level is of primary importance. A large number of agricultural extensionists is needed to ensure that the knowledge accumlated in Africa's first-rate research institutes reaches the farmers. Many observers consider the shortage of such officials to be one of the most serious factors limiting agricultural progress. This, indeed, is one reason for the emphasis the Israeli program places on extension work. At least a fifth of the Africans trained in Israel in 1961 were in the field of agriculture. The program, administered through a special department for foreign training in Israel's extension service, included seven courses on agricultural extension, irrigation techniques, poultry, and farm mechanization. These were to be repeated in 1962, along with courses on cattle husbandry and citrus growing, all to be taught in both English and French, with the possible addition of Spanish in 1963 to accomodate trainees from Latin America.

The agricultural instruction program in Israel was inaugurated in August of 1960 with a ten-month course for twenty-two trainees from Liberia and Sierra Leone under the auspices of the foreign ministry. A few months later the foreign training department was organized within the Extension Service, and took over all training activity in agriculture. The course was organized in response to a recommendation by a highly placed Israeli agronomist who has made a survey of the two countries. Its aim was to provide general training in agriculture and some specialized knowledge in one selected branch. The course opened with a three-week introductory session at the Ruppin Institute, an agricultural training center in the heart of Israel's farm area. It serves as a base for all foreign agricultural training activities, and all "theoretical" lectures are offered there. The trainees were then dispersed throughout northern Israel for eight months of work and study on the settlements. The remaining period was spent in summary sessions which included the study of village and regional planning.

This was one of the longest courses in the field. Most others ranged from four to six months and were devoted either to general agriculture or to a specific branch.

1961 Courses in Agriculture

Subject	Countries Represented	No. of Trainees	Duration Of Course	Language Of Instruction
General Agriculture	Liberia and Sierra Leone	22	10 months	English
Agricultural Instruction	Ethiopia	20	5 months	English
General Agriculture	Congo	10	6 months	French
Irrigation Techniques	Asia and Africa	25	4 months	English
Irrigation Engineers	12 countries	19	6 weeks	English
Agricultural Instruction	East Africa	19	4 months	English
Poultry Rearing	Ghana and Nigeria	17	5 months	English
Poultry Rearing	Ghana, Sierra Leone, India, Cyprus, Laos, Persia	14	5 months	English
General Agriculture	Central African Republic	25	10 months	French

Most courses consisted of four or more parts. The first and third phases were usually theoretical studies at Ruppin, while the second and fourth ones involved practical work combined with observations on the agricultural settlements. In addition to affording experience in a chosen branch, the practical work period offers an opportunity to observe at first hand the structure and operation of Israel's rural cooperatives. At least some of the trainees in each course remain for a further period of specialized work following the regular session. Appendix III, which contains the programs of three of the courses, shows that about two-thirds of the time is usually devoted to the practical work.

Although the short courses constitute the bulk of the training in agriculture, a few students get individual training. Thus an official from Mali was attached to an agricultural experiment station for a year to study citrus growing, and several students from Thailand, under USOM sponsorship, underwent special training in irrigation methods. Likewise several Africans are enrolled in the graduate and undergraduate programs at the Agricultural Faculty of the Hebrew University. Since the biggest impediment to academic studies in Israel is the need to learn Hebrew, a language of very limited scientific usefulness, the institutes of higher learning plan to offer courses in English and French that are especially tailored to the needs of developing countries.

One such offering, a four-year course, in English, leading to a BSC in agricultural engineering, was inaugurated in November, 1962, at the Technical College (Technion) in Haifa.[1] The program is reproduced in Appendix IV. African students receive individual guidance from Israeli graduate students assigned to them. They also learn elementary Hebrew so as to be able to communicate with all strata of the local population. In the summers students will be given an opportunity to engage in practical employment. It is expected that a few of the professors teaching in the course will visit Africa to familiarize themselves with the problems which their students are likely to face upon their return home.

ELEMENTS OF STRENGTH

Despite a variety of problems which will be discussed in the next section, this program has been widely praised for its effectiveness. On numerous occasions senior African officials expressed their preference for Israel over Europe as a training ground for their juniors. F AO officials, familiar with training facilities the world over, have voiced similar views.

Such commendations arise for three main reasons. First, the courses are well staffed and managed. Each group of up to twenty trainees has a professional and a social guide, and is rarely left without supervision. The instruction program is carefully tailored to the needs of the students, and painstaking efforts are made to meet their social requirements. With few exceptions, the instructors are competent and dedicated. The principle of teaching by example extends all the way to the man in charge of the program. His active participation and willingness to lend a helping hand often drew the admiration of students. "In my country a department head in government service would never dirty his hands like this one," is a statement made by a trainee and echoed by many others.

Secondly, not only are most courses well structured, but they are being

---

1. The first time the course was given it contained thirty students from twelve countries in Asia, Africa, Cyprus and the West Indies. They lodged at the Student's Hostel, each sharing a room with an Israeli. (The Jerusalem Post Weekly, November 30, 1962.

continuously improved as more experience is gathered. The theoretical and practical parts are usually well integrated, with each phase based on knowledge acquired earlier. Great emphasis is placed on practical work, and as a general rule classroom instruction explains what has already been seen or felt. This minimizes the need for abstract thinking, in which most African trainees are rather weak.

Considerable importance attaches to the requirement of actual work on the farm. As a rule, when Africans return from courses abroad they feel prepared to be bosses or administrators, or at best to teach others to till the soil. They almost invariably shun physical labor, considering themselves above it. Israel's emphasis on practical work changes this attitude at least in part. In one case where two Africans, one trained in Israel and the other in Britain, were employed on the same project, their difference in attitude toward manual work was so apparent that the latter had to be discharged. An American expert in another African country who had sent a trainee to the poultry course in Israel, said: "He came back full of energy and know-how and became very alert to situations regarding management practices on the farm." In the words of a senior agricultural officer in Kenya who had sent some of his underlings to be trained in Israel:

> The students sent to date have been mostly Africans of mature field experience, but limited educational background, for whom the most instructive and practical courses are particularly suitable. No other country caters so well to this type of trainee. Those who have been sent have returned with a marked enthusiasm and a belief that great difficulties of climate and physical conditions can be overcome by hard work, 'know-how' and united effort.....The general ecological conditions in Israel are to a large extent comparable to those obtaining in much of Kenya.....The short courses for Africans at a low educational level, as mentioned before, are excellent, and we would welcome any opportunity to make greater use of the facilities offered.

In a similar vein an FAO official said: "The courses in Israel are excellent because they are practical and able to document points under conditions similar to Africa. They do not give you arguments and counter-arguments, but go right to the main point and demonstrate its practicality. With the exception of Norway, most European institutions are more similar to universities." And an Israeli agronomist remarked, "Our strength is in translating theoretical knowledge to practice. We can help solve practical problems in planning, extension, settlement and certain agricultural branches. Theoretical knowledge can be acquired more easily elsewhere."

Thirdly, Israel itself has important advantages as a training ground. Her agricultural development since independence has been at a rate and of a quality that many African countries hope to match. During the decade ending in 1958, the output of various products in Israel increased from two to five times, and in industrial crops it jumped thirty-eight times. While it is unlikely that other countries can attain such a rapid rate of growth, the knowledge that it can be done gives them hope. They can attempt to adapt the techniques and organization which made it possible. The combination of modern methods and smallness of scale is indeed instructive to many students. This is one reason why the United Nations agencies select Israel as a location for some of their courses. For example, because "Israel has made outstanding progress in the dairy production field, particularly in relation to yields per animal under extreme climatic conditions," FAO, UNICEF, and WHO are planning to hold a three-week dairy training course there. Officials from Cyprus, Ethiopia, Greece, Israel, Italy, Kenya, Malta, Poland, Spain, Tanganyika, Turkey, Yugoslavia, Hungary, Bulgaria, Czechoslovakia, and Rumania will study improved methods of milk production, milk hygiene, control regulations, and other ways of improving the quality of milk production and handling.

While the offer of hope is certainly a commendable ingredient, the building of false aspirations has to be avoided. Special pains must be taken to point out the conditions of availability of human and capital resources under which Israel's progress was made, and to indicate that the accomplishments of the past fifteen years were built on a solid foundation laid during a period of fifty years before independence. This will induce visitors to moderate their own goals, and thus prevent possible disappointment.

Israel acquired considerable experience in introducing relatively primitive people to modern farming. During the decade from 1948 to 1958, the number of people employed in agriculture more than doubled. At least half of the new farmers were immigrants from Asia and Africa who had very limited educational backgrounds. It was therefore necessary to organize an efficient training establishment, and devise extension methods and aids suitable for the newcomers. The following are the impressions of two African visitors of Israel's extension service:

> Owing to many immigrants who previously had no contact with agriculture, Israel developed a highly efficient extension service. The approach is essentially a direct one, with immediate practical applications whenever possible. Audiovisual aids, in particular, have been extensively used and are imaginative and practical. Charts, diagrams, posters, film strips and flannelgraph model have all been used in the campaign to familiarize potential and practicing farmers with the techniques to be applied in obtaining maximum production. They are combined with farm demonstrations, farmers days, discussion groups, competitions, exhibitions and other methods, and this approach has been found to be highly successful and preferable to formal classroom lectures.

Our agricultural personnel used to wear such officialdom which made them repulsive, thus gaining little confidence of the farmers. A farmer looks upon an instructor as a prosecutor and not a friend. We suggest therefore, that ways be sought to change the attitude of these officials. It seems to me that agricultural instructors in Israel have a completely different spirit of approach to farmers. They have known that the best way of helping the farmer is to plan with them and not to plan for them. Through this way they have gained farmer's confidence, and the farmers feel the need of their instructions.

Some of the training facilities in Israel are no longer used. The decline in the immigration rate and the increased educational level of the settlers have freed a large number of instructors from pressing duties. They can now be used for instructing foreign trainees in several languages.

African trainees in Israel can see newly established villages still struggling to attain economic and social viability, as well as settlements in advanced stages of development. Through a cross-section of such villages it is almost possible to follow progress from one stage to the next. Consequently one can learn how problems are being solved, instead of merely hearing about how they were solved. A recognition of the dignity of agricultural labor, so totally lacking in Africa, can still take place in Israel.

Not only does the contribution of cooperation to rural progress assume a very tangible meaning in Israel, but the joint effort of many disciplines in solving development problems can be observed. For this reason the FAO chose Israel as a suitable location for an international seminar for agronomists and irrigation engineers which was designed to show the engineers the problems of water demand and explain to the agronomists the limitations on water supply. An FAO representative to an Asian country said:

One of the most outstanding features and main reason for the brilliant success in the utilization of the country's soil and water reserves is the perfect cooperation of all services concerned (pedologists, hydrologists, irrigation engineers, economists, sociologists, settlement experts, agronomists) — A tremendous contrast when compared with the one-sided approach by hydrologists and irrigation engineers only in developing countries.

Finally, Israel's climate is more similar to that of Africa than conditions obtaining in Europe. Israelis are used to working in the heat, and grow some of the same crops. East Africa finds Israel's geographical proximity and accessibility by sea important in cutting transportation costs. A senior British official in Kenya who chose to send a trainee to Israel in preference to a more attractive scholarship from Europe justified his decision in words which may serve to summarize this discussion:

Israel is a small country but possesses technical services of a very high order. Every effort is made to develop intensive agricultural production under conditions which in many cases are difficult. There is a determined effort by all to work hard for the rapid development and prosperity of the country as a whole. A very wide range of crops is grown; many of these are the same as in Kenya.

PERSISTENT PROBLEMS

The program is good, but like any other training venture it could be improved. Some of the problems which have plagued it in the past and the issues they raise follow. (Social problems, which are common to all trainees regardless of field, will be discussed in Chapter 12.)

Selection of Candidates

Short courses, conducted away from home, can be of value only to students with an adequate background in the subject. Alternatively, if the topic studied is a branch of agriculture not yet developed in their country, trainees should be given in addition expert supervision upon their return home. In all cases, each sponsoring African country (or agency) ought to send to Israel a group having a homogenous background, and possessing a common intellectual and practical denominator on which to build the course. Unfortunately, this does not always happen. Students in many contingents vary in age, experience, and education, which poses considerable difficulties for both the organizers and the instructors. In describing one group, an Israeli official said: "Their only common denominator is that no one knows anything about the subject."

Selection of students has, at times, been a hurried process, based on nepotism and favoritism as much as on merit. Thus, a brother of one African minister was sent over for a course "because the minister does not want idle people around him." Israeli officials rarely take part in the selection, and sometimes do not even receive adequate information on the trainees' background. An Israeli minister, while attending the independence ceremonies of a new African state, offered fifty fellowships for training in Israel. No further communication on the subject took place for months. The next news Israel received was a telegram announcing that fifty trainees were on their way in a chartered plane for a year's training. Their questionnaires, including information on both backgrounds and interests, arrived with them. It is to the credit of Israel that, under such trying circumstances, adequate courses were hurriedly prepared for them. In another case, fragmentary advance information indicated that a forthcoming group wished to study banana growing. A study program was prepared accordingly, but when the group arrived it was discovered that its interest lay primarily in poultry. In still another case a few students arrived in the winter to learn methods of raising cotton -- a crop which grows only in the summer. A frequent occurrence is a trainee who claims he was promised at home a longer stay in Israel or a different specialization than he was actually granted. In contrast to such instances, one of the most successful courses was provided for agricultural instructors from East Africa, and its success was due in no small measure to the personal selection of candidates by the Israeli at the head of the program.

Both Israel and the sponsoring countries must tighten up the selection procedure and be more precise and prompt in the exchange of preliminary information. Israel should demand adequately qualified candidates even at the risk of getting fewer trainees. In countries where there are no Israeli representatives to take part in the selection process, use can be made of the FAO country representative. Likewise, the better African graduates of Israel's programs could help both in choosing the trainees and in preparing them for their experience abroad.

On a general policy level, the sponsoring governments should see to it that the training fits into their overall development plan. If returning trainees do not have jobs waiting for them in their area of competence, much of the training effort is wasted. In one case a contingent of returning students found themselves completely out of work, and in another the African government asked for an Israeli official to return with the group to help determine their future assignments. It would be helpful if each contingent of students could be accompanied by a senior officer familiar with the country's needs. He could help steer the training program to suit the most urgent of these, determine the future jobs of the trainees, help them adapt their newly acquired knowledge to home conditions and, last but not least, exert his influence and prestige to counter possible resistance at home to changes the returning trainees propose. On many occasions the students are on such a low level in the administrative hierarchy that they are unable to put into practice what they have learned. "I wish my boss was here with me" is a desire frequently expressed by African students in Israel. And there would be merit in fulfilling the wish, at least in part.

Effectiveness of Practical Work

Despite its importance, the practical work phase of the program presents a variety of problems. Some students simply find manual work too difficult. They are not used to working a whole day, or even half days, under the blazing sun. In a course such as poultry rearing, for example, it is impossible to work for half a day and study the other half. For technical reasons the student must go through the different phases of an entire day's work in order to get all-around training. Others resist it and still feel it is shameful. One group of graduates, for instance, asked that their diplomas omit any mention of their having done practical work. Another contingent avoided all manual labor to the point that the Israeli students in the same agricultural school referred to them as "People of work and peace (Shalom) -- when they see work they say good-bye (Shalom)." (Shalom, in Hebrew, means both peace and good-bye).

The attitude towards work appears to be related to the trainees' background. As might be expected, the extension agents are more willing to do it than the clerical personnel, and the latter tend to have a stronger feeling for the "proper" distinction between ranks. Nevertheless, in most cases the problem is overcome by the Israeli's patience, tact, and firmness. The following explanation of the need for work is given to trainees:

> The object of the practical work is not to turn you into a good labourer. The object is to enable you to prove to the farmers, whom you will train back at home, that your method is workable. This you can do by taking the tool from his hand and showing him yourself that the job can be done.

On the Israeli side it is not easy to find settlements which are ready and willing to absorb the trainees properly, namely, to agree to instruct them while they work. Since a village can absorb only a few trainees, the students are usually dispersed throughout the country, with the result that their professional instructor cannot visit them more than once a week. Consequently, students must turn to their village hosts for answers to questions that crop up during the daily work. Often, the villagers are unable to answer the questions, or do not know the shared language well enough or have time for discussion.[2] Students are expected to benefit from the mistakes of farmers, but how can they learn if such errors are not pointed out to them? While special lectures are occasionally organized for trainees in the village, not all of them come up to expectations. For example, one student complained, "In a lecture on cattle breeding, instead of talking about technical considerations, the lecturer discussed the cattle business of his village."

The Kibbutz versus the Moshav

For the greatest effectiveness of instruction, working on a Kibbutz is preferable to a Moshav. Agriculture in a Kibbutz is a highly specialized operation. The individuals responsible for each branch are more knowledgeable in their field than the small-holder whose farm consists of a little bit of everything. In addition, many trainees prefer to train on a Kibbutz because the work is easier there than on a Moshav.

---

2. To a lesser extent this problem exists also in the theoretical study phases at Ruppin. Many lectures are given by "outsiders" on an ad hoc basis. This prevents contact with the lecturers, and bars sufficient opportunity to ask questions after the lecture. But at least it is partly rectified by the continuous presence of the professional guide on the premises.

There are, on the other hand, numerous considerations wherein the Moshav is superior. As a small-holder's farm, it is more similar in scale to what the trainees are likely to encounter at home. (In some branches such as poultry it is desirable to study both scales of operation, since the Kibbutz provides a close parallel to commercial production.) Second, trainees on a Moshav live with individual families and become attached to them. By contrast, in a Kibbutz they are given their own living quarters, eat in the communal dining room, and have rather impersonal relations with the members. Finally, in a Kibbutz trainees are more likely to encounter adverse attitudes toward religion.

On balance most observers rate the Moshav as the superior training ground. Some think it would be desirable to concentrate all training in newly formed Moshavim where the similarity to African conditions would be the greatest, but such a concentration presents difficult problems of accommodation.

Familiarity with African Conditions

While conditions in Israel may be more similar to those in Africa than those prevailing in Europe, the differences are still vast. Observe, for example, irrigation problems. In Israel, with its severe shortage of water, the main restraint on water use is economic. By contrast, in countries outside the arid zone, the limit to the application of water is technical; that is, it is possible to apply water to the point where it begins to damage the crop. Consequently, the African trainee would find that the Israeli farmer applies less water than is optimal for his own country. Furthermore, Israel has acquired unique knowledge in sprinkling irrigation, a technique which requires too heavy a capital outlay for most developing countries. In Africa the problem is mainly one of supplemental irrigation during the dry season. Only where an arid zone must be developed for an economic or other reason, and where the topography does not permit an open irrigation system, is there a need for the sprinkler technique. Finally, Israel has little to offer trainees who are interested in flood control.

In poultry, Africa's generally higher humidity and higher minimum temperatures require more ventilation in the cages, dryer litter, and feed furnishing less energy, than is needed in Israel. Also, content of the poultry-rearing course should be confined to fundamentals. For example, trainees were carefully taught about a rare vitamin until an Israeli expert returned from an African survey and suggested that this was not essential information. Finally, when it comes to tropical crops, it takes a specialized scientist or an Israeli immigrant who has served in the Belgian colonial service to know enough about them.

These differences underscore the need for using instructors who are familiar with conditions in Africa -- something which is rarely done. True, the number of such persons is still limited, but even experts who have had African experience are all too often overlooked when instructors or guest lecturers are selected. One example illustrates the point. An Israeli poultry expert stationed in Nigeria was at home on two months' leave when a poultry course was given to west African trainees. Since no one in the program knew of his presence in Israel, he was not asked to participate in the course in any capacity (although he would have gladly done so.)

Even an occasional half-day seminar conducted by such experienced individuals is useful. I was present at one session in which an expert who had just returned from a two months' survey in Tanganyika was able to offer penetrating answers to problems raised by east African students. Their queries centered around the applicability of what they saw in Israel to their own countries, and the possibility of introducing social and economic reforms to overcome the impediments to growth resulting from longstanding traditions. Since there is a growing number of Israeli agricultural experts operating abroad, greater efforts should be made to utilize them, upon return home, in the instructional program.

Closely linked to this problem is that of continuity. Trainees who, before their training in Israel, had had very little experience with agriculture, are prepared at graduation only to be effective counterparts or assistants to mature experts in their country. They are rarely equipped to work independently under different conditions from those under which they studied. Returning trainees usually want to copy rather than adapt what they learned. A story is told about one African who studied dairy and then wanted to adopt a milking machine in his own labor-abundant country. The ideal solution is the "integrated project" wherein the trainees would be sent for training by Israeli or other foreign experts operating in their country. Upon return they could become counterparts to such experts in preparation to taking over the project.

PROPOSAL FOR A PERMANENT INSTITUTE

A number of the issues raised above could be resolved by setting up a permanent training institute with long-range planning, instead of running the courses on an almost ad hoc basis. Indeed, Israel and a few African nations have proposed such an institute, for which they requested support from the United Nations Special Fund.[3] The proposed center would offer six-month courses to groups of twenty-five participants from one or two adjacent countries. Each group would be led by a senior official, and upon

---

3. State of Israel, Proposal for the Establishment of an Agricultural Training Center for Participants from African and Asian countries. Jerusalem, 1961.

completion of their training would take an Israeli expert home with them to help adapt what they had learned to local conditions. Over a five-year period the center would train 750 officials from thirty countries in organized courses, while 250 officers would undergo specialized individual training. The estimated total cost of the program was $4 million, of which $2.3 million was requested from the Special Fund and the balance was offered as Israel's contribution. The courses proposed for the first five years were:

Course	Number of courses to be given
Training for Agricultural Instructors	13
Poultry Rearing	5
Cattle Raising	3
Training for Irrigation Technicians	2
Agricultural Cooperatives	5
Mechanization in Agriculture	2
Total	30 courses

Although the proposed program would resemble the courses offered in the past, the permanent facility might obviate some of the observed shortcomings while still retaining the advantages of training in Israel. In the first place, students in each course would be from countries having similar climatic conditions. Each contingent would be led by a senior official from their own country who was charged with the responsibility for increasing group cohesion during the training period, helping to select the fields of specialization, and giving other sorts of professional assistance. Through the facilities of the FAO a better selection procedure could be implemented, with admission restricted to experienced officials who would benefit most from a refresher course in an environment different from their own. The continuity of the program, extended by having Israeli instructors accompany the trainees home, would insure better adaptability to local conditions. At the same time, the backing of a foreign expert would lend prestige and strength to the attempts of returning students to introduce technical or social changes.

Second, a small farm would be attached to the institute, making possible immediate demonstration of methods discussed in the lectures. Various types of equipment like incubators, which trainees are not allowed to use on the settlement for fear of damage, would be available for supervised experimentation. Thirdly, permanent accomodations would be built at a few selected Moshavim to house the trainees during the period of practical work.

This would make it unnecessary for each group to be dispersed throughout the country, and enable the course supervisor to be in constant touch with his trainees and answer their questions as needed. At least some of the facilities might be attached to new agricultural settlements, where conditions are still relatively primitive. Finally, an institute with a long-range program would require the employment of permanent teaching personnel who would have all the fringe benefits enjoyed by civil servants, making it easier to recruit the best available talent.

The proposed center won the support of the FAO on grounds of merit. However, the Special Fund considered it outside its proper jurisdiction, and suggested that Israel apply for Foundation support. It is unfortunate that to date no steps have been taken in that direction.

TRAINING CENTERS IN AFRICA

Training overseas is relatively expensive. It costs the sponsoring government up to $500[4] to defray the cost of transportation for each trainee going to Israel. To be sure, the exposure of Africans to Israel's agriculture has considerable merit, but the opportunity is of full benefit only for senior, experienced officials. For junior grade officers separation from the home environment for any length of time has certain risks. In the words of the Committee for Technical Cooperation in Africa South of the Sahara:

> As far as possible, middle-grade officers should be trained in the continent where they will be called upon to work. Their training would thus be better adapted to their future working conditions. Furthermore a grave danger would thus be avoided which comes about when young persons, sent overseas for their technical training, return unsettled, psychologically affected, unwilling to take up the duties for which they were trained either in urban or rural areas. Experience has generally speaking proved that the sending of immature young people overseas for elementary technical training is inefficient, costly, and sometimes dangerous.[5]

The point applies with particular cogency to agriculture, where climatic and environmental conditions are important. Apart from experienced personnel, training abroad can be beneficial for lower grades in activity areas

---

4. For east African trainees going by sea to southern Israel, costs are considerably less.

5. Training of Personnel (Middle Grade), Report of Committee for Technical Cooperation in Africa South of the Sahara, Abijan, 1962.
    The Report recommends that regional training centers be established for accelerated courses in various vocations, each to serve a few adjoining countries.

which do not exist in their country. Poultry is a case in point. Countries which want to introduce modern poultry production need access to training institutes overseas. But once the method has been introduced, training facilities can be attached to one of the new poultry farms. Thus Ghanaians and Nigerians can obtain their best basic training in poultry at home, and go abroad only for advanced specialization in subjects such as nutrition, breeding, marketing, and extension methods. East Africans, on the other hand, must still go overseas for basic information.

Recognizing this point, Israel has gradually directed its efforts toward the establishment of training and demonstration facilities in Africa. Two centers have been proposed thus far, one in Senegal, and the other in the Upper Volta to serve the four Entente countries (Ivory Coast, Dahomey, Upper Volta, and Niger). While the two plans vary in detail, the concept underlying them is the same. Financial support for the first plan was requested from the Common Market Fund, while the second was submitted to the Special Fund of the United Nations with a request for a $0.9 million grant. The Governing Council of the Special Fund approved the program at its May, 1962 session.[6] (Appendix V reproduces the text of the request by the Upper Volta.)

As far as Israel itself is concerned, the idea was originated by an agronomist making an agricultural survey in Senegal.[7] In connection with a large-scale drive to organize marketing and other rural cooperatives, the government of Senegal requested Israel to supply one expert for each region to help set up agricultural planning centers. An Israeli agronomist was dispatched to study the feasibility of the proposal. Upon surveying the field he concluded that, rather than trying to integrate Israeli personnel into a foreign and unfamiliar administrative machinery, his country's advice would be more effective in other areas and could be best utilized in setting up training and demonstration centers. He suggested that such a center, operating as an independent administrative unit, could perform three functions: training local extension personnel, improving agricultural techniques, and developing new branches of agriculture. The developmental function is designed first to enrich the nutritional value of locally-consumed food (which is a prerequisite for improvement in productivity) and, second, to replace imports and increase exports. At the same time, new crops can be planned in such a way as to contribute to the reduction of disguised unemployment — forced idleness during the long dry season.

---

6. Personal letter from Paul-March Henry of the Special Fund, dated August 9, 1962.

7. See R. Agmon, Compte-Rendu D'une Etude Agricole Au Senegal, Tel-Aviv, May, 1961.

How would the proposed center at the Upper Volta perform these functions?

Training

A two-year course would be offered to young school graduates who had some agricultural experience. Outstanding students would be admitted to a third year of specialized study. About two thirds of the course would be devoted to supervised practical work on the Center's farm in all branches of agriculture, while the remaining third would consist of theoretical studies, with emphasis on agricultural subjects such as soil science, vegetation, animal husbandry, field crops, agricultural bookkeeping, and extension methods. Training would be carried out on both irrigated and non-irrigated land. A model farm for each of three prototypes would be attached to the Center and operated by second-year students with the elementary equipment appropriate to small-holders' farms (e.g., work animals). The model farms would be used for experimentation with various types of farm composition and serve as bases for future planning, such as planning a farm with a well-balanced work load throughout the year. Produce from the farms would be sold in the city.

Graduates would be given a choice of several pursuits: establishing modern farms in traditional villages, thus serving as demonstrators to their fellow villagers; working as instructors in designated villages; establishing new villages in new development regions; joining the staff of experiment stations; or becoming grade-school teachers in agriculture. All these alternatives are useful in bringing about rural progress, but the last might be the most beneficial in terms of its long-run "multiplier effect" and its impact on the social values of the community.

An Indian minister once described the educational system introduced by the British in their colonies as "designed to lubricate the wheels of government", namely, to produce civil servants. As a result, graduates of the school system turn to administrative, clerical, and commercial jobs, and are neither inclined to nor equipped for agriculture and industrial trades. In the agrarian economies of Africa the change in attitude toward farm work must start on the lowest educational level. Exposing primary-school pupils to elementary changes such as the cultivation of crops in straight rows (as against the customary cross-checking) or the use of a plow would be of great value. Likewise, school children can engage in a small but modern poultry project; it would require little capital or land, bring quick returns, and be valuable for soil fertility. Such a project would produce an appealing and nutritious food from which the children themselves would benefit and for which there is a ready market.

An African trainee in Israel described how improved farming methods can emanate from a rural school:

In the past few years Sierra Leone has produced a few Agricultural Education Teachers to teach Agriculture in the form of Gardening, Rural Science, or Natural Science, in order to get the children more interested in this field. This would improve upon the standard of agriculture which the children would take home to their people, as well as the standard of the children themselves when they leave school.

Another kind of training which could be offered in the proposed Center is agricultural instruction for high school teachers. Two or three teachers in a high school, trained to teach agriculture, could produce a strong impact on the surrounding villages. A teacher from Sierra Leone who had been trained in Israel, proposed the use of his school for instruction and demonstration of banana growing, in order to improve the methods used in the entire region. Should such teachers receive additional training in community development, the secondary school would be in a good position to become a spearhead for rural progress.

At this early stage it would perhaps be presumptuous for the proposed Center even to contemplate such a program. On the other hand, a start could be made by offering an intensive two-year course for high school teachers in Israel, with a gradual transfer of this function to the Centers in Africa. Israel herself has an effective system of agricultural high schools; in addition, the field of agriculture is well integrated into the primary school curriculum.

Demonstration

Groups of farmers would be brought to the Center for instruction and demonstration under two programs: 1) short courses concentrated in one agricultural branch, to be held four times a year during the slack season, and 2) study days devoted to practical demonstration in a specific field, such as modern methods of cultivation, use of work animals, pest extermination methods, treatment of fruit trees, irrigation, preparation of hay and silage, and the like. Five such days are envisaged each year, involving a total of 500 farmers.

For both programs a follow-up by extension agents is contemplated. But, in particular, the farmers undergoing the first type of course would be carefully selected and intensively advised afterwards until each of their farms became an example to the village. This is one extension method practiced in Israel for the benefit of new immigrants which made a deep impression on African visitors. In the words of a Liberian trainee:

Farmers will care little if they are taken to a government farm, but they will be impressed if they see the same thing on an individual farm. This will give at least some of the farmers the incentive to make a trial. Those farmers who are willing to try must be given every assistance and advice to ensure success.

New Crops and Techniques

The Center would serve as an experimental farm for the development of new agricultural techniques and new crops. In addition it would disseminate seeds, seedlings, chicks, and artificial insemination, and maintain a farm machinery station to serve the local farmers.

"Adopted" Villages and Farmers

In coordination with the agricultural extension service, certain villages as well as single farmers in the area would be chosen for direct collaboration with the Center. They would be selected according to their ability to adapt to modern methods and given intensive instruction and basic farm implements. Once sufficient progress had been achieved, they would yield their places to other farms or villages.

Inasmuch as the government wishes to promote agricultural cooperation, the Center could establish and sponsor an experimental cooperative village adjacent to its land.

For eventual fulfillment of the Center's objective it would have to be well integrated into the existing national agricultural services. Full cooperation with the extension service and the research stations would have to be secured; primary schools would have to agree to employ the Centers' graduates as agricultural teachers; and credit agencies would have to support the farmers who cooperated with the Center. Without such collaboration the Center could not have a full impact on the community. Likewise, unless it were integrated into the bureaucratic structure of the country, it could not survive the departure of the foreign technicians.

It is anticipated that the Center would be run by a team of eight Israeli advisors.[8] Promising local experts, as well as graduates of the Center, would be sent to Israel for training. Upon return they would serve as counterparts to the Israeli technicians, and in time would take over the management of the Center.

Emphasis in this program is on instruction and demonstration. Land settlement would merely be a by-product of these functions, and is contemplated on a much more modest scale than the projects outlined in the last chapter. Similar demonstration Centers are being set up in other areas such as Tanganyika, as part of a youth organization program. However, because they vary in purpose from the ones described here, they will be discussed in Chapter 7.

---

8. From the FAO point of view this is a unique arrangement. They consider it an essentially bilateral program, yet financed by the United Nations. That is one reason for their insistance on a non-Israeli expert as head of the center.

CHAPTER 6 ADVICE IN
AGRICULTURE

In addition to the training of Afro-Asian personnel, Israel extends technical assistance in a variety of agricultural subjects and attempts to diversify rural economies through the introduction of new types of activity. In choosing new agricultural branches, preference is given those that can yield quick results, improve the country's trade balance, and add protein to local diets which now consist mainly of root crops. In most cases the experts shy away from too-advanced production techniques such as mechanized agriculture. They concentrate on simple methods which can be easily employed, yet be very useful in improving local practices. These include the introduction of new seed varieties, pest control, the use of fertilizers and work animals, and the development of small-scale irrigation projects.

SELECTED PROJECTS

Commercial Poultry

One successful line of assistance offered by Israel was the introduction of commercial poultry-raising to Ghana and Western Nigeria. The project in Ghana began in 1959 on the recommendation of an Israeli survey expert, and in three years local production had expanded sufficiently to replace all imported eggs (which had exceeded five million a year), and to lower prices significantly. In 1962, the project was taken over by a carefully selected Ghanaian. Having been trained in poultry husbandry, he was sent to several countries (including Israel) to observe more specialized practices such as breeding, artificial insemination, and farm management before he replaced the Israeli technician.

In Nigeria the project began a year later, but the results were similar. Furthermore, one of the Israeli advisors there went beyond the call of duty and developed a goose plant in the country. Realizing that conditions in the western region lend themselves to the raising of goslings, and that livers of fatted geese command high prices in Europe,[1] he spent part of his vacation studying the feasibility of the project, and finally received government backing for it.

The line of approach to poultry rearing was the same in both west African countries. It consisted of the development of a modern poultry branch on a government farm, and the use of this farm for instructing extension workers and local farmers interested in starting poultry production. At a later stage the central farms were equipped with incubators and mixing plants, thus making the import of chicks and feed from Israel no longer necessary.

Farmers interested in developing a poultry branch received government loans, and did the construction and installation under the supervision of the Israeli expert. Poultry extension in Nigeria takes the following forms: a) visits by farmers to the government farm, where a permanent exhibition aids in the learning process; b) four-month courses for potential extension workers, of which three are devoted to practical work on the farm; c) visits to farmers, followed by letters and reminders concerning farm practices (the central farm keeps a record for every farmer under its supervision); d) monthly public lectures to farmers; and e) publication of a monthly bulletin, the Poultryman's Companion, which explains farm management practices, answers questions, and announces news of importance (it has a circulation of 350 copies).

Most of the growers thus far are owners of large poultry farms near the big cities who emphasize efficient production and rapid expansion. Consequently, while making a few people quite wealthy, the project has contributed very little to the general improvement of indigenous agriculture. To overcome this main deficiency, the experts in charge intend to make an attempt to reach the small farmer. For that purpose they would switch from imported and fairly expensive batteries, to the use of deep litter cages built from local materials.[2] In Nigeria, a poultry branch is also being added to the new settlement scheme.

Government backing was essential to the success of the projects in both Ghana and Nigeria. Whenever it was not forthcoming, progress was slowed down. Indeed, the activity of an Israeli poultry advisor in a third African country is in jeopardy because such support is lacking. Once the projects become viable, some of the poultry husbandry experts can be withdrawn and transferred elsewhere, but Nigeria and Ghana will still need assistance in specialized areas such as marketing, genetics, nutrition, and veterinary medicine.

---

1. Incidentally, these livers will probably be sold on the French market in direct competition with like products from Israel.

2. Batteries are claimed to be more suitable for commercial poultry production since they facilitate disease control.

Farm Mechanization

To the extent that the initial clearing of land or other agricultural tasks call for the use of machinery, most underdeveloped countries are hampered by a shortage of maintenance technicians. One of the first Israeli experts to go to Burma was a mechanical engineer; he served from 1954 to 1958, and was followed by two others in the same capacity. His main task was the maintenance of available agricultural machinery and the training of Burmese in their use. Upon his arrival, he found one hundred poorly maintained tractors scattered throughout the country. He had them assembled in one area near Rangoon, where he built a maintenance workshop and a school. [3] During his second year he organized three courses: a one-month course for Ministry of Agriculture officials; a three-month course for tractor operators, and a four-month course for mechanics. In addition, he supervised the mechanical work on the nearby experiment station. Once a hard core of operators was trained, he started establishing tractor stations throughout the country, with adjoining maintenance sheds. Twenty such stations were set up over a three-year period, staffed largely with his trainees. His school also supplied mechanical technicians for various agricultural development projects like the settlement scheme at Namsang.

This is an example of what one competent person with the right attitude can accomplish in a few years. In fact, this same individual was at the same time involved in a variety of other projects, including the setting up of experimental farms, helping in land settlement, and the building of a poultry farm. His successor, on the other hand, confined himself to work in mechanization: He planned tractor stations, organized courses, maintained machinery, and estimated the type and amount of modern agricultural equipment necessary for the Burmese development plans.

Production Farms

Various countries have developed large-scale, centrally managed farms to expand agricultural production rapidly.

At times it is not clear whether such farms are an end in themselves, or if they are regarded as a convenient stepping-stone to land settlement. These farms may be used for experimentation with new crops and techniques as well as for demonstration. But, unlike the Instruction Centers discussed in the last chapter, their training function is usually secondary. Israel has, on occasion, supplied advisors to plan or manage such farms. Also, an International Water Resource Development Company [4] (WRD) established in Israel with government and other funds, has a special division which

---

3. Funds for equipments were obtained from the FAO, the Colombo plan, and the Ford and Asia Foundations.

4. See Chapter 10, below.

contracts for the development of such farms in Afro-Asian countries, especially on irrigated land.

A team of five Israeli advisors have planned two government farms in the Accra plains of Ghana which are to be used for increasing production, experimentation and, to a certain extent, demonstration purposes. The project grew out of an Israeli report proposing the reorganization of Ghana's Ministry of Agriculture. Among its recommendations was the establishment of such large experimental farms. While very little came of the reorganization plan, the author of the report was asked to head a team and implement his recommendation to set up large farms. Each farm will contain about 700 acres devoted to extensive agriculture (mainly grain and root crops), 300 acres of irrigated land, 100 acres of tree crops, as well as dairy and poultry branches. Once the plan has been implemented, the team will be replaced by two farm managers.

Another Israeli team is running a large farm in the Philippines devoted primarily to growing cotton. Their idea is to develop it as a nucleus for the instruction of the neighboring farmers in modern techniques and supplying them with seeds. They hope to help expand production to a point of completely replacing imported raw materials for the island's textile industry.

Seven demonstration farms, mainly for cotton and sugar beets, have been organized and managed by WRD in Iran. Furthermore, a large dairy farm is being built and a poultry farm is planned. In Cyprus WRD is planning two farms, 2½ acres each, to demonstrate irrigation techniques. The same company also plans to manage a 15,000 acre (irrigated) demonstration and production farm in Ethiopia which will be financed by the International Bank for Reconstruction and Development. Finally, in Thailand Israeli technicians will use 100 acres for demonstration projects in irrigation techniques, employing Israeli equipment.[5]

Two farms were planned and managed by an Israeli team in the dry zone of Burma. Primarily using sprinkler irrigation, they experimented with a variety of field crops and attempted to train Burmese technicians in irrigation methods. Other farms set up in Burma were connected with the army settlement project. The Israeli mechanical engineer mentioned earlier helped establish two experimental farms for the training of future settlers. They were planned with full mechanization, sprinkler irrigation, and a large poultry branch (managed by another Israeli advisor).

In the Namsang region, there was at one time a plan for a joint Burmese-Israeli project to cultivate one million acres of wheat. A four-man Israeli team, dispatched in 1957, discovered that the project was not feasi-

5. In some cases the main purpose of the demonstration is the sale of irrigation equipment by Israeli manufacturers.

ble because of lack of security in the area, opposition from the Shan State, and absence of adequate transport facilities to the main markets. Instead, they constructed a large experimental farm and used it for demonstration and training as well. The results of their experiments were later utilized by the advisory team in its preparation of the regional settlement scheme.

Surveys

The numerous surveys undertaken by Israeli experts in the field of agriculture fall into three categories. The least useful type, from the viewpoint of the receiving country, is a general survey of the agricultural economy. For individuals unfamiliar with local agricultural conditions and with tropical crops, it is next to impossible to identify crucial problems and make recommendations in a two months' survey. It is even more difficult to integrate such recommendations into the overall development scheme. The usual outcome of such a survey is a report that is filed away and forgotten.

More useful are surveys concerning a particular problem or branch of agriculture, like the two conducted by an Israeli dairy scientist in Western Nigeria and Liberia.[6] In both cases he recommended the expansion of dairy farming with breeds immune to the TseTse fly, coupled with experiments to develop new breeds which would be done mainly in the experiment stations and at the universities. He also suggested intensified training in dairy management. His reports led to the dispatch of an Israeli advisor to organize the veterinary services in Liberia. Another example of such fruitful endeavors were the fisheries surveys carried out in Burma and Western Nigeria by an expert who had served in 1952 in Haiti under FAO auspices. On the basis of his recommendations the United Nations has approved aid in fish processing and marketing to Western Nigeria, an Israeli expert is advising the Burmese army on the development of fish ponds, and seven Burmese have been trained in this field in Israel. In addition, Israel cooperates with Ethiopia in the development of fisheries, and a similar avenue of cooperation is contemplated with Mauritius.[7]

Other surveys of this type have been undertaken in various countries in the growing of corn and citrus. The latter is an area in which Israel is particularly qualified to render assistance. One citrus advisor has been working in Western Nigeria for three years, and others are likely to be sent in the future.

---

6. Y. S. Goor, Proposals for the Establishment of Dairy Farming in the Western Region. Nigeria (Ibadan: April, 1960), and Proposals for the Establishment of a Bureau of Animal Health and Production in Liberia. (Jerusalem: October, 1961).

7. Reported in The Jerusalem Post, July 21, 1962.

The third kind of survey involves an investigation into what Israel can do to help an African country in its agricultural development. Such surveys resulted in the first agricultural course in Israel for trainees from Liberia and Sierra Leone, and in the poultry development project in Ghana. The plans for establishing training and demonstration centers are also outcomes of such investigations.

Development of Seed Varieties

A final avenue of cooperation is the interest of the Israeli Seed Company (Hazera) in developing disease-resistant varieties of maize and sorghum which would grow well in Africa. The semi-arid zone provides ideal conditions for such experiments, if an African experiment station would agree to do justice to the seeds and institute prompt reporting procedures.[8] Thus, Hazera hopes to set up a working arrangement with the Richard Toll station in Senegal.

So far, excellent relations have been established with the East African Agriculture and Forestry Research Organization (British) in Serere, Uganda. The east African researchers experimented with hybrid varieties of Israeli and African sorghum and obtained good results. Their reports have been accurate, prompt and purposeful, and enable Hazera to follow through with increased supplies of the successful varieties for further experiments.

PROBLEMS OF IMPLEMENTATION

Competence of Experts

The overwhelming majority of Israel's agricultural advisors abroad are competent in their fields, as has been recognized by African and FAO officials alike.

But like most generalizations, this too has its exceptions. Perhaps the most glaring was the planning of a large irrigated farm in an arid area. The entire project seems to have been poorly conceived, and grave doubts have been cast on its economic usefulness, although the project has a strong emotional appeal to its government and a high prestige value. Its technical execution was also very poor. In planning a network for sprinkler irrigation the engineer ordered materials for 1,300 acres, but only 900 acres were cultivable, and water was available for only 350. The plans had not been shown even to other Israelis in that country. However, it is to the credit of the Israeli sprinkler factory that it sent a team of irrigation and field crops men to salvage whatever was possible from the blunder.

In other cases, criticisms have been leveled against some particular

---

8. European interests in Africa sometimes oppose the introduction of Israeli seeds, and may set up experiments with them under deliberately unfavorable conditions.

phase of an expert's work. One person effectively organized the marketing of a certain fruit in an African country, and trained local counterparts to take over. Unfortunately, his performance was not so generally admired when he remained for an additional period as a general consultant. Another advisor was criticized for preferring materials from Israel which could have been obtained for almost half the price elsewhere. Finally, some experts have been condemned for a lack of tact which prevented effective team work or amiable relations with local officers. And one expert was charged with refusing to cooperate with Israelis working on another project in the same country, although such cooperation would have been functionally useful.

But these cases are few and far between; they can be regarded merely as isolated incidents. Generally the Israelis are widely commended for their technical expertness, efficiency, and practical approach.

Prior Preparation

Technical competence notwithstanding, every expert sent abroad requires extensive preparation before undertaking his assignment. He needs data on climatic and argo-technical conditions (especially if he is going outside the semi-arid zone)[9] as well as social and anthropological information. "How much do we know about tropical crops or mechanized work in tropical areas?" asked one expert. "True, a great deal can be learned from the local research and teaching institutions.[10] But we could accomplish much more if we received some advance preparation."

Experts invariably complain that except for an hour's briefing at the foreign ministry, they were given no background information. Occasionally extensive discussions took place with individuals who had returned from service in the same country (even in the same line of work), but those were based on personal acquaintance. Since most persons going abroad do not have such contacts, they often leave for their assignment inadequately equipped. The following possible means might be instituted to rectify the situation:

(a) The least that could be done would be to give the expert a month of paid free time before his departure to investigate written materials on the country of his service (in Yugoslavia experts are known to get three months for that purpose), and put him in contact with some individuals who have already served there. (b) The Faculty of Agriculture of the Hebrew University might consider incorporating into its program an elective course

---

9. Certain FAO officials criticized Israel for extending itself too rapidly in the rain forest area, where conditions differ so vastly from those in Israel.

10. For example, some Israelis in Burma benefited greatly from contact with the university at Mandalai.

on tropical agriculture and African conditions which experts going abroad could take. (c) Alternatively, the government might set up a special course which would teach such experts the demography, sociology, and history of the country, as well as conditions pertaining to their field of activity.

Some progress has been made in the training of farm managers intending to serve in Africa. With the growing demand for such managerial personnel, a four months' course was instituted by Israel's extension service on an ad hoc basis. Thirty graduates of agricultural high schools with experience in farm management either on a Kibbutz or with a private organization were trained in agriculture, management, planning, and a foreign language, preparatory to taking on overseas duties. A further step in the right direction was taken by the National and University Institute of Agriculture in organizing monthly study days for potential African advisors. These monthly seminars are, however, too superficial and give only a cursory treatment of a wide range of topics.

Support from Home

Once in his assigned location, the expert is faced with a variety of technical problems which are compounded by an unfamiliar social structure and a slower work-pace. The size of Israel's program precludes the establishment of a far-flung organization with outlets in each country (à la the USOM), and often the Israeli expert has no access to other foreign advisors. In his isolation he depends on professional and general guidance from home. This is particularly true in the field of agriculture where technical problems abound, and the expert does not always have a language in common with local research institutions.

But support from home is rarely forthcoming. One advisor wrote: "Things are not moving well, and one of the reasons is lack of contact between us and Israel." Others complained that their letters and reports were not read, that their queries went unanswered, and that there was no central agency in Israel on which they could depend to refer their questions to the proper professional authorities for prompt reply. Likewise, a Hebrew University researcher invested a lot of time and money in the "African project." Not only was he not reimbursed for his efforts and expenses, but he did not even receive replies to his letters of inquiry.

Perhaps the problem lies not so much in lack of goodwill as in the inability of the foreign or agricultural ministries to cope with the pressures of this rapidly expanding program. However, some progress toward a solution was made with the establishment, at the end of 1961, of the Center of Comparative Studies in the Agricultural Faculty of the Hebrew University. The Center was set up as a research and coordination agency. Its purpose is to gather material on agriculture in African, Asian, and Latin American countries, and analyze the reports of Israeli agricultural experts operating in them. The material will then be made available to individuals preparing for foreign assignments, and to other interested persons. Ideally, questions from the field would be channeled through the Center to the appropriate authorities, and the activities of the various organizations engaged in agricultural assistance would be coordinated by it.

Cooperation of the Foreign Government

Despite good intentions, all too often problems arise from lack of proper communication between governments, and experts find themselves in situations where necessary support from local authorities is not forthcoming. The government requesting technical assistance from Israel does not always have a definite idea of what the expert can or should do, and does not provide a clear-cut definition of his assignment. One country, for example, requested an advisor on tree crops. The expert arrived to find that by "tree crops" the government specifically meant coffee and sugar cane, neither of which is grown in Israel, and of which he had no knowledge. If that government had only consulted the Israelis already working there, the mistake could have been prevented.

Administrative red tape and delays in release of funds already appropriated for a project are frequent obstacles to progress. And sometimes tractors or bulldozers may not be available because a highly placed official has ordered their use in the construction of a race track or golf course in which he has a personal interest.

Even collaboration in the field is not always forthcoming. Experts are sometimes forced to do things against their better judgment -- they may find a local farm manager working against them because their success would reflect poorly on him and, most important, local counterparts are frequently very poor or non-existent. It would be very useful if Israel could insist, as a condition for each project, that qualified Africans be sent to Israel for study so that they could effectively assume the function of counterparts for the Israeli experts.

Use of the Experts at Home

In view of the scanty Israeli knowledge of African and Asian conditions, it might be expected that returning experts would be asked to contribute to the foreign instruction program and the planning of further projects. Unfortunately, this is not the case. One high level official whose surveys had yielded fruitful results lost contact with the program altogether. Another agricultural advisor compiled a thick volume of impressions, plans, and other revelant professional material, and was not even asked to come in for discussion. An agricultural planner literally had to put pressure on the foreign office to get an audience to which he could relay his experience. "It's a pity to lose all the accumulated experience", said a machinery expert, "no one can imagine what it is to serve in a tropical country."

And an irrigation adviser stated: "I invested many hours in learning that country's conditions, and still keep up by reading newspapers and corresponding with people in the field. Yet when an issue comes up I am not consulted, and I am never invited to talk to visitors from the country with whom I have much in common."

A paradoxical situation thus exists in which the possessors of valuable knowledge are anxious to share it and have it put to use, but the agencies which desperately need their information seem to be unaware of their existence. Both the instruction program and the planning of projects are the consequent victims. But proper leadership exercised by the foreign and agricultural ministries can easily rectify the situation.

7 COMMUNITY DEVELOPMENT AND YOUTH ORGANIZATION

Community development is a movement to promote better living for a community with the active participation of all its members. Activities in social welfare, education, health services, and youth clubs all fall within its realm. By virtue of her own efforts in the absorption and rehabilitation of immigrants, Israel is eminently qualified to render technical assistance in this area. Most of the work done so far has been in youth organization with particular reference to agriculture, but other activities are expanding at a rapid rate.

ISRAEL'S YOUTH ORGANIZATIONS

In Africa a serious problem is the village youth who drifts to the city and ends up in a purposeless existence; Israel, on the other hand, has developed a vast network of youth clubs to cope with not too different problems. While many of the clubs are sectoral or affiliated with political parties, and their social concepts, intellectual ideas, or organizational feasibility may make them unsuitable for African adoption, the two national youth organizations, the Gadna and the Nachal, have long attracted the attention of African and Asian governments for possible adaptation to their countries.

Gadna – Youth Battalions

Administered jointly by the Ministries of Education and Defense, the Gadna is a national youth movement which is combined with some paramilitary training. Through study sessions and camp activity it tries to develop the social and civic consciousness of its members, and instill in them a national purpose; it also offers, for those who want it, training in such specialized areas as aviation, seamanship, signals, and marksmanship.

In the post-elementary school the Gadna offers supplementary education in hobbies, sports, physical training, and manual work, while for immigrants and working groups it offers local club activity. Indeed, it is the only youth movement which, thanks to state support, has been able to work effectively with neglected young people in the poorer strata of the population. As a national organization the Gadna performs such public services as instruction in immigrant villages, road construction, help in hospitals, first aid, and fire fighting services.

In addition to weekly training in clubs or schools, the Gadna operates various field camps during school vacations, where children go through more concentrated programs. It also manages a farming estate in the arid zone where groups of young members work and train on a rotation basis.

Nachal — Fighting Pioneering Youth

Nachal is a formation within the Israeli Army which combines military preparedness with agricultural training and settlement pioneering. After they complete basic training, Nachal groups are assigned to farm settlements for a nine months' period of combined agricultural and military training. Each group occupies a specially erected camp which, though within the settlement, preserves for it a separate social and military identity. During this period the soldier adjusts himself to agricultural labor. While maintaining military preparedness, the group becomes a socially cohesive unit, and helps implement the production plan of the settlement to which it is attached. For the balance of his military service the Nachal soldier is assigned to a frontier settlement where he lives and works as a civilian. [1] In some cases, soldiers erect and colonize new settlements where conditions are not yet suitable for a permanent civilian village, but where there is urgent need for colonization.

Since Nachal transcends the normal sphere of military interests, the attainment of its objectives requires an intensive educational program. This is particularly true when a Nachal unit consists largely of new immigrants. The program is carried out mainly during the second phase of military service, after basic training, and includes general orientation, instruction in Hebrew, courses in folk dancing and singing, training in agriculture, and cultural activities. Special emphasis is placed on fostering group spirit, as many a unit forms the nucleus for future settlement. Quite a few groups belong to a pioneering youth movement before military service, intending eventually to set up a settlement. This arrangement preserves the group as a unit through its years in the service. By the end of military service the group is ready, both in spirit and in technical competence, to form a settlement if it wishes. Indeed, scores of new villages have been established by Nachal soldiers in areas essential to the development and security of the state. Similarly, nuclear groups of Nachal have reinforced more than 130 of the border settlements which suffer acutely from shortage of manpower.

---

1. Compulsory military service in Israel is 2½ years for men and two years for women.

Initial Contact With Africa

The first introduction of Africans to these youth organizations took place in a six-week International Seminar for Socialist Youth Leaders of the International Union of Socialist Youth held in Israel in the spring of 1959. Participants, hailing from twelve countries on four continents, were people active in socialist youth organizations, political parties, trade unions, cooperative movements, national liberation movements, and student and professional organizations. The program was divided equally between lectures, work on a Kibbutz and a Moshav, and study tours.

> Israel was considered a good location for such a seminar because of the important role that youth movements have played and are still playing in the national and social structure and character. Therefore, in planning the program, what was termed the Israel Case Study was to be central in the lectures and discussions at the seminar.[2]

Some of the subsequent African interest in the Israeli youth movements stemmed from this seminar. The Tanganyika National Union (TANU) Youth League, for example, established close contacts with the Gadna and Nachal as a result of the participation of its leader, Joseph Nyrere, in the seminar. Later in 1959 a Gadna delegation visited Ghana, Liberia, and Nigeria. Their meetings with Presidents Nkruma and Tubman underscored the need to do something about African Youth, and the desirability of Israel-African cooperation in this field.

GHANA'S BUILDERS BRIGADE AND YOUNG PIONEERS

Ghana attempted to cope with its youth problems by setting up the Builders Brigade (now the Workers Brigade) in 1957. Established originally under British command, the Brigade was designed to absorb veterans, school leavers, and other unemployed, and to prepare them for productive life. For a variety of reasons, its first two years were not marked with success.

In September of 1959, a high-ranking Ghanaian delegation paid a visit to Israel. Impressed by the accomplishments of the Nachal, the mission recommended that its pattern be adopted by the Builders Brigade. Shortly after the visit John Tettegah, a member of the delegation, was named commander of the Brigade, and one of his first actions was to invite a team of four Nachal officers to advise and guide his organization.[3] In addition to its

---

2. Report on the Seminar, p. 3.

3. He was later replaced by Mr. Arabio, who paid a two week visit to Israel in August of 1961, thus continuing the cooperation between the two countries.

head, the team consisted of specialists in education, agriculture and engineering.

Preliminary study revealed to the advisory group that the Brigade's main problem was lack of purpose. It is next to impossible to prepare an effective training program when no one knows what the training is for. The objectives of such a national organization must be determined by the economic planning or other governmental authority. Drawing on their own background and experience, the Israeli advisors proposed the goal of cooperative agricultural settlement, but although the Ghanaians did not accept the proposed objective they offered no alternative in its place.

Lacking a final objective toward which to guide the Brigade, the advisors had to content themselves with intermediate purposes. The program they instituted consisted mainly of work and training in modern agricultural techniques, and in fighting against illiteracy. But training is also offered in various other useful vocations: building construction and tractor operation and maintenance for men, and weaving, embroidery and other crafts for women. All courses are given at a central school, where group leaders are also being trained.

Operating as an economically independent unit with an annual budget of G£2 million (= $5.6 million), the Brigade numbers 12,000 members, of which 2,000 are women. They work, but do not reside, in thirty camps scattered throughout the country. While most of the work is in agriculture, some groups are engaged in a variety of public works such as laying sidewalks in Accra. Land for the camps is provided free by tribal chiefs who are interested in having a camp nearby, for they appreciate its demonstrative impact as well as the income it yields to the villagers. The most impressive camp is in Somaya, thirty miles north of Accra, where one thousand acres have been put under permanent (as opposed to shifting) cultivation with modern agricultural techniques. An interesting system of bush clearing was developed whereby the trees were retained to mark off ten-acre plots and at the same time to prevent floods and erosion where the land slopes. Plans for the future include the construction of housing for members, operation of resthouses in which the women members can be employed, participation in the Volta Dam project, and perhaps the establishment of a few model cooperative villages.

Absence of a clear-cut final objective remains the central problem of the Brigade. "It is a training program - but for what?" said one FAO official. Further, some feel that the Brigade is not well integrated into the rural economy. The Ministry of Agriculture is not kept informed of its activities, and lack of marketing channels hampers its agricultural expansion and diversification. This is one reason for the concentration on the production of indigenous foods such as cassawa and yams. New crops are introduced only when the demand warrants. For example, vegetables are grown for sale to the armed forces and, it is hoped, will also be purchased by Europeans employed on the Volta Dam project.

Against this background, the Brigade can point to an impressive list of achievements. It has mobilized technically untrained and partly delinquent individuals, and converted them to disciplined and organized workers' groups who are ready for any national task and very proud of their organization. [4] It operates thirty well-administered farms, employing modern methods and equipped with heavy machinery for which ample maintenance crews have been trained ---- the camp at Somaya is one of the show places to which visiting foreign dignitaries are brought. Among its members are people who have received training and experience in essential technical vocations. And, last but not least, the Brigade's farms have a strong demonstration effect on the surrounding villages and on the neighboring countries. Farmers in the vicinity of the camps attempt to put into practice new methods they have seen there, and on many occasions have even asked to be drafted into the Brigade. After seeing the results of the Brigade's work, many west African countries turned to Israel for assistance in youth organization. One measure of the Brigade's success is that it can now plan to dispense with Israeli aid in the near future. Four Ghanaian officers are to be sent to a youth-training course in Israel and subsequently to specialize in irrigation, agricultural equipment, and farm management. Upon return home they are expected to assume central technical positions in the Brigade.

Another Ghanaian organization which for some three years could not gain momentum is the Ghana Young Pioneers. Working with teenage youth, it was trying unsuccessfully to emulate the activity of the British Scouts. In 1960, the commander of the GYP visited Israel and was impressed by the Gadna. Under Israeli advice he decided to revitalize the movement by introducing attractive technical subjects like seamanship, establishing a leadership training school, and integrating the movement's activities into the school system.

YOUTH LEADERSHIP TRAINING IN ISRAEL

At the request of the Builders Brigade and of other west African nations, Israel has instituted courses in youth leadership for Africans based on Gadna-Nachal principles. Two four-month courses were offered in 1961 in parallel English- and French-speaking classes. The first course included thirty students from five English-speaking countries and twenty-seven students from five

---

4. A body of 12,000 disciplined people can, of course, be misused. But it is not for their use that the Israeli advisors are responsible.

French-speaking nations. In the second course the respective figures were twenty-six and forty-eight. Close to a third of the participants were women. The same number of courses was planned for 1962. In view of the increasing demand, it is planned to make this a permanent school and add a class in Spanish for Latin American countries. The first Spanish-speaking class, to be attended by students from eleven Latin American countries, was to be opened in the fall of 1962.

The objective of the youth leadership program is to train youth organizers at the regional level, on the assumption that trainees will first work for at least one year as local instructors. Held at the central Gadna training camp, it combines theoretical discussions with practical work, covering the following subjects: field activities, sports and physical training, social activities, principles of education, and administration and organization of youth movements. The program in detail is reproduced in Appendix VI.

The courses were well planned and efficiently executed. A final report giving a comprehensive analysis of the results enabled the organizers to learn from past mistakes and improve various practices in subsequent sessions. In the first course, for example, theory and practice were handled separately. In the second they were well integrated under each of the functional subjects to make possible immediate documentation and demonstration of theoretical points. Since, for some reason, the first group of trainees seemed to feel they were in a privileged position and therefore demanded special concessions and were not respectful toward the staff, stricter discipline was instituted in the second course and a final paper was required of all participants. These measures improved the students' attitude and raised their level of achievement.

As in other training enterprises, the courses were hampered by improper selection of students. About half the participants had no intention of engaging in youth work at home (most of them preferred office jobs) and many had inadequate backgrounds. One country invited an Israeli instructor to participate in the preliminary selection of candidates, but even there favoritism prevailed over his judgment in many cases, and some of his appointees were replaced by less suitable trainees. Nevertheless, slow and consistent progress is being made by insistence on higher standards, and by using the better African graduates of the courses to help in the selection of candidates. It is hoped that teachers and youth leaders will eventually constitute the bulk of the participants.

An important issue concerned the semi-military atmosphere in which the course was conducted, as evidenced by camp surroundings, uniforms, and the inclusion of such subjects as target shooting and topography. Several trainees expressed dissatisfaction with the idea of a military camp. But, on balance, the consensus seems to favor the present arrangement. First, the Gadna is the only prototype of a national youth organization in Israel, and is therefore the only vehicle through which understanding of such a movement can be imparted to participants. Second, given a certain autonomy and flexibility within the military establishment, the Gadna can run the course more efficiently and at lower cost than any outside organization. It can provide adequate logistical support, and some of the best instructors are to be found within its ranks. Thirdly, some African countries are actually interested in a para-military organization. Those who are not can easily dispense with all the semi-military aspects. And finally, as one African ambassador stated, "Some military discipline is actually good for the trainees."

Still, attempts are made to minimize the military atmosphere. There is no military discipline, and most rules are enforced by the trainees themselves through their national group leaders. Where that is not possible, the Israeli officers resort to tactics of persuasion, using such phrases as: "Why did you come here?" "You are a representative of your country." Only as a last resort are trainees threatened with being sent home. Also, trainees are free to come and go as they please whenever no program is planned for them. However, their access to the city is limited by most of their time being taken up by study, work, or social activities at the camp.

The main problem, as seen by instructors and students alike, is that of continuity. Although trainees receive all the material in writing, they cannot easily apply it upon their return home. Not only are conditions vastly different from those in Israel, but course graduates find they seldom have an opportunity to put what they learned into practice. Often they need the prestige and support of a foreign expert if they are to introduce the newly acquired methods. The course itself "creates an appetite without satisfying it," says one Israeli instructor.

In order to solve the continuity problem Israel is gradually shifting some of her training activity to Africa. In most cases an Israeli instructor accompanies the contingent of graduates of the youth leadership course when they return home, to start executing a pre-conceived plan. Rudimentary plans already exist in several countries, but their execution is most advanced in Tanganyika, Togo, and the Ivory Coast.

Progress of the Tanganyikan contingent in the second Gadna course was closely supervised by an Israeli instructor who subsequently assigned them to additional special training. Upon completion of their training he returned with them to Tanganyika to set up a Pioneer Training Center, the plan for which had been delineated earlier by an Israeli survey mission and approved by the government. The Center will offer training programs in three fields: youth leadership; domestic science and vocational subjects (women's section); and agricultural subjects. In the first year each of the three branches will be headed by an Israeli advisor, but the instructors will be the Tanganyikans trained in Israel. The educational director will also be an Israeli, but the administrative head of the Center is to be a Tanganyikan. Adjoining the Center is a model 45-acre farm which is to be cultivated by the students themselves. The Center will also include six classrooms, two workshops, a laboratory, a library, an infirmary, a central dining room, and lodging facilities. It is hoped that it will serve as a model for similar centers to be set up in other parts of east Africa.

In Togo an Israeli survey expert offered a plan for establishing a pioneer agricultural youth movement which is now being executed by seven Nachal officers. The three-phase plan calls first for the introduction of a Gadna-type movement in the last two years of primary school, with emphasis on the creation of cohesive social groups. Second, upon graduation these groups are expected to undergo agricultural training on two 400-acre farms. Using semi-modern methods they would raise industrial crops, vegetables, livestock, and indigenous crops. Upon completion of the second phase, they would be settled in model Moshavim on land adjoining the training farms.[5]

The Ivory Coast has requested Israeli assistance to transform its entire army to a Nachal pattern where soldiers, following basic training, will perform a variety of developmental tasks and public works. It has also indicated an interest in establishing Gadna units in the school system with the help of the graduates from Israel's Youth Leadership course. The following report describes the progress made in this program by November of 1962:

> Seven Israeli and three African officers are now training groups of cooperative settlement leaders in the Ivory Coast jungle. The first group of 128 privates and non-commissioned officers has already completed its training for leadership in the villages... aimed at turning African soldiers into farmers capable both of defending their country and developing its economy.
>
> The Ivory Coast French-language daily Fraternité recently carried a story by a correspondent who visited the jungle camp, which is based on the principles of Nachal...The Israelis are training the Africans in technical matters and citizenship, while the three Ivory Coast officers are responsible for military training. The group has begun clearing the jungle around the camp, and has built an irrigation dam and canals under the guidance of one of the Israelis. Vegetables, cotton, corn and rice grow now in the area.
>
> The students are divided up into groups, each under the guidance of an Israeli officer. One...is training his group as foremen, and teaching them to plan working schedules, organize workers,

---

5. While these plans are still very preliminary, the limitations on land settlement as a solution to youth problems (discussed in Chapter 4) apply here, too.

estimate costs and choose equipment. Another is training some
20 Africans in basic engineering and building—how to construct
small-scale irrigation networks, plan villages, and clear under-
growth. The third Israeli is a poultry expert and is teaching his
group to care for 8,000 chicks, which were flown in especially
from Israel, and how to plan poultry farms.

The African soldiers are learning the ABC's of cooperative
life: cooperation, tolerance, discipline, and respect for manual
labor, Fraternité wrote. The paper's correspondent was particularly impressed to see sergeants working side by side with pri-
vates, and the Israeli officers also lending a hand on the job.[6]

Other countries which have expressed an interest in setting up national
youth organizations patterned after the Israeli prototypes include Nigeria,
Dahomey, Upper Volta, the Central African Republic, and Liberia. Likewise,
the heads of the national youth movements from Mali, the Malagasy Republic,
and Senegal visited Israel to study the structure of the Gadna and Nachal.

An interesting by-product of the youth leadership course was Israel's
involvement in organizing a sports festival in Brazzaville on the Congo's
third independence day. The festival was suggested by Congolese trainees
who had witnessed a similar affair in Israel. The three-man Israeli team
trained twenty-one instructors who in turn prepared 2,000 children from thirty-
three schools for a mass calisthenics exhibition (as a result, physical education has since been introduced to the school system). Another feature of
the widely publicized event was folk-dancing by seven tribal groups. After
some observation, the Israelis discovered that there were several steps
common to all groups (although the same step had a different meaning for
different tribes). It took considerable persuasion, but eventually all the
troups appeared together in a dance built around the common steps as a
demonstration of national unity.

While the training programs discussed in this chapter have some semi-
military features, their main purpose is in the area of youth development. By
contrast, a new dimension was added to Israel's assistance program in 1963,
when sixty East African officer cadets concluded an Israeli army training
course. They will form the nucleus of the armies in their newly independent
states. These trainees were followed closely by 228 Congolese soldiers,
who came to Israel for paratroop training under United Nations auspices. [7]

---

6. The Israel Digest, November 23, 1962.

7. The Jerusalem Post Weekly, September 18, 1963.

COMMUNITY DEVELOPMENT

In other phases of community development, the vast network of social welfare institutions Israel had to establish over a short period to cope with her own pressing problems have attracted the attention of many interested observers. The International Union for Child Welfare, for example, selected Israel as a site for its 1961 international seminar, which was held in Jerusalem from April 12 to June 19. Fifteen participants came from both French- and English-speaking African countries, and nine from Asia. In the words of Mr. Mulock-Houwer, secretary of the Union.

> We chose Israel because it combines ideals with practicality; because the cooperative ideas with which it is imbued is more important for community development than the organization chart; and because it has achieved (or in places striving to achieve) a balance between oriental tradition and modern western techniques. Such a balance will somehow have to be struck in most African countries where the youth must learn modern techniques and still retain respect for the elders.

Indeed, most of the twenty-four participants in the two-month seminar found something of professional value to observe and learn. Agricultural instruction at a young age, vocational training, treatment of delinquent children, community services in the regional village center, education of the handicapped child, and the close cooperation between curative and preventive medical workers are some of the subjects that interested them. The problems common to most seminars existed also in this one: diverse educational background of participants, the need for simultaneous translation into two languages, and the question of adaptation of Israel's methods in their own countries. However, the emphasis on observation tours, on individual study in the social agency of his interest, and on rudimentary rather than the most advanced facilities available in the country, went a considerable way toward minimizing these problems and yielding satisfactory results. Note, however, that at times trainees did not receive adequate attention in the social agencies, either because they were not equipped for instruction, or because none of the employees knew English or French.

Israel itself sponsored one six-week seminar in the spring of 1961 in the area of community development. Entitled "The Role of Women in a Developing Society," the seminar was planned for women who work in the educational, health, and social welfare fields and for those active in public life in general. Its director had attended the UN-sponsored international conference in Addis Ababa on "The Participation of Women in Public Life" to gather ideas for the seminar. Sixty-six women from eight French-speaking and fourteen English-speaking countries attended, some of whom occupied prominent positions in their lands. Forty lecturers, of whom eight were guests from abroad, took part in the program, and five tutors assisted the participants in their work. Sixteen days, spread out through the seminar's six weeks' duration, were devoted to study tours and excursions to historical sites. The participants visited various types of institutions and organizations: kindergartens, schools, health centers, housing projects, agricultural settlements, and labor women's organizations; they also met with the students of the Child Welfare Seminar, and with African trainees at the Ruppin Institute.

One tutor termed the seminar "a trial shot." It provided a bird's-eye view of every aspect of community life, and included many theoretical discussions which used Israel as a background.[8] But except for the ten participants who remained for further specialized training in selected agencies, it was not a functional course. Rather, it served as a basis for developing operational courses to be offered in a permanent community development school in Haifa. Four such courses were held in 1962, a four-month course for rural community workers (see Appendix VII for the program), a six-month accelerated course for kindergarten and nursery teachers, a three-month course in home economics, and a one-month seminar for volunteer community workers. In addition to offering functional training, the school serves a useful purpose in advancing African women in both knowledge and status. In the words of one male agricultural trainee, "Women have an important role to play in the development of our country. It is inconceivable that they should be left behind while men advance through training and education."

---

8. Lectures and discussions are available from the organizers in mimeographed form.

PART **III**

PART *III* ASSISTANCE IN OTHER FIELDS

Israeli technical aid in fields other than agriculture covers a wide variety of subjects. Much of it involves the training of personnel required for industrial expansion and the service industries. Although some of the activities almost defy any logical classification, they have been grouped under the four topics which comprise this part.

CHAPTER 8 VOCATIONAL AND
MANAGEMENT EDUCATION

NEED FOR TRAINING OF INTERMEDIATE-LEVEL PERSONNEL

An educational system oriented entirely toward the training of civil servants deprives agriculture of competent personnel; it also fails to supply trained technicians to lubricate the wheels of expanding industry. One observer of the African scene has remarked that the usual emphasis on humanistic education is unsettling to social equilibrium, since it gives Africans increased wants but not the ability to satisfy them. At present, next to agricultural education, the promotion of technical training is a most important need in Africa. While high level technical advice can usually be secured by employing foreign consultants, any developing nation needs to produce an indigenous core of intermediate-level personnel:

> The training of middle-grade and junior personnel is particularly important during the first years in the life of a newly independent country which is anxious to accelerate development. In fact, at this stage in its life the shortage of personnel of this category is particularly acute. Many of those who held posts at this level before independence have taken up posts in political, administrative or trade union spheres; and many others have been enabled to undertake advanced studies. Far from increasing in keeping with the needs of new development programmes and keeping up with the rate of training of senior staff, the numbers of middle-grade personnel remain stationary and in some cases are even reduced. The position has become even more critical with the decrease in technical assistance: junior personnel of the colonial powers were withdrawn soon after independence.[1]

In some European countries, notably the United Kingdom, technical training takes place in industry through an apprenticeship system. But in Africa, as in Israel, the conditions for such training are lacking: well-developed industrial plants, and a tradition under which the interests of

1. Training of Personnel (middle-grade), Report of the Committee for Technical Cooperation in Africa South of the Sahara (Abijan, 1962).

education and production are fully harmonized. Israel, like certain European countries, obtains its technicians from special technical schools at the secondary level, and most African countries will have to do likewise. Thus, in a widely acclaimed report on vocational training in Eastern Nigeria, an Israeli survey expert added his voice to those recommending a shift to an educational system which would consist of a six-year primary school followed by a three-year junior high school and a three-year senior high school.[2] Under his proposal, some of the senior high schools would have a technical orientation while, at the same time, the teaching of crafts at the primary school level would be emphasized with a view to raising the general esteem of technical vocations.

Several African countries already have training facilities in the form of trade centers, and various foreign assistance agencies are engaged in setting up new vocational schools.[3] But "the great problem which faces the expansion of technical education is the lack of qualified staff to teach technical subjects, and this shortage is apparent at all levels."[4] Coupled with this is the need to "Africanize" the graduation requirements and adjust the curriculum to local requirements. Constant coordination between the schools and local industry is necessary if the curriculum is to be adapted to the changing needs of industry. Pupils in Nigeria, for example, in order to earn their certificate of graduation, had to prepare for the London City Guilds' examination, spending much time and effort on subjects not usable in Africa at all:

> I have seen building technicians spending a considerable amount of time studying the building and structure of open fire-places, which are rather scarce in Nigeria. The instructor who was teaching this class admitted that between one-third and one-half of the subjects taught are not applicable to local conditions. But, he added: "I have to teach them these subjects, for without them they will not succeed in the examinations for which they are sitting, and the Certificate is very important."[5]

---

2. M. Goldway, Report on Investigation of Vocational Education in Eastern Nigeria, 1961.

3. The United States Agency for International Development, for example, has opened a technical training center at Port Harcourt, Eastern Nigeria (a rapidly industrializing city) and in Conakry, Guinea (The New York Times, August 5, 1962).

4. "Technical Education in Nigeria," Nigerian Trade Journal (January/March, 1962).

5. M. Goldway, op. cit., p. 33.

VOCATIONAL TRAINING

Less than a decade ago Israel was on the receiving end of United States' technical assistance in vocational education, but over a period of a few years she developed her own training facilities to a point where the United States now uses Israel as "third country" -- as a training ground for students from other underdeveloped nations. Her vast network of four-year vocational secondary schools enabled Israel to inaugurate her own foreign training program.[6] In so doing the government had the full cooperation of ORT (Organization for Rehabilitation Training) — an organization devoted to the rehabilitation of Jewish children through vocational training.[7] ORT, one of a few vocational high school systems in Israel, has been operating training facilities throughout the world for more than eighty years, and has a network of its schools in Israel. Most, but not all, of the foreign training activity is conducted in ORT schools. Of particular importance is ORT's experience in working with children from primitive backgrounds, and with accelerated courses for new immigrants.

The center of activity in vocational education for African students is an ORT technical high school situated near Natanya, a medium-sized industrial town about twenty miles north of Tel-Aviv. In 1961, training and lodging facilities for about one hundred pupils were added to the school, and the following "one-year accelerated" courses were initiated (the school already had a Ghanaian pupil studying in the regular Hebrew course):

Metal Work (taught in English and French): This is a course intended to train skilled tradesmen for jobs in the building industry such as fitting windows and doors, installing gates and fences, railings of different types, and the like. Electrical Work (taught in English and French): Students are trained to handle (under supervision) the repair, maintenance, and instal-

---

6. Here too, Israel has shown a capacity to improvise in order to meet her own pressing social and economic needs. The lack of adequate schooling facilities in many immigrant centers induced the Ministry of Education to inaugurate an accelerated post-primary vocational training program. Fifty-five two-year vocational schools were opened throughout the country which have a combined enrollment of 4,000 pupils, mainly of Oriental origin. The Ministry has also contacted various industries in order to coordinate the teaching program with projected industrial needs and provide supplementary on-the-job training under supervision. As the social pressures wear off, steps are being taken to replace some of these small schools with comprehensive regional schools where general studies will not be "crowded out," and where a wider choice of vocations can be offered (The Jerusalem Post Weekly, October 19, 1962).

7. In embarking on this program ORT has agreed to deviate from its principle of confining its educational activity to Jewish children.

lation of domestic appliances and industrial instruments. These include lighting and power systems, heating systems, electric motors and control panels, and the mechanical work needed for these jobs. Carpentry (taught in English): The course is intended to train carpenters for the building and the furniture industries. A course in agromechanics will be added to the program in the near future.

Altogether, forty-eight students from three English-speaking countries (thirty-six of whom were Nigerians) and twenty-two from four French-speaking countries registered for the first year. Average class size was ten to fifteen pupils, and each class received twelve hours of theoretical instruction and thirty hours of practical training in the school's workshop per week — all taught by the same instructor. Studies were intensive and completely concentrated on the subject. Half of the students were to remain for two years of additional training, after which they could become foremen or instructors at an African trade center. At the same time, seventy new pupils would be accepted. Third-year students are expected to tutor freshmen as part of their training.

In addition to this permanent facility, Israel has sponsored ad hoc courses in a variety of subjects. These include automechanics, telecommunication, radio broadcasting, woodworking, linotype operation and printing, education for the blind, physical education, and construction. Information about the courses is provided in Appendix VIII.

Israel's qualifications for instructing Africans in these subjects stem from a high level of technical competence coupled with small-scale plants and lack of extreme specialization. Thus a printing instructor, who taught two Liberians for one year, made the following remarks about his vocation:

> We in Israel are twenty years behind the United Kingdom, while Liberia is fifty years behind. Consequently students can learn here with less effort than at a comparable British institute. Furthermore, Liberian newspapers print about 5,000 copies, compared to our 25,000. Why should they learn techniques at the "Daily Mirror" with a circulation of four million? They do not need methods advanced enough to produce that many newspapers, neither do they have the money to buy expensive machinery. The equipment used in the United States or the United Kingdom costs six times those used in Israel. Liberia does not need such large and modern machines which will merely stand idle most of the time.

Likewise, several telecommunications students said: "Israel was selected for training because we can see here the process of building up a system. In the United States they can only show us what they have." Also, Israel's small radio broadcasting service faces the problem of broadcasting news in many languages, as do many African countries.

Most of the courses enumerated above have been successful in carrying out their intended purpose. The students exhibited an unusual desire to study. "I never saw such enthusiasm and appetite to learn", said one instructor. Whenever background was lacking they willingly invested extra time and effort to make up the deficiency. Most of the instructors were competent and strongly motivated. In many cases, beyond the call of duty, they gave freely of their time to help the students advance faster or make up missing material. Several of the teachers had a particular interest in teaching Africans, and intended to serve in Africa at some future date.

While the arrangement (at the permanent facility) which keeps the instructor continuously with the same class taxes the teacher's endurance to the limit, it also has important advantages. In addition to encouraging an intimate relationship between teacher and student, it assures complete coordination between the theoretical and practical phases of the course. As a general rule the African students are unaccustomed to abstract thinking, and are consequently better able to learn through practical work than absorption of theoretical material. Having the same teacher for both makes it possible to get theoretical points across with the help of continuous demonstrations and observation. Indeed, the progress of one ad hoc group, where pupils were dispersed among several schools and taught by many teachers, was not marked with success. Contributory causes, however, were the group's lack of advance preparation and an attempt to turn novices into instructors in fifteen months.

A related element of strength in most vocational courses has been the stress on practical work. Performance of such work in the school's workshop under the instructor's supervision enhances its value. Again the exception demonstrates the rule, and in this case the exception is the construction course for construction foremen. Employers and sponsors of the trainees voiced strong objections to its theoretical orientation which, they felt, made the training inadequate on the practical level and, in addition, made the students who returned feel they "knew enough to be elevated out of manual work." The trainees were ill prepared to absorb the theoretical material, so the level had to be downgraded to the lowest common denominator. Furthermore, stated one lecturer, the students had no use for that much theory: "They received 45 hours of statics calculation which foremen do not need, and the 45 hours of drawing could have been cut down by half just teaching them how to read plans." He felt that more time should have been spent on various phases of practical work. "In Africa, where there is less reliance on subcontractors, more is expected of the foreman."

However, the over-emphasis on theory resulted partly from the lack of a vocational school for the construction trades, so that all practical work had to be done on the job where it was difficult to find good foremen able and willing to instruct in English. This latter difficulty has been compounded by

Israel's use of the metric system which trainees cannot readily convert into inches and feet, and by other differences in working conditions between Israel and Africa. Two printing and linotype students who received outside practical training at The Jerusalem Post complained about the same sort of thing. Similar problems were encountered in attempts to give the students in electricity, carpentry, and metal work on-the-job training outside the vocational school. Regrettably, none of the instructors in the construction course had worked in Africa, although engineers who returned from African assignments were consulted in the planning stages. Consequently, the course management has decided to set up a mobile foreman-training course in Africa as a service to the joint African-Israeli construction companies.

Even the basically successful courses were often beset by the participants' inadequate backgrounds. As a rule, the more experienced and the better educated the student, the greater the benefit he derived from the training. This was very apparent in the case of two Liberian trainees in linotype and printing. They had the same enthusiasm and aptitude, but the one with four years of prior experience benefited much more from the course than his friend, who had had only six months' experience. Diversity of background created problems in several theoretical classes. In one course, where some students were conversant with logarithms while others had difficulty with simple fractions, it was necessary to free the advanced students from the mathematics classes for a couple of months until their friends caught up.

While the ad hoc courses were instituted in response to specific requests from African governments, the permanent training facility near Natanya will in the long run recruit students for standard courses. Its objective is highly commendable, but is this the most efficient way to fulfill it? Is it worthwhile to incur the expense of training semi-skilled workers in a foreign country? Would not the teaching of novices in a foreign environment severely curtail the usefulness of such instruction? Most observers believe that basic instruction is best offered right in Africa, and that the Israeli facility should confine itself to the training of instructors. The present method of selecting such instructor-trainees, by simply choosing the top half of the first year's graduates, is expensive and inefficient. In addition, it has created bitter feelings among the unchosen. Not only do they face the possibility of being considered failures when they return home, but in vocations such as electricity a year's study is insufficient even to qualify them for semi-skilled status.

It would no doubt be preferable if graduates of the post-primary trade centers with experience in their field could be brought to Israel for an instructorship course. Where trade centers do not exist, an alternative requirement could be eight to ten years education plus a few years experience in the trade. The length of the course could vary between two and four years depending on the vocation, but the curriculum should not be planned in a vacuum. Since Israel itself does not contemplate opening trade centers in Africa, the program should be coordinated with existing trade centers and with agencies engaged in opening new ones. Only thus can the curriculum be made to fit the requirements of African industries, and teaching jobs be assured for the course graduates, making the "multiplier effect" as large as possible. In addition, it would be useful to employ in the course teachers who have worked in Africa. At the time of writing there were twenty Israeli secondary and vocational school teachers instructing in Ethiopia, Mali, Guinea, Niger, and Togo. When they return home, some of them could be used in this program. Other potential teachers of such courses should endeavor to gain experience of African conditions.

The twenty Israeli teachers working in African schools are employed individually, and are not part of a self-liquidating institutional arrangement which would have a lasting effect beyond the period of their service. By contrast, Israel has successfully established two technical institutions in Ghana, a Flying Training School and the Nautical College.

With the help of fifteen instructors from the Israeli air force Ghana opened its flying training school in September of 1959. Fifteen cadets were trained over a two-year period, receiving 1,500 hours of technical instruction and 120 hours of flying (of which 60 were "solo" flights). In addition to the ten successful graduates, the course produced a cadre of supporting Ghanaian technicians, trained on the job. When the first course was ended the Israelis were replaced by British instructors for a political reason: Israel uses French planes; as a reprisal against French atomic tests in the Sahara, Ghana severed diplomatic relations with France, and decided to switch from French to British planes.

In connection with the establishment of Ghana's shipping company, the Black Star Line (established as a joint company with the Israeli Line, Zim; see Chapter 10), the government saw the need of training Ghanaian crews. Impressed with what Israel has been able to accomplish in the few years since independence, it contracted with the Israeli navy for assistance in setting up a Nautical College.[8] During 1959-1961, the College concentrated on the training of "other ranks" in nine-month courses open to graduates of primary schools. Since the seventy-two graduates of the first two courses satisfied existing needs, the college turned to the education of officers. At the time of writing forty high school graduates were enrolled in two classes of the two-and-a-half-year course (the Ghanaian fleet would require a total of one hundred officers). In a future class it is planned to include

---

8. Israel has one four-year naval secondary school. Its graduates are ready for service in the navy as second lieutenants, and as third officers in the commercial fleet.

ten students from east Africa who are expected to serve mainly in lake shipping. In addition to these regular courses, the school occasionally engaged in ad hoc operations, such as a six-month course for crews of fishing boats and a seamanship course for volunteers from the Ghana Young Pioneers. A Ghanaian officer is now being prepared to take over command of the school.

SCIENCE AND ENGINEERING

On a higher level, Israel provides scholarships for study in its institutions of higher learning. Because of the necessity for learning Hebrew, the number of students enrolled is small. Consideration is now being given to expanding the offerings of special English-speaking courses beyond the fields of medicine and agricultural engineering to which they are now confined. It is likewise hoped to increase the number of post-graduate research fellows where, since no class attendance is required, the knowledge of Hebrew is not mandatory.

A rather unique contribution was made by the Weizmann Institute of Science in 1960 in organizing a two-week conference on "Science in the Advancement of New States." Its purpose was to explore the potentialities of science and technology as instruments for guiding and promoting the development of new states. The announcement of the Conference read:

> The scope of the Conference is to present a general picture of the achievements and prospects of the scientific and technological revolution in our time. The emphasis will be on the practical application of new techniques to the scarcities and disabilities of new societies in Africa and Asia. These include agriculture, energy and power, nutrition, public health and medicine, education, and the role of science in furthering the economic, social and political development of new states.

To that end, 120 scientists and statesmen from forty countries convened in Israel. The results of their deliberations are now available in book form, and have already stimulated considerable discussion on the subject.[9] Partly as consequence of the conference the Weizmann Institute, in collaboration with the Hebrew University, is considering the opening of a special post-graduate department for students from Africa and Asia. It would combine study and research, and the instruction would be given in English.[10]

---

9. Science and the New Nations, edited by Ruth Gruber (New York. Basic Books, 1961). A summary is also available in a pamphlet entitled: The Rehovot Declaration (Israel, 1960).

10. Another conference worthy of note was a seminar organized by the Israeli Student Association in 1962 on the role of students in developing countries.

A few Israeli professors, mainly from Israel's Institute of Technology, have taught in such African universities as the University of Liberia, (in its Pre-engineering Program) the Kumasi College of Technology (Ghana), and the Imperial College of Engineering in Addis Ababa. In the latter two cases they took charge of the engineering program. Their effectiveness was attested, among other things, by the success of the Kumasi students on the London examinations. However, these professors were hired as individuals by the respective African institutions. Israel's only contribution was in helping to locate them and evaluating their competence. A more effective arrangement would have been the "adoption" of an African institution by Israel's College of Technology (a procedure often followed by the U.S. AID.) This would involve the dispatch of Israeli professors to the African institutions, and the preparation of Africans in Israel to take over the teaching responsibilities. It is hoped that Israel's aid to the creation of a new university in Yaoundé, the capital of the Cameroons, will take this form. An agreement specifying Israel's role in this new venture was signed in the fall of 1962.

MANAGEMENT AND ECONOMICS

As a general rule, new countries are in dire need of public administrators and economic planners. Israel's contribution toward these needs has consisted of sponsoring courses in public administration, accepting individual trainees, and furnishing experts in such fields as transportation, investments, foreign trade, and statistics. Because of the great diversity of these activities, they are listed in Appendix IX; only two selected projects in the field of banking will be reviewed here.

The Bank of Israel has on occasion accepted individual trainees from foreign central banks. Officials from Madagascar, Burma, and Ghana, for instance, have taken specially tailored courses at the Bank, for durations ranging from three to ten months. The success of these programs has depended to no small extent on the officials' background. "Ill-prepared trainees simply waste their time and ours," said one Israeli official. Well-prepared trainees, like the two from Ghana's central bank, had a worthwhile learning experience.

The Ghana trainees arrived in 1961, after the deputy director of their bank had made a short preliminary visit to Israel. One of them, an economist, studied monetary and balance-of-payments problems in the research department of the Bank of Israel. Under the guidance and supervision of a senior Israeli research officer, he carried on analyses of Israeli data, and subsequently of data from Ghana supplied by mail. The second trainee concentrated on state loans, and familiarized himself with all the relevant phases of the Bank of Israel's work in that area. Both received considerable attention from the Bank's staff, including being given translations of forms into English and detailed explanation of work processes. "Some of the problems they tackled are still non-existent in Ghana," said one of their instructors, "but when they do arise the trainees will at least know that there is a solution."

Israel does not have the eminent tradition in central banking which the trainees could have found in England. It also had, for the men from Ghana, a language barrier not easy to overcome. Yet, when asked why they chose Jerusalem over London, they offered two reasons: "First, the combination of small-scale central banking operations and first-rate technicians makes Israel appropriate for Africans. And second, unlike many advanced countries, the focus in research and government loans is on economic development -- and that suits our needs best." Indeed the group of six officials from Madagascar spent part of its six months' study program in Israel in the Industrial Development and Agricultural Banks.

Turning now to work in banking abroad, a team of two Israelis was called upon to manage a bank in Burma for the Defense Service Institute, and another Israeli took over the management of the African Continental Bank in Nigeria. Their performance was highly regarded by the host governments. Yet, a remark by one of them brings up a common problem: "At the end of my second contract I would like to return home. But the Nigerians will not hear of it, since it would be difficult to maintain the improvements and innovations I introduced after my departure." Indeed it is impossible for one person, however competent, to change long-standing practices in two to four years, and expect the changes to outlast his presence. Management and training must go hand in hand. Here, as in the case of a hospital or a university, the proper solution is "institutional adoption" for a specified period of time. Under a pre-conceived plan, a team from an Israeli bank would take over the management and training functions in the African bank, while Africans would be sent to Israel for specialized training at the "adopting institution." Upon their return the Africans would gradually take over the management functions. Under such an arrangement the adopting institution would have to be responsible for the replacement of its team at proper intervals, until the assistance project was phased out.

CHAPTER **9** TRADE
UNIONISM

ISRAEL'S LABOR MOVEMENT

Because of certain unique features, Israel's Federation of Trade Unions
(Histadrut) has long attracted the attention of labor leaders throughout
the world. The succession of distinguished visitors representing the trade
union movements of Asian, African, and Latin American countries demonstrates the attraction it holds for the newly emerging nations.[1] Like their
own labor movements prior to independence, the Histadrut was a bastion of
resistance against colonial rule. But it differs from them in its structure,
orientation, and breadth of activity.

Unlike those in many western countries, the labor and cooperative movements in Israel did not spring up as a counterforce to the exploiting power
of private capital, nor as an instrument in a class struggle. Rather, they
started as a constructive tool of economic and social progress. In the words
of A. D. Gordon, one of the Histadrut's founders, "We are not going to
change anything or improve anything. We are going to begin from the beginning." The Indian Government Delegation (see Chapter 4) was struck by
this fact, and its report states:

> .....very little private capital existed in Palestine when the early
> Jewish settlements were set up. Hence the cooperative movement
> as well as the labor movement in Israel was shaped primarily as
> an instrument of economic development rather than as a safeguard
> against exploitation. In the words of Margaret Digby, the Coopera-
> tive Movement in Israel is 'engaged not in transforming an exist-
> ing economy but in creating an economy.'

Starting from this premise, the Histadrut evolved a structure and activities to meet the economic challenges of its time and locale. As a trade

1. The following is a sampling of such visitors: John Tettegah of Ghana
(1957), Dr. Goh Keng Swee of Singapore (1959), Dr. S. Tania of Indonesia
(1959), Seril Adoula of the Congo (1960), R. Binto of Katanga (1960), high-
level delegations from Mali, Cyprus, India and Senegal (1960), Tom Mboya
of Kenya (1962), N. Kazimoto of Tanganyika (1962).

union in the narrow sense of the word, the Histadrut is centrally organized, based on individual membership rather than the affiliation of separate unions. [2] The worker joins the General Federation directly and, through his membership in it, is also a member of a particular union. The Histadrut itself is the center of authority and delegates certain powers to its unions, most of which were formed by its initiative. This is rather different from many national trade union federations, which derive their powers from largely autonomous affiliates. Collective agreements are negotiated by individual unions, but within the framework of an overall policy laid down by the executive committee of the Histadrut. Dues are paid to the central body (by the check-off system) which allocates a percentage of them to the individual unions.

In unity lies strength. And while power can be misused, in the case of the Histadrut it made possible the pursuit of policies in the national interest. For example, according to a visiting Ghanaian delegation, "On such basic questions as wages, the Histadrut can take into account not only the immediate interest of the workers but the need of the national economy and the interest of all labor." [3] In other areas, the Histadrut has sponsored adult vocational training programs to help alleviate unemployment which is highest among the unskilled, and has launched a productivity drive to make Israel's products more competitive abroad. [4]

Furthermore, the Histadrut maintains a vast network of social services. All members automatically benefit from the Sick Fund which runs 900 outpatient clinics and sixteen hospitals throughout the country (almost half of the membership fees are earmarked for health services). A variety of welfare institutions give assistance in various types of social need, while a whole array of educational services and cultural programs operate on both the local and national levels.

A final feature of the Histadrut is the economic enterprises which it holds or supervises. The far-flung cooperative movement, paramount in agriculture and transport but prominent also in certain industrial and service branches, is affiliated with it. [5] In addition, it owns a large number of

---

2. For a detailed analysis of its structure, see Margaret Plunkett, "The Histadrut: The General Federation of Jewish Labor in Israel," Labor and Industrial Relations Review, II, No. 2 (January, 1958), 155–183.

3. Ghana's Trade Union Congress (TUC), The New Charter for Ghana's Labor, Accra, p. 5.

4. The Histadrut participates in the National Productivity Institute, encourages incentive pay based on norms and premiums, and consults with the manufacturers on production problems.

5. See N. Malkosh, Cooperatives in Israel (Tel-Aviv, 1958).

industrial, construction, and service enterprises through its holding company Solel Boneh.[6] The "business arm" enables the Histadrut to play an important role in the development of the country. As a rule such enterprises began on a very small scale as ad hoc solutions to immediate problems. Solel Boneh started as a small building company at a time of economic depression in 1925 to help create jobs for construction workers. A similar employment crisis in the rural areas led to the formation of an agricultural contracting company, now Yahin-Hakal. The consumer's movement grew out of supply difficulties during the First World War, and the Agricultural Marketing Company, Tnuva, was started to help the workers' villages dispose of their produce. In recent years Histadrut industries have largely been located away from the main population centers, in immigrant towns which faced grave unemployment problems. Also, large capital has been invested in the exploration of natural resources. Profit from these enterprises is always reinvested.

Visiting delegations from several countries have expressed interest in adopting some of these features of Histadrut. Thus the Boodhan mission from India stated: "The structure of the Histadrut should be studied carefully by some prominent and imaginative workers of the trade union movement with a view of finding out how far things can be borrowed and applied to our own labor movement." Premier Okpara of Nigeria's eastern region was impressed by the Histadrut's role in developing the economy, as was a delegation from Senegal. Other visitors have evinced interest in emulating the Histadrut's activities in the social and educational fields. Tom Mboya and N. Kazimoto, leaders of the Kenyan and Tanganyikan trade unions, concluded agreements for technical cooperation with the Histadrut, which also advises the Malagasy labor movement. But Ghana's Trade Union Congress (TUC) went furthest in actually borrowing much of the Histadrut structure and accepting Histadrut advice on the introduction of basic reforms.

GHANA'S T.U.C.

Following his 1957 visit to the Histadrut John Tettegah, the General Secretary of Ghana's labor movement, decided to centralize the structure of his organization. He dispatched six department heads to examine closely the activities of the Histadrut.[7] On the basis of their reports, and with the help of three successive Israeli advisors on loan from Histadrut, Ghana's

---

6. Solel Boneh will be discussed in greater detail in the next chapter.

7. Following are the topics studied by the delegation: a) General Structure, Solel Boneh (Histadrut Construction Co.), Housing; b) Economic Enterprises of Histadrut; c) Trade Union and Histadrut Accounting; d) Trade Unionism; e) Educational and Cultural Activities, Health Services, and Insurance; f) General Structure of the Histadrut, Cooperative Settlement.

trade union movement was changed to conform more closely to that of its Israeli counterpart, "different in structure and in aims from labor movements in Western industrial countries, similar to the Histadrut in aims but in structure a Ghanaian movement as such." [8]

A centralized structure holds considerable appeal for labor leaders in newly developed countries as a means of strengthening their movements. That such strength is now lacking, and that the weakness of many African unions results in no small measure from their small size, is attested by the following account:

> These unions are typically small.....because they are small, they are weak—too weak, in some cases, to be able to exercise even the rudimentary functions of trade unionism. By the time the one or two necessary officials, say the chairman and secretary-treasurer, of a small union have collected their expenses and honoraria, there is very little dues money left for extension work. And in small, largely illiterate groups, it is seldom possible to find those who are skilled in negotiation, the making of agreements, and the settling of disputes.....
>
> Being small, weak and on the defensive, most African unions devote a large part of their time to the redress of individual or collective grievances against plant managements, and to seeking to improve plant working conditions. Accordingly, in function, at any rate, they are not very different from the labor-management committees or works councils that many companies have set up. [9]

By contrast, a number of powerful unions have developed in recent years in French-speaking African countries. These include the Confédération Générale du Travail which muster almost two thirds of all the trade unionists in the territories formerly constituting French West Africa, the Confédération Africaine de Travailleurs Croyants, the Force Ouvrière, and the West African Fédération des Cheminots Africans. Their strength is quite closely related to their size:

> Not the least reason for the power of these French unions is that they are large enough.....to have a decent income from dues. This enables them to maintain both a field staff and a headquarters staff. With the former they can keep their members well informed of the work of their union and so disposed to go on supporting it. With the latter they can keep government and management apprised of their demands, and see to it that these demands are continually put before the public in speech, newspaper and pamphlet. [10]

---

8. Ghana's TUC, The New Charter for Ghana's Labor, Accra.

9. Kimble, Tropical Africa, op. cit., Vol. II, pp. 214, 216.

10. Ibid, p. 217.

Prior to the reorganization Ghana had over 100 independent unions, joined together in a loose federation, some with a membership of just over fifty. These could not "hope to provide any service to the membership except protecting them from dismissals and victimizations."[11] The loose federation pattern widely practiced in the industrial nations of the west was deemed inadequate for the labor movement of an essentially agrarian nation. A centralized movement would not only contribute strength, but would be able to play an active role in the country's economic development.

Consequently, Ghana's trade unions were amalgamated first to twenty-four and then to sixteen national unions, affiliated with a strong federation.[12] The movement is governed by the Supreme Congress which meets annually and delegates authority to an executive committee of twenty-five, consisting of sixteen leaders of the national unions and nine heads of departments of the General Secretariat.[13] Membership dues are collected by the federation through a check-off system, and are allotted as follows: 50 per cent to the national unions, 15 per cent to the TUC for general administration and education services, 30 per cent to special social security and economic enterprise fund, and 5 per cent to the national strike fund.

During his short stay, one of the Israeli advisors witnessed sincere efforts by the TUC on behalf of all workers. He observed: "A few years ago there were 125 trade unions in Ghana which spent most of their energy in internal conflicts and intrigues. Today the artificial barriers have disappeared, and Ghana's workers are united in one TUC composed of sixteen unions. Its growing membership today is 400,000."

But the "new structure" was not achieved strictly through voluntary

---

11. New Charter, op. cit., p. 2.

12. These are: 1) The Building Trades Industrial Union; 2) Union of Distributive, Retail and Allied Workers; 3) National Union of Agricultural and Plantation Workers; 4) General Municipal and Local Government Employees' Union; 5) Civil Service Clerical and Administrative Staff Union; 6) National Maritime, Lighterage and Dockworkers' Union; 7) Public Utility and Allied Government Industrial Union; 8) National Union of Railway Workers; 9) Ghana Mineworkers' Union; 10) Amalgamated Timbers and Woodworkers' Union; 11) National Ghana Teachers' Union; 12) Ghana Health and Hospital Workers' Union; 13) Ghana Postal and Telecommunications Workers' Union; 14) National Journalists and Printers' Union; 15) National Union of Ghana Oil and Petroleum Workers; 16) National Union of Domestic, Restaurant, Hotel and Bar Workers.

13. The TUC Departments are: International Organization; Finance and Accounts; Publicity and Information; Education; Legal; Economic; Political and Social Affairs; Trade Development and Business Enterprises; Research Department.

action. Not only was it imposed from above, but it was supported by legislation. From the beginning Mr. Tettegah realized that some leaders of the independent Unions would not willingly give up their leadership.[14] Thus, along with the reorganization came the Industrial Relations (Amendment) Act of August, 1959, which made the existence of unions outside the amalgamated sixteen practically impossible. It thereby forestalled the withdrawal from the TUC of unions opposing the centralized structure.

The Ghanaian movement hopes gradually to introduce several of the social and educational services practiced by the Histadrut, as well as activities in the economic sphere. Paragraph 9 of the New Charter reads:

> From the Social Security and Business Enterprises fund, money will be invested in starting productive enterprises, e.g., Building and Construction Companies, Cooperative, Wholesale, Retail and Distributive shops, Harbour Management Catering Services. In short, subsidiary companies will be chartered by the Trades Union Congress on its own or in partnership with other labour institutions internally or abroad without dividends, the profits being used to increase the economic strength of the Labour Movement.

Although some enterprises were taken over from the government, little progress was made in this direction during the first three years of the new TUC.

Can any inferences be drawn from this experience as well as from statements of labor experts in other countries? There is good reason to believe that certain features of the Histadrut can be beneficially borrowed by underdeveloped countries. Some amalgamation of extremely fragmented unions would be helpful in strengthening the labor movement, in making possible education activities and social services, and in conserving and bettering the utilization of scarce competent union personnel. Consideration of the national interest in the formulation of wage and other union policies is another essential feature for countries engaged in development. Furthermore, the establishment of consumer and credit cooperatives by individual unions and their ultimate affiliation with the national labor movement can be of benefit to the membership.

But blanket emulation holds dangers. Especially if imposed from above, a centralized movement lends itself to undemocratic exploitation. While the belief of some observers that government-inspired trade unionism is bound to become government-controlled may not hold in all cases, the danger of such an eventuality should be guarded against. Although the initiative for centralizing a labor movement must often come from above, any action in that direction should be preceded by careful consideration by the constituent unions.

---

14. The Histadrut never had to face such a problem, since it started with a clean slate.

They should be given a feeling of active participation in the reorganization process. As the centralization process progresses, there are always dangers arising from conflicts of interest among heterogeneous groups. The Histadrut itself has not always been able to resolve such conflicts in recent years–and demands by professional unions for larger wage differentials between themselves and the majority of the membership have led to "unauthorized strikes" and threats of secession. Similarly, the teachers' strikes in Guinea and the Takoradi port strike in Ghana were against the will of the Federation.

Some features of the Histadrut which other labor movements want to adopt may properly belong elsewhere. Ghana's TUC, for example, absorbed the labor exchanges. But even in Israel these have been meanwhile transferred to the Ministry of Labor. The Sick Fund, which is the envy of many an African labor leader, may some day be transferred to the Ministry of Health.[15] Finally, the companies controlled by the Histadrut were created before Israel's independence, and one may ask whether in independent states their functions do not properly belong in the development and other ministries.

Almost any African emulation of the Histadrut involves changes in the status quo under conditions totally different from those which prevailed in Palestine forty years ago. The obvious point of the above illustrations is not that certain modifications are not worthwhile, but there is need to temper enthusiasm with careful study before undertaking any changes of social importance. The USOM motto, "Adapt -- not adopt," applies here with particular cogency. It is with this motto in mind that the Histadrut has set up the Afro-Asian Institute for Labor Studies and Cooperation.

THE AFRO-ASIAN INSTITUTE

Unlike its forerunners, the courses in cooperation (see Chapter 3), this Institute is a permanent center of learning. Its purpose is "to train the leadership of labor movements in Asia and Africa.....with an emphasis on practical experience."[16] Housed in a newly constructed building[17] at the

---

15. At present the Ministry of Health and the Histadrut maintain parallel curative and preventive health facilities, and there is considerable agitation in Israel for concentrating all publicly-owned health facilities in the hands of the Ministry.

16. Avrech, "Afro-Asian Institute for Labor Studies", Educational Institutions and International Labor, Proceedings of a Conference at Michigan State University, March, 1962, p. 109.

17. Costing a quarter of a million dollars, the building includes a dormitory, classrooms, halls, offices, and a dining room.

heart of Tel-Aviv, its annual budget of over half a million dollars is financed by the Histadrut with a generous scholarship contribution from the AFL-CIO. It offers four-month courses, taught in English and French, and has a permanent staff of fourteen officials consisting of the director, a deputy director, an organizational assistant, four tutors, two outside advisors, a registrar, a librarian, and three secretaries. Most lectures are given by outside specialists, but they are supplemented by intensive discussion sessions under the supervision of the Institute's tutors.

The Institute gates were opened in October of 1960, and through the spring of 1962 it offered three courses of varying duration. Table 9-1 provides essential information about the student body and the content of the courses (for a detailed program see Appendix X).

Table 9-1

Session	Duration	Number of Students	English-Speaking	French-Speaking	Number of Countries Represented	Number of Outside Lecturers
First	6 months	71	39	32	24	40
Second	4 months	50	25	26	26	40
Third	3½ months	48	48	0	19	23

Distribution of Days

	First Session	Second Session	Third Session
Lectures	81	40	40
Excursions	22	31	15
Work on cooperative settlements	12	11	9
Specialized observations	12	6	6

Division of Lecture Hours

	First Session	Second Session	Third Session
Cooperation	196	40	60
Trade unionism	166	84	90
Economics	66	60	50
Israel and its people	34	20	10
Total	462	214	210

Studies are conducted five and a half days a week. The mornings are usually devoted to lectures, while the afternoons are left free for independent work, largely under the supervision of the tutors. On Sundays and Fridays arrangements are made for Christian and Moslem students to attend their own religious services. All living expenses are borne by the Institute, which in many cases also covers transportation to and from Israel. Recruitment of students is facilitated through Israel's diplomatic representatives in Africa and Asia, in cooperation with trade unions and cooperatives in Afro-Asian countries.

To varying degrees the courses in the Institute suffer from the problems common to other training programs. Many of its students never went beyond primary school. Consequently, quite a few of the lectures are well above their heads, while in some subjects the students force a reduction in the standard of instruction to the lowest common denominator. The latter consequence produces bitter complaints from the sizeable minority of better-educated participants who feel, rightly, that it makes little sense to have university graduates and primary-school leavers in the same class. The great diversity among the students in experience, age, and general orientation only aggravates the situation.

But the Afro-Asian Institute is burdened with unusual problems, partly because it deals with broad social issues rather than strictly technical matters like cattle-breeding or carpentry. And its conflicting aims make these problems difficult to cope with.[18] Two such conflicts may be readily perceived -- the combining of cooperation and trade unionism, and the attempt to make a miniature university out of the Institute

An examination of the program shows that cooperation and trade unionism played equally important parts in the first and third sessions. To a lesser extent this was true even of the second session, allegedly devoted solely to the latter subject. The composition of the student body illustrates the same phenomenon. Most participants are drawn from the ranks of middle-grade officials in the labor and cooperative movements and in the appropriate government departments.

The alliance of cooperatives with the labor movement in Israel is a source of strength to both — unique as it may be. It can perhaps be beneficially adapted by African countries, but the students who come to the Institute are not qualified to pass judgment on the feasibility of such emulation. Their background is much too inadequate for comprehension of a social transformation of that nature, and their position in their various organiza-

---

18. It must be emphasized that the following discussion is based on the first two years of the Institute's activities. The 1962 attempts to introduce significant changes in many phases of its operation are not included in this account.

tions is too low to allow them to exert significant influence in that direction. Essentially their horizon does not reach much beyond their own often small union or cooperative. As such they resent having to devote much time and energy to the study of a subject that does not directly concern them. The trade unionists fail to see any value in practical work on cooperative settlements. "This is not a course in rural planning," complained one of them. Cooperators exhibit equal annoyance at having to study trade unionism. The one African student out of thrity interviewed in one course who liked the mixture of the two subjects switched from union to cooperative work as a result of the course, which is certainly not an objective of the Institute.

This is an unsatisfactory state of affairs. The teaching of cooperation to trade unionists should be confined to superficial treatment in a few lectures on the Histadrut structure. Beyond that it should be strictly oriented toward aspects having a direct potential benefit to the student. The organization of a consumer cooperative or a credit society by an individual union is one such aspect. Likewise, there is little point in exposing secretaries of small marketing societies to extensive work in trade unionism. The clearer the separation between the two subjects, the better the results will be for the students.

An unconscious but fairly perceptible attempt to give university status to the Institute has resulted in a serious gap between the level of the lectures and the level of the students' capacities. This is manifested first in the reliance on a large number of outside specialists. An occasional guest lecturer is usually a good thing, but to run a permanent Institute on that basis is of questionable value. The resultant fragmentation of topics deprives the course of a focus, prevents direct and frequent contact between student and lecturer, and causes repetition and sometimes conflicts. For ex-example, students complained that the section on economic development was covered before they had completed its prerequisite, introductory economics. To be sure, the outside-lecturer system exposes the trainees to the best specialized knowledge in each field, but since they are not graduate students, all too often such knowledge is well above their heads. Consolidation, focus, and good instruction on a high-school level are far more important, and can be attained by greater reliance on the excellent tutors, and on a few good high school teachers who are conversant with the subjects and able to lecture well in English and French. It would also be worthwhile to employ an African instructor for each language. Finally, the course could be structured so as to devote, in succession, two weeks to classroom instruction and practical observation for each subject.

A further evidence of a tendency toward a university orientation is the emphasis on broad social subjects. The teaching of economic theory and development on a fairly sophisticated level in thirty hours is a hopeless and unwarranted effort that yields negligible results. The same holds true of close study of the structure of the Histadrut and other broad labor problems by students who cannot comprehend how these matters might apply to Africa. Several African labor leaders felt that the Institute was too removed from African conditions. One of them said that "those who returned from the Afro-Asian Institute were useless at home and could not do a thing because they were always thinking in terms of a structure which does not exist here."

By contrast, the Labor Institute at Kampala, Uganda, run by the International Confederation of Free Trade Unions (ICFTU), is based on east African conditions, and concentrates on topics which are of direct value to the students' daily work. Its program includes:

Philosophy of Unions	Workers education
Unions and Society	Speech
Office management	

Organizational Problems of Unions:

membership	auditing
elections	accounting
strikes	conducting union meetings
publicity	grievance procedure
finances	

Israel's Ministry of Labor planned a two-month international course in Industrial Relations for the spring of 1962 with a similar orientation. Designed for African labor officers in government, unions, and industry, it was to consist of twenty-five days of lectures, seventeen days of practical work and excursions and ten days of directed studies with the help of tutors. Judging from the printed program (reproduced in Appendix XI), the lectures would be directly focused on carefully-restricted practical problems.

It would be well for the Institute to adopt a more practical orientation. [19] With it should come greater reliance on visual aids, purposeful field trips, and workshops in the instruction program, and the devotion of some attention to foreign and international trade union movements. The director and tutors should visit Africa and study its labor problems at first hand. They should also meet with the African labor leaders and arrange for them to share the responsibility for the courses. This would make it easier to enforce discipline on students who fail to apply themselves by sending them home or denying them the graduation certificate. To the extent that labor problems

---

19. On May 10, 1963, the Jewish Observer and Middle East Review reported (p. 15) that "the ambitious courses were replaced by simpler, more practical material, which were readily assimilable and of direct use to students when they returned home."

vary between different regions of Asia and Africa, segregation of classes by geographical groups would make for more effective teaching.

The study of broad social issues must be reserved for students with university educations, and one place to recruit such students is from the number of young Africans attending schools in western Europe. In 1961, 2,760 students from tropical Africa were enrolled in British universities, of which 1,210 were studying in the Arts faculties. At the University of Paris there were over 3,300 students from the overseas French Union countries, of which close to a quarter were in the social sciences and law. Selected students in the social sciences, preferably after their junior or senior year, could be brought to the Institute for a summer program. They could come to Israel by sea, which would lower the cost of such programs and make orientation possible en route. The programs should instruct them in broad subjects in which Israel possesses unique features, and which are related to their university studies.[20] If Hebrew university professors were enlisted to teach the courses, the students could perhaps get credit for their work at their own universities.

Because of the unique structure of its labor movement, Israel lacks the setting for teaching "classical" trade unionism to middle-grade functionaries. But at least as important is the Institute's inability to provide opportunities for practical training and observation. Such training is considered by many African leaders to be the most important part of any course. Ideally, each student should be assigned to the organization of his choice (which should be related to his work at home) for the duration of his stay, and learn in depth the operation of at least one or two of its departments. As it is, such training is not integrated into the course; only one meager week is reserved for it at the end. And even that week presents problems. Often the ill-prepared student does not quite know what he wants to observe, or his preference may be totally unrelated to the course work. Statistics, the stock market, and the fire department are examples of irrelevant specialization requests made under these circumstances.

For the subjects closely related to the study program, the Institute does maintain close contact with thirty trade unions and other organizations in the Tel-Aviv area.[21] But the training there is very superficial, and the Institute does not attempt to follow it up by receiving and examining progress reports. Language is a severe handicap. Since collective bargaining is carried out in Hebrew, the students cannot follow the sessions at first hand.

---

20. I made this suggestion to the Director of the Institute, who at the time promised to pursue it.

21. The question has been raised as to whether Tel-Aviv or a new, small development town is more suitable for such training.

Often it is impossible to provide an interpreter for every small group of trainees. Finally, students do not always arrive for practical training with adequate backgrounds, and the Institute seldom provides the "training organizations" with advance background information on their trainees. In sum, says one Institute instructor, "the practical training degenerates into a week of pleasant sightseeing tours."

While the practical training is too short and too loosely supervised, a disproportionately large part of the course is devoted to Israel — in both lecture and tour. Said one serious student: "While justly proud of their achievements, the Israelis are carried away with their zeal and devote too much time to Israel and its people. This is supposed to be a seminar on trade unionism and not on the problems of Israel." The Institute tutors feel that too much emphasis on Israel and its problems gives the students an exaggerated feeling of importance — "as if they were brought here to be converted to Israel's side." Important guest lecturers merely enhance this feeling. It got to the point where one student threatened to say "anything he liked" about Israel if his demands were not met.

An attempt to train trade unionists who hold central positions in their countries' labor movements was made by the Histadrut in 1961. A two-week seminar was organized in Israel for seventy-three east African labor leaders, but half of their stay was spent in touring the country, leaving less than a week for substantive lectures. As a consequence, while some of those interviewed before departure favored their movement's adopting a centralized structure, they did not seem to realize the full implication of such action. That it would sharply curtail the freedom of action of their individual union and limit its right to strike without federation approval appears to have escaped them. An apparent attempt at a deeper understanding of the Histadrut was undertaken by twenty-five labor leaders from twelve Latin American countries during a five weeks' study-visit in the fall of 1962.

The following recommendations appear warranted on the basis of this study. First, the regular 3½ month course at the Institute should be confined to specific branches of cooperation. Coupled with an insistence on a homogeneous student body, and with the adoption of a practical orientation, this would make for a program which the intermediate-level participants could absorb and apply. Indeed, one of the better courses in the field was the one on agricultural cooperation for east African cooperative officers discussed in Chapter 3. Second, in the area of trade unionism the Institute should organize three-to four-week seminars for high-level, well educated labor officials. Among other topics they should study the structure of the Histadrut and decide which, if any, of its unique features they might wish to adopt. Only after the spadework was done would it be profitable to teach lower-level courses on trade unionism.

CHAPTER 10 JOINT COMMERCIAL VENTURES

"Speed and Joint Ownership" are the key factors to which The New York Times attributed the popularity of Israel's projects in Africa.[1] Indeed, the great majority of Israelis who work in Asia and Africa are attached to companies organized as partnerships between an arm of the local government and a semi-public Israeli company. These enterprises engage primarily in construction, water resource development, and shipping; the local government always owns the controlling share -- either 51 or 60 per cent -- of the stock. There are also plans for setting up industrial plants on the same basis, but none has materialized so far except a company for the export of uncut diamonds, established in partnership with the Central African Republic in mid-1962.

THE FACTS

At the request of the Ghanaian government, Israel's national shipping company, Zim Lines, entered into a 40-60 per cent partnership with Ghana to establish the Black Star Line (with a registered capital of G£1/2 million.[2] This joint venture, embarked upon at the end of 1957, was the first undertaking of its kind in west Africa. (Nigeria has since set up a shipping line in a similar partnership with a British company). The partnership lasted for three years. In 1960, as part of an overall policy to terminate all partnerships between the government and foreign interests, Ghana bought out Israel's share, but retained Zim on a management contract through 1965. Similarly, Burma invited Zim to take over the management of its Five Star Line on a five-year management-contract basis. The contract also provided for the training of Burmese officials at Zim's headquarters in Haifa.

In the field of water development, a subsidiary of Israel's publicly-

---

1. October 16, 1960.

2. Equals U S $1.4 million.

owned corporation, Water Resource Development - International, Ltd., entered into partnership with the governments of Eastern and Western Nigeria to form water resource development companies. They engage in well drilling, dam construction, building of sewage systems and similar projects. In eastern Nigeria, the operational company is also the planning consultant to the government, while in the west an independent consulting company was formed by Israel (not in partnership), to advise the government and supervise the execution of its water plans.[3] An Israeli planning office was also set up in Ghana, with an initial assignment to plan water-supply systems for five cities between Accra and Takoradi. Functional separation of the contractor from the planner, with the latter supervising the former on behalf of the government, is considered a healthier arrangement, although not always warranted by the scale of operations. The planning offices were established by Israel's Water Planning Authority (Tahal), and many of the detailed plans are actually drawn in Israel.

By far the greatest number of the joint commercial ventures is in the construction field. Solel Boneh, the construction company of the Histadrut and the largest contractor in Israel, has been engaged in overseas operations in Turkey and Cyprus since the end of World War II. In May of 1958 it entered into partnership with the Ghana Industrial Development Corporation to establish the Ghana National Construction Company (GNCC) on a 40-60 per cent basis. Subsequent partnerships were formed in Western Nigeria (Niger-Sol), Eastern Nigeria (Eastern Nigeria Construction and Furniture Company), and Sierra Leone (National Construction Company). In East Africa, Solel Boneh is active in Ethiopia and plans joint companies in Tanganyika and Kenya, where the partnership will probably be with the trade-union movement, while Nepal and Burma are its strongholds in the far east. Plans are under way to set up joint construction companies in the Upper Volta and the Central African Republic.[4]

By the fall of 1962 the joint construction companies had reached a combined annual turnover of $40 million. They employed a total of 33,000 local workers and 350 Israeli engineers and foremen. Annual turnover of individual companies ranges from $3 million in Sierra Leone and Eastern Nigeria to $10 million in Western Nigeria. The latter company employs seventy Israelis and 7,000 Nigerians. With a few exceptions, such as a highly successful furniture factory in Eastern Nigeria, the companies special-

---

3. The Jewish Telegraphic Agency reported on March 8, 1963, that Israel and Brazil have set up a joint water development company, capitalized at $210,000, with the majority share owned by Brazil.

4. An Israeli construction company, the Meir Brothers, operates in Liberia and the Ivory Coast as a private expatriate firm.

ize in construction projects that include houses, hotels, roads, airports, public buildings, a fishing harbor, and dams. Some of their more impressive performances were the completion of the parliament building in Sierra Leone in ten months (in time for Independence Day) and of the Black Star Square in Accra in time for the queen's visit in 1960. Many companies have their own ancillary services such as carpenter shops, machine shops, maintenance units, quarries, building materials yards, and departments of heavy e-quipment, transport, and technical activities.

All partnerships are subject to a time limit after which complete ownership is to be turned over to the local interest in return for fair compensation. In Ghana the partnership was terminated in February of 1962, two years ahead of schedule, when the government bought out Solel Boneh and assumed the management of the company. However, the Israeli technical staff was retained in an advisory capacity for several years, at the end of which the Ghanaians are expected to take over all technical positions.

In line with the desire to separate construction from planning, a planning and design company, AMI, was set up as a subsidiary of Solel Boneh to serve as a consultant to foreign governments. Jobs performed thus far include the design of the Parliament building in Sierra Leone, the university campus, at IFE, West Nigeria, four hotels in Nigeria, an airport in Nepal, factories, housing projects, and office buildings. The activities of AMI may or may not be related to those of its "sister contractors."

A final example of semi-commercial activities are the management contracts in the hotel industry. Israeli companies are managing hotels in Ibadan, Monrovia, Rangoon, Abijan, and Dar-Es-Salaam. In most cases these luxury hotels were built by an Israeli or joint construction company, while the one in Rangoon was constructed by Russian builders. Training of indigenous personnel, which would eventually take over the management, is provided for in all the contracts.

THE ROLE AND MERITS OF JOINT ENTERPRISES

All the companies mentioned above involved the respective African governments in more than negligible expense. In addition to the initial investment (which varies considerably from one country to another), the host government often commits itself in advance to award the new company negotiated contracts, which are sometimes compensated for at above-market prices. It may rightly be asked what these jointly-owned companies contribute to the development of the countries in which they function.

In several cases the new enterprise supplied a service which had not existed before. None of the African countries had an organization specializing in the development of water resources, yet this is an activity of considerable direct benefit to the people. The drilling of wells in remote villages, where drinking water has had to be carried by human power over a considerable distance, has a favorable impact on the rural economy. Both the technician who executes the project and the politician who is credited for bringing him to the village are widely appreciated and acclaimed. Similarly, there are countries in which no modern construction company existed before the joint venture, which meant considerable delays in the execution of development plans. So, for example, a United Nations representative in Nepal said, "The joint company met a badly felt need since several UN-designed projects have in the past not been executed. This will now be the only up-to-date construction company in the country." Finally, while it might be argued that Ghana has not yet reached a state of development which warrants large investment in shipping, ownership of the Black Star Line gives Ghana a voice in fixing freight rates (through participation in the shipping conference in which such rates are determined) on which her own foreign trade depends.

But several of the construction companies (as distinguished from those concerned with water development) did not add any new services. Large expatriate firms have long been in existence in some African countries, and by virtue of tradition and experience were capable of meeting international standards in the construction trade. In fact, the newly created companies, lacking knowledge of local conditions, often suffered "teething problems" during their first year. The negotiated government contracts were indispensable for setting them on their feet.[5] Thus the main justification for establishing them is their potential for creating indigenous firms. This, in most cases, is the overriding objective of the African government, and it is also the stated aim of the Israeli partner. In the words of a high-ranking official of Solel Boneh: "The avowed aim is to set up construction companies able to compete effectively with the expatriate firms operating in the respective countries; companies which will eventually be transferred to local ownership, and which will be capable of executing the countries' development plans." It is for this reason that all agreements contemplate the termination of the partnership at a specified future date.

What is the advantage of the partnership arrangement over the formation of a strictly indigenous enterprise with the help of foreign technical consultants? The overwhelming majority of the African officials interviewed felt that as partners the Israelis would be more devoted and committed to the success of the new ventures. To this Israeli officials added two reasons of their own. First, "the role of an advisor is to answer questions, and often

5. Even there the new companies (once they became viable) often served the important purpose of injecting competition into a semi-monopolistic market.

the Africans would not know what questions to ask, or how to derive full benefit from the advice given. The only solution lies in handing over both management and execution to the foreign technicians." Second, the creation of a new company is usually superior to the gradual modernization of an existing agency or company through foreign technical advice. It makes possible the introduction of a new organizational framework and new ways of executing contracts, while freeing the foreign consultant from administrative red tape. It sets up a new body, capable of making independent decisions and taking vigorous action, which will remain viable after the foreign interest has pulled out. This point may be illustrated by the experience of an Israeli hydrologist and a driller who were invited as consultants to an African government to help supply water in certain remote locations. They were unable to convince the government that drilling equipment does not belong in a separate department, but should be attached to the driller in the field. Often they were frustrated by an inability to use funds which had already been appropriated, because releasing them required signatures of two officials who were not on speaking terms. And quite frequently they were hampered by cumbersome administrative procedures whenever it was necessary to order new equipment. As a consequence, they recommended that an independent company be hired to do the job.

Viewed in this light the joint ventures embody important elements of technical assistance. They are potentially self-liquidating. And their objective is to leave behind a viable indigenous organization, supplying essential services and engaged in basic developmental activities. To that end each project calls for the training of local personnel at both the intermediate and university level who will gradually, under supervision, assume central positions within the organization.

A combination of factors have made Israel attractive as a partner to African governments. By virtue of her small size Israel poses no threat, and could not possibly use the partnership as a means for long-run economic exploitation. The ease with which the Ghanaians were able to terminate the partnerships ahead of the date originally agreed upon underscored this point. And considerable importance attaches in the African mind to the temporary nature of the partnership. "Do whatever you deem necessary – but do not build synagogues here," said one African official. At the same time Israel possesses the required technical and managerial skills and is willing and eager to share them. Her outstanding record in developing a large, modern, and efficient commercial fleet in less than a decade, and in meeting challenges in both water development and construction, were undoubtedly instrumental in drawing the attention of African leaders. Finally, Israeli foremen and engineers are known for their hard work and practical approach. "Where else would I get such donkeys?" said one official, comparing them to the British, whom he called "sit-at-tables engineers." Indeed, the Israeli technicians who went from one village to the next drilling wells twelve hours a day, or the men who worked on road construction for equally long hours, demonstrate his point.

The typical pattern is for the Israeli partner to supply the core of managers, engineers, and foremen, and to recruit locally as many technicians and skilled workers as are available. As time goes on, more indigenous personnel is trained (locally and overseas) to assume positions of responsibility in the firm.

That the joint venture is a valuable tool of assistance and advice is demonstrated by the unqualified success of Ghana's Black Star Lines. By 1961 that company was lucratively operating seventeen ships in three lines (to Europe, the United Kingdom, and the United States), and was planning a fourth line to the Mediterranean. An intensive training program was instituted in Accra and in Zim offices in Israel and London. Administrative positions are gradually being transferred to Ghanaians, and it is hoped that by the end of the current management contract Israel's aid can be terminated. In the equally difficult area of manning the ships, there are already one Ghanaian captain and thirteen officers, and Ghana's Nautical College, also aided by Israel (see Chapter 8), will eventually supply all the necessary manpower.

Similar observations can be made about the Ghana National Construction Company. Capable and enthusiastic directors, and competent and experienced engineers and foremen came from Israel to set up the company. Once the initial hurdles were overcome, the company's performance met international standards in quality and was competitive in price. There is also evidence that it brought about a price reduction by injecting a competitive element in an otherwise semi-monopolistic market.

Right from the start a training program was inaugurated at all levels. Ten scholarships were awarded to engineering students at the Kumasi Institute of Technology, and Ghanaian students in British universities were approached regarding future employment with the company. A dozen skilled workers were sent to Israel for special training; from those were later drawn the heads of a carpentry shop, a storage unit, a quarry, and a mechanical workshop. Various specialized courses were offered by the company in Ghana, and at times special instructors were brought from Israel. One such course raised the productivity of brick layers by 200 per cent and, in another, thirty foremen were instructed in soil mechanics by an Israeli professor at Kumasi. In addition, on-the-job training was carried on at all levels, and even the chief architect of the company was trained as a counterpart to the Israeli architect. All Israeli holders of central positions had Ghanaian understudies, facilitating an orderly transition in 1962.

These success stories illustrate the tremendous potential of the jointly-owned enterprise for transferring technical and organizational know-how. But not all of the companies mentioned have met with such a high measure of success, and some are beset by more serious problems than any other Israeli aid project.

No one company faces all the difficulties to be discussed next --- they have been assembled from the records of several firms --- nor are they designed to discredit the joint venture as a vehicle for extending technical aid, nor to cast doubt on Israel's ability to use it. Rather, the objective is to identify the factors that have prevented some of the companies from realizing their full potential, and to explore possible avenues for correcting them.

CRUCIAL PROBLEMS

The Competence of Israeli Technicians

No company is better than its central staff, and the qualities of the core of Israelis who inaugurate a joint enterprise are vital to its success or failure. In the opinion of most participants and observers, these central positions in Africa demand of their holders a higher level of competence, more experience, and greater tact than they would need in equivalent posts in Israel. The following is a composite of remarks made by several people in the field:

> In Israel there is more team work, and foreman and engineer alike can count on research, statistics, personnel, and other departments for advice and guidance. Here the foremen must determine salaries and promotions and check all the financial accounts. A foreman in Africa is not only the organizer who tells skilled workmen what to do. He must also show them how to execute the tasks assigned to them, and therefore ought to be able to instruct and demonstrate in a foreign language while working. Instructions must be given in the simplest fashion, and the check on performance must be continuous, since one cannot assume that his instructions will be carried out properly. All this calls for much tact and forbearance. Engineers should have had field experience because much of their work is in the field. In general, the distinction between engineer and foreman gets blurred. To top it all, technicians have to get used to different methods, new construction standards, and larger scale projects.

In some cases, such as the GNCC, these requirements were met; in others they were not. Three factors may account for the difference. First, the enthusiasm for the first venture in west Africa wore off somewhat as more companies were set up. Second, manpower resources in Israel are not un-

limited, and as activities expand into new countries and more companies
are formed, lower-quality personnel must be used. Sooner or later, the bot-
tom of the barrel is necessarily reached. The leadership of Solel Boneh,
for example, explicitly recognizes the relative scarcity of highly qualified
technicians in certain phases of civil engineering.

Thirdly, organizational changes in Solel Boneh seem to have accounted
for a good deal of the trouble. Because of its rapidly increasing size, Solel
Boneh was subdivided in 1958 into three independent units: the Building
and Public Works Company in Israel, which engages in domestic construction,
and owns several large subsidiaries producing building materials, cement,
lime, and stone; the Industrial and Craft Holding Company (KOOR) which
is responsible for a range of important factories including a complex of
iron and steel plants, ceramic works, glass works, fire-brick plants, and
plywood factories; and Solel Boneh Overseas and Harbor Works Company,
which is the arm engaged in all foreign operations and in harbor services in
Israel.

GNCC was set up before the three-way division. Its top quality managers recruited their staff from within Solel Boneh on the basis of personal acquaintance. By contrast, the partnerships entered into after 1958 were
contracted by the independent Overseas and Harbor Works Company which,
except for port works, does not engage in construction in Israel. It is a
company operating abroad without a "home base," and consequently cannot
institute an internal rotation system for its personnel. Foremen and engineers
must be recruited in the marketplace, without the company having first-hand
knowledge of their professional and other qualities. True, both the overseas
and domestic construction companies are arms of Histadrut, and the former's
turnover is only a fifth of the latter's. But since cooperation between the
two units is lacking, the domestic company does not provide the necessary
"home support" for its sister organization which is involved only in overseas activities. [6]

As a general rule, engineers and foremen are offered a two-year contract with one possible renewal (it is unusual for anyone to stay longer than
four years). There is no commitment to the individual beyond the period
of the contract, and he must upon return find his own employment. Coupled
with the limited job contract is the disadvantage that the job itself demands
harder work under more taxing circumstances than is expected of similar
workers in Israel. [7]

6. The lack of cooperation was also harmful to the construction of a
new port in southern Israel.

7. Most people show signs of exhaustion in the second year; it has
been suggested that employees should be given longer vacation periods to
counteract that phenomenon.

What, then, are the attractions of the overseas jobs? Some people are drawn by challenge, the new experience, the higher level of responsibility, the broadening of professional and intellectual horizons, and the opportunity to travel. Members of Kibbutzim, who get no personal benefit from the wages they earn, tend to fall into this category. For some others the attraction lies in higher social and professional status. But the overwhelming reason most people undertake overseas assignments is money, and what that money can buy. Not only are salaries more than twice as high as they are in Israel.[8] but after two years' absence from the country one can bring in durable consumer goods free of duty which might otherwise reach 100 per cent on some items.

Despite the financial advantage, few experienced engineers are willing to give up permanent and respectable positions for a two- to four-year adventure in Africa, beyond which nothing is promised them. Furthermore, most men of experience are middle-aged, and the education of their high-school-aged children would suffer from a job overseas.[9] As a consequence, engineers must sometimes be recruited right out of college, or following a couple of years of office work. Thus the ideal qualifications of maturity and field experience are not always met. Similar observations can be made about foremen, especially during Israel's period of severe housing shortage (caused by waves of immigration) when the domestic demand for their services is highest.[10] Managers of the joint companies often complain about the caliber of their staffs, as do several of the competent African officials. "Many of their personnel is unqualified and inexperienced," said an African construction engineer. "Quite a few of the Israelis brought here are far from first class," said another. Conversely, on a couple of occasions when close deadlines had to be met, the Overseas Works company asked and received, "on loan" from other public bodies[11] in Israel, complete construction teams; it is notable that they successfully carried out their assignments. Not only does the lack of a "home base" prevent procurement of first-rate technicians

---

8. Since salaries in Israel are low by Western standards, with engineers averaging less than $200 per month after taxes, Israeli technicians can be attracted to Africa for much less than Americans or Europeans with similar skills and levels of competence.

9. Israel does not have a "boarding school tradition," and the "Israeli communities" in Africa are not large enough to operate Hebrew schools beyond the eighth grade. For further discussion, see Chapter 12.

10. Some of the foremen were small contractors in Israel who took jobs in Africa in order to get out of debt.

11. E.g., the Public Works department of the government — but never the domestic construction company of the Histadrut.

from within the company, but it makes adjustment to fluctuations in business turnover overseas very difficult. Whenever a company accepts a new contract, it must make a commitment to each Israeli technician it employs for at least two years; unless it is virtually assured that the expanded operation will last that long, it dares not accept the contract. Indeed, one of the construction companies suffers from a chronic excess of capacity, while others have had to turn down contracts because of the time limitation. All these points apply more to the construction than to the water development companies which are usually smaller, fewer in number, and better equipped to recruit technical personnel internally. Their usual procedure is to hire new staff for the home office, thus releasing experienced personnel for overseas duty. But even there technicians may sometimes be sent abroad after only a short "internship" at the home office.

Having recruited a significant number of ill-qualified people, the companies do virtually nothing to train them for the overseas assignment. Many of the Israelis arrive quite unprepared for the totally new conditions. The inability of many of them to speak English only compounds the problem, since attempts to communicate with Africans in Yiddish or Hebrew are usually fruitless. Occasionally an Israeli foreman approaches the African workers directly, rather than through the African foreman, an encounter too likely to result in shouting and insults. The following statement, made by an Israeli concerned about the situation, is perhaps too strong. Nevertheless it helps drive home the point: "The new honor and high status go to the heads of many Israelis who at home are so accustomed to social equality."

Training of African Personnel

If the main criterion for the success of the joint venture is the establishment of an indigenous firm, then the training of local personnel to the point where they can assume central positions in the company is of crucial importance. Most joint companies are in fact conscientious in this regard. In addition to on-the-job training, they have sent workers to be trained in Israel and have organized courses in Africa. A six-month course for draftsmen in Nigeria and the planned mobile school for construction foremen in west Africa illustrate the point. A good example of technical training on a higher level is the three engineering fellowships granted by the Eastern Nigerian Water Development Company to the University of Nigeria at Nsukka, only forty miles away. In addition to summer internship with the company, the fellows are expected to join the company's staff upon graduation, and gradually to assume positions of responsibility. This is indeed an excellent way to overcome the shortage of indigenous technical personnel.

But with a few exceptions the joint companies do not do enough toward equipping indigenous personnel to fill key posts. Even the purely expatriate firms tend to do more to train local technicians than the joint companies do. Furthermore, some of the companies extend too few grants for university study for their size, and are at times reluctant to give fellowships to local universities which are in many ways superior to overseas study.[12] And even Africans trained in necessary skills do not always find the sailing smooth. All too often the Israelis lack initiative in introducing Africans to technical jobs, and are reluctant to entrust them with positions of responsibility. In one case, it was necessary for the head of a company to compel one of his engineers to employ as a foreman an African who had returned from taking the construction course in Israel. The claim made by some Israelis that there are just not any qualified Africans to be hired for technical positions is in many cases unfounded, and is denied by Africans and Israelis alike. But even where indigenous personnel is almost nonexistent, it is a responsibility of the joint company to inaugurate a training program in the necessary skills no later than the first year of its operations. That many Israeli directors and holders of other central posts had no African understudies after three to four years of activities, and the tendency of some managers to wait until the last year of the partnership to select and train counterparts, show that the joint companies do not always fulfill the objective of transfer of authority to local hands. The general image several of these companies project to the public is that they are Israeli enterprises. Although well aware of African sensitivity to the "Africanization" process, they don't even attempt to give the impression of doing much about it. Apparently the purely expatriate firms at least have better public relations techniques. Hardly a day goes by without a mention in the press that some of their positions are being turned over to African hands.

Position in the Market

"The Israelis entered this market and maintain their position only through political contacts. They cultivate friendships instead of attempting to be competitive." This accusation, or variations of it, can be heard in African public works departments. In its support, officials point to a country in which the joint construction company received, through negotiated contracts, £3.2 out of £5 million worth of work awarded by the government in one year. Although the quality of their work remains undisputed, the companies are sometimes blamed for obtaining above-market prices through political contacts. "Israelis often use political pressure on us. They threaten to go to the Minister to get our decisions overruled," stated one African engineer.

While there is an element of truth in these allegations, it is also true that political support at the initial stages is absolutely essential

12. A full fellowship at the University of Nigeria at Nsukka, for example, costs only £160 ($450) per year.

if the new company is to surmount the natural impediments as well as the artificial obstacles thrown in its way by expatriate government officials. Moreover, such support, if it leads to the formation of indigenous companies, is justified. But all the joint enterprises should strive to attain commercial viability, as some have successfully done. Having entered the market through agreements on a political level, they ought to bend over backward to maintain an impeccable record. One senior Israeli official of the companies has indicated that this indeed is their aim, and that he regards their political dependence "as only a passing phase."

Finally, the joint companies are sometimes criticized for combining execution with planning and design: "The separate consulting outfits are not really independent of the contractors. The separateness is purely fictitious." Observers also point out that drawing many of the detailed plans in Israel leads to delays in execution and financial losses. Here again the evidence is not conclusive. Israeli officials reply that they "have been bending over backwards to observe the very strictest separation." They also emphasize the advantages to the client, in both quality and time, of having the detailed design work done in Israel:

> In quality, because designing abroad makes it impossible to get the full guidance of the top specialist on every problem; the local office is no better than its best men, who obviously cannot be the parent company's best men for each and every facet of design. In time, because it is not possible to send out a sufficiently large number of men to do each job in a short time and then to have them hanging around waiting for the next rush job. Concentrating a large number of men for a short time on an urgent job is only possible in the office of a large organization such as our head office, which is sufficiently flexible to make this realizable.

Lest there be any misunderstanding, the point made on page 139 above will bear repetition. The issues raised in this section are not inherent in the joint venture device. Some of the companies so established are quite free of these problems, and none is beset by all of them. Moreover, the joint enterprise is an excellent vehicle for the transfer of technical and organizational know-how in a wide variety of fields, and is very well suited to a small aid-giving country like Israel. There is no doubt that they have contributed considerably to the development of the countries in which they function. But correction of the imperfections wherever they are found would enable the companies to realize their full potential.

PROPOSED REMEDIES

Recruitment of Israeli personnel is the first problem to attend to. One reason for the success of the Black Star Lines and the GNCC was the

supply of the core staff from within Zim and Solel Boneh. The Overseas
and Harbor Works Company should not continue without a "home base". It
must be amalgamated, or at least cooperate closely with, the domestic
construction company of the Histadrut. This would make it possible to place
overseas duty on a rotation basis. Not only would the joint companies then
be sure of the competence of new staff members, but experienced engineers
could easily be lured abroad once they were certain that an equivalent position awaited them at home. If personal feuds are hindering such an agreement, it is incumbent upon the highest echelon of the Histadrut to inter-
vene and resolve them.[13]

Even when selected from within the company, men and their families
should not be sent abroad without considerable preparation. According to
one experienced engineer, they should be exposed to "knowledge of the
country, its people, and their mentality, working conditions abroad, slower
pace of work routines, lower efficiency of workers, and the like." Another
engineer even wanted to subject all candidates to a psycho-technic examination in order to test their reactions to the situations they are likely to
encounter in Africa.

While on the job, Israeli technicians should be able to count on technical advice from their home office. Technical contact with home must be in-
stitutionalized; it cannot depend on personal friendships. This indeed is
being done by the water companies, where "such support is being steadily
streamlined."

The number of partnerships undertaken at any given time should be
geared at least in part to labor supply conditions in Israel. For example,

---

13. It is gratifying to note that in March of 1963, the Histadrut (which
had been in possession of this chapter since November 1962) decided to
merge the two companies. Commenting on the merger, the Secretary-General
of the Histadrut stated:

> The main problem encountered by the Overseas Company
> is shortage of skilled technical and managerial personnel, and
> that problem is inherent in its severance from the home base. It
> cannot possibly offer permanent jobs to engineers, managers,
> technicians, and so on, on the basis of shifting contractual work
> carried out in various countries, in any case not as easily as it
> is required in order to obtain the necessary number of people —
> and the people must be good. For an engineer doing his job in a
> foreign country is also a representative of the Israeli nation, and
> must be fit to bear that responsibility as well. The number of
> people both ready and able to undertake such overseas jobs is
> necessarily limited, and the Company has been put at a disadvan-
> tage by the split which made it impossible for it to engage in
> operations at home. (The Jerusalem Post Weekly, March 1, 1963.)

when a wave of immigration forces an acceleration of Israel's housing program, it will inevitably interfere with the availability of first-rate construction technicians for overseas service. Conversely, the completion of the Jordan river conduit, diverting the water of the Jordan to irrigate southern Israel, is certain to free many water engineers for operations abroad. Here again, a policy of internal recruitment would enable the company managers to adjust their operations in accordance with labor-supply conditions in Israel.

At the same time, the host country should insist that the contract include a timetable for the transfer of authority to local hands. A six-year partnership should be ample for recruiting and training understudies, even if there was no competent technical staff available when the firm was set up. No later than the first year each company should begin to furnish scholarships at a local college for a number of engineering students who would agree to work for the company on an internship basis during the summers and join its staff after graduation. Where there is no local university, competent high school graduates could be sent to study in a neighboring country. As soon as the supply of adequately trained personnel permits, each Israeli should be assigned a local understudy. The tendency of some managers to wait until the last year of the partnership to select and train a counterpart must be guarded against in the contract. After the management is transferred to local hands, Israeli technicians can stay on in an advisory capacity for as long as they are needed.

CHAPTER **11** MEDICINE

In practically no field are Israel and Africa so diametrically opposed as in medicine. Africa, with a fantastic need for medical and health services, has a pitifully small proportion of doctors, of whom a not inconsequential number turn to politics in search of power and prestige, and inadequate facilities for training more. By contrast, Israel has the highest ratio of doctors to population in the world (one per 400 people); it has a first-rate medical school with professors from many countries on its faculty, and a student body which includes immigrants from east and west; it has an excellent and well-developed health service, and a rather recent experience in stamping out diseases such as malaria which are rampant in Africa. It is therefore quite natural that medicine has become an important area in Israel's technical cooperation. In terms of number of government experts sent abroad it is second only to agriculture.

MEDICAL TRAINING

Israel's most outstanding contribution to the training of African medical personnel was the opening in 1961 of a special course for Afro-Asian students at the Hebrew University medical school.[1] Seventeen students were enrolled in the first year: five from Nigeria, two each from Tanganyika, Ethiopia, Kenya, Sierra Leone, and Liberia, and one each from Basutoland and Nepal. Eleven of them were recipients of WHO[2] fellowships, and six were financed by the Israeli government. In addition to having secondary educations, they had all passed a special advanced science examination. Candidates were first screened in their respective countries by three-member committees on

---

1. In the past the medical school accepted several African students in its regular course, taught in Hebrew. But for a variety of reasons, not the least of which was the language problem, these experiences were not marked with success.

2. World Health Organization of the United Nations.

which the World Health Organization, the Israeli embassy, and the local ministry of health were represented. About half of those so chosen were subsequently selected by the Hebrew University.

As presently constituted, the medical training program consists of four phases: a year and a half of pre-medical studies in the basic sciences and the humanities, two and a half years of pre-clinical subjects, a two-year clinical program and, finally, one year of internship in a hospital in the student's country of origin. (A detailed description of the curriculum is reproduced in Appendix XII). The M.D. degree will be awarded by the Hebrew University upon successful completion of the seven years. While the initial phase is taught in English, there is some hope that the students will gain a sufficient knowledge of Hebrew during the first year and a half to make it possible to integrate them into the regular curriculum. In any event, the students will certainly have to know sufficient Hebrew by the third stage so that they can converse with patients.

Setting up the course placed a considerable academic, financial, and organizational burden on the medical school. Laboratories and equipment had to be provided, English-speaking instructors recruited and the students' social life provided for. It is unfortunate that the number of doctors that can be trained in this commendable and highly useful enterprise is only a drop in the bucket compared to Africa's immense needs.

Although medical education overseas has long been an accepted practice in underdeveloped countries, its utility might be questioned on several grounds. First, tropical diseases are a rare phenomenon in most Western countries, and Israel has nothing equivalent to London University's School for Tropical Medicine in Great Britain where African students can specialize (although mature Israeli doctors can still remember treating malaria cases). Second, the uprooting of students for six years from their home environment holds a variety of dangers. And finally, after having worked at the ultra-modern Hadassah-University hospital in Jerusalem, the students' willingness to practice in remote rural areas, if it ever existed, is likely to disappear completely. They would all prefer to practice as specialists in the capital city. All this applies with particular cogency to countries like Uganda and West Nigeria which have good medical schools (at times with unutilized facilities). Considerations of prestige and personal preference undoubtedly motivate many African students to go abroad, even though it would be better for them to study in the environment in which they will later practice. For this reason, WHO does not give foreign scholarships to nationals of countries with medical education facilities.

The final solution must lie in the opening of medical schools in Africa. And the contribution of the Hebrew University would have the greatest impact if it worked toward an institutional "adoption" of such an African school, training its present African students as the nucleus of a local faculty. In the meantime, preference must be given to students from countries lacking training facilities, and every effort should be made to recruit as faculty men who have experienced African conditions. The number of top medical practitioners with tropical experience in Israel is small, but they are far from non-existent. They were not completely utilized in the planning of the medical course, an oversight which must not be repeated at the pre-clinical stage.

Finally, the possibility of confining the training in Israel to the first two phases and sending the students home for the clinical stage deserves serious consideration. The suggestion is embodied in a report by an outstanding Israeli eye specialist on his return from an east African survey:

> There is a great need and desire to increase rapidly the number of doctors in Kenya, it being appreciated that the medical school of Makerere is not in a position to supply the requisite number of graduates. The following opinions seemed to meet with general acceptance regarding plans of undergraduate teaching.
>
> Plan A: A local medical school in Nairobi is desirable. The difficulties in the way are lack of pre-clinical and pre-medical teachers, and the lack of finance. The potential clinical teachers impressed one as being of good standing.
>
> Plan B: Sending undergraduates abroad for seven years is fraught with severe social tensions. Moreover there is a danger that the newly qualified doctor will not be in a hurry to return to his own country.
>
> Plan C: It would abviate the difficulties mentioned in A and B above if the undergraduate studies pre-medical and pre-clinical subjects abroad and returned to his country (in this case Kenya) for the clinical course, rotating housemanship and final examination.[3]

There are similar problems in the training of nurses. A group of girls from the Congo (Brazzaville) and Mali underwent nurse's training in Israel (the students from the Congo had been selected by an Israeli medical survey mission) and plans are under way to establish permanent training facilities. The effectiveness of such a program would be considerably enhanced if it could be made to lead to the creation of training schools for nurses in Africa.

None of these inherent limitations apply to post-graduate specialization. Thus, three experienced Thai specialists came for one year of study and work in Israel (one opthalmologist, two dermatologists). They were com-

---

3. Professor Isaac Michaelson, Report on Ophthalmic Services in Kenya, Jerusalem, December, 1961.

pletely integrated into their respective departments at the medical school, participated in academic seminars, made the rounds with Israeli doctors, and treated English-speaking patients. They felt that Israel offered numerous advantages for specialized work, among which are the great variety of nationalities and points of view represented in its medical profession, and the free access of trainees to specialists of outstanding reputation.

Likewise, a medical practitioner and a public health expert from Mali spent six months in Israel to learn measures for combating malaria and bilharzia. They were intelligent and adequately prepared, and derived considerable benefit from their two months' study of Arab villages where conditions approximate their own. Furthermore, they were able to benefit from the conclusions an Israeli medical team drew from a survey in Mali. Its expert on malaria and bilharzia discussed with them his ideas on what could be done in Mali in these areas.[4]

PROVISION OF MEDICAL SERVICES

Israel's work in Africa ranges from the setting up of new operational clinics and service in existing medical institutions to high-level planning and advice. Of all these methods of rendering assistance, the first has proved most effective. It enables the foreign expert to establish and function within a new organizational framework. Not bound by long-standing institutional traditions, he can introduce new practices and expect them to outlast his presence. Nothing demonstrates this point better than the case of the Monrovia eye clinic.

At the request of the Liberian government, Professor Isaac Michaelson of the Hebrew University conducted a survey of eye diseases in that country. He recommended the setting up in Monrovia of a twenty-bed well-equipped eye clinic with an outpatient department. An Israeli team consisting of two eye specialists and an optician (the wife of the head doctor) was dispatched to open and run the clinic, and two Liberian nurses came to Israel for work in ophthalmology under Professor Michaelson. Now famous all over west Africa, the clinic is a referral institution and performs many cataract and glaucoma operations.[5] Work is well organized, and the staff became ac-

---

4. Examples of suggestions he made are: Since the malaria mosquitos multiply in standing water, he proposed over turning at night all the boats on the Niger River and other water-containing objects. Similarly, he called for plugging all holes in trees in which water can accumulate, and for opening up a drainage canal to eliminate a big swamp near Bamako.

5. It is interesting to note that Theodor Herzl, in his futuristic novel Altneuland, written in 1902, visualized the future contribution of Israel in curing eye diseases in other countries.

customed to promptness, night duty, and other practices which might be difficult to introduce in an already-existing hospital. The head nurses, upon return from Israel, are performing their supervisory and training functions well, while the Israeli optician has already trained Liberian assistants to work with her. In addition, the team engages in research in tropical eye diseases at the clinic and at the West African Research Institute for Tropical Medicine, in coordination with a parallel research program at the Hebrew University.[6]

Although the agreement called for a Liberian doctor to come to the Hebrew University for specialized training under Professor Michaelson prior to taking over direction of the clinic, such an individual has not yet been found. Most Liberian doctors prefer private practice, where they can make more money than they can expect in government service. It is now anticipated that Israelis will staff the clinic for five years on a rotation basis, during which time an appropriate Liberian candidate will be selected from the next crop of graduates of medical schools in the United States.[7]

This fruitful combination of treatment, teaching, and research within a single framework should have lasting effects after the foreign assistance is phased out. It is an outstanding example of technical aid which, it is hoped, will be duplicated elsewhere. A similar clinic is now planned for Tanganyika; in addition, Israel will staff a trachoma research and treatment institute in Addis Ababa, and perhaps send a trachoma researcher to Kenya to work in coordination with the Hebrew University program.

By contrast, the five Israeli medical specialists who work in Ghana function within existing government hospitals at Accra and Kumasi. Although the original plan called for their lending a hand to raise the professional level of the entire hospital, they were assigned upon arrival to routine medical tasks. Thus they have no authority to modify institutional practices nor to raise the level of "support" of para-medical personnel. Their work is beneficial while it lasts, but it is unlikely to have an enduring impact.

Between activities like the newly established Monrovia clinic and the service in Ghanaian hospitals lie a variety of cases in which Israeli specialists are entrusted with the responsibility of introducing organizational and other changes in existing institutions. Israeli physicians direct a hospital in Massawa, Ethiopia; run a tuberculosis clinic, an obstetric department and a psychiatric hospital in Monrovia; manage a maternity hospital in Freetown, Sierra Leone; and head up various hospital depart-

---

6. Another Israeli specialist was for four years employed in research at that institute.

7. A suitable candidate was found in 1963.

ments in Burma. Most of these doctors are well-qualified and render very satisfactory service.[8] The permanence of their contributions however, rests upon their finding a good local successor -- and as often as not such counterparts are not available.

In all operational assignments, the more independent the framework within which the foreign expert operates, the higher his chances of success. By contrast, the possibility of success is rather remote when a foreign expert, however competent, is invited to supply high-level advice on the reorganization of ministries or national services. At best such assignments should be left to appropriate United Nations agencies like the FAO and WHO. The few cases, in both agriculture and medicine, in which Israel undertook such tasks demonstrate this point. The well-meaning expert almost inevitably comes up against national customs which frustrate his attempts to introduce any changes.

In one instance a high-level Israeli advisor proposed a complete overhaul of a national health service, and was given authority over budget and personnel to carry out his recommendations. His objectives were to raise medical standards, to decentralize the service and place responsibility on a regional basis (so that the minister would not have to deal personally with every problem), and to define the "chains of command," thereby streamlining the operations.

Yet the advisor encountered insurmountable difficulties within the administration which were compounded by an unexpected ten per cent cut in the budget. When many appointments are based on nepotism, favoritism, and political pressure, any changes are likely to result in hostility from people whose cooperation is essential. For budgetary reasons the Israeli had to dismiss twenty messenger boys; one of them, the son of an important treasury official, had been absent from work all too often. When the Israeli did not yield to direct pressure to restore the boy's job, his office began to encounter continuous difficulties with the treasury. Another case was a cousin of the President who never showed up for work. When asked for an explanation, she replied that the "President does not expect his relatives to neglect their private affairs."

Deeply-rooted social traditions under which each person is responsible for the well-being of his extended family are often the reason for this kind of attitude toward public service. Any prominent government official is expected to help his relatives, and he can best do this by giving them jobs

---

8. Some of the host countries prohibit foreign doctors from engaging in private practice. Israel applies that rule to all her doctors practicing abroad, in order to avoid friction with local physicians. The one case in which the service of Israeli doctors was terminated by the host country resulted from a breaking of this rule.

whether they are qualified or not. Foreign advisors must work within the existing social framework, and can hope to change it, if at all, only over an extended period of time. Tact, patience, and support from a prestigeous international organization are imperative ingredients for success in any such endeavor.

On various occasions Israelis have undertaken short-range medical assignments. A team of thirteen doctors was sent to the Congo during a period of emergency, in quick response to a call from the WHO. (They were recruited in a matter of forty-eight hours.) For three months they staffed three regional clinics and organized short-term courses in public health and nursing. A two-man survey team spent two months in Sierra Leone, planning a new medical center for Freetown. Their proposed center includes a 500-bed hospital, a medical school, a training school for nurses and midwives, and a school of pharmacy, at an estimated cost of £3½ million.(The project was proposed without regard to its priority in the country's development plan, which was not a part of the team's term of reference). A year later another expert made a survey of the health services in Lagos, and left behind a set of recommendations for their improvement.

RELATED SERVICES

Apart from direct medical advice, Israelis have worked in such related areas as nurses' training, environmental sanitation, and drug production. The nursing branch of the Histadrut's Sick Fund undertook to render advice in the establishment of a nurses' training school attached to the army hospital in Burma. The head of the branch, accompanied by the director of a large nursing school, inaugurated the project and were subsequently replaced on a rotating basis. Their duties consisted of advice and teaching. Simultaneously, a scholarship was offered by the Sick Fund to a Burmese nurse, by means of which the School Matron spent nine fruitful months of study in an Israeli hospital. The general feeling is that within three years Israel's advice can be dispensed with.

A number of Israelis work in environmental sanitation (a branch of preventive medicine) under WHO auspices. Among these are public health engineers in Liberia, Ghana, and Nigeria. Their tasks vary from one country to another, with the expert serving in West Nigeria having the most comprehensive terms of reference (perhaps too broad for one person.) His duties are: the establishment of a sanitation department in the Ministry of Health and the training of a counterpart to head it up (WHO usually provides a foreign study scholarship for that purpose), the introduction of sanitation to the curriculum of local teaching institutions (university, teachers' college, and nurses' training school), and the improvement of sanitary conditions in several cities. Only in Ghana was a suitable counterpart readily available.

Finally, Israeli pharmaceutical experts took over the management of a drug factory owned by the Defense Service Industries in Burma. In January of 1957, two Israeli experts were invited by Burma to survey the local drug market and to look into the operation of the factory which had been erected and run by a European company. A year and a half later, when the Burmese army took over the government, Israel was requested to carry out the experts' recommendations. Three successive teams, each consisting of two advisors, served between 1958 and 1961, and in two years converted the factory to a money-making proposition. Essentially they found the plant too modern for Burma's needs, with only one-tenth of its capacity utilized. They introduced new products which could be manufactured with the same machines, curtailed imports, and changed the packaging to suit local conditions (e.g., smaller packages of Aspirin). By mid-1961 the management was gradually being transferred to Burmese hands. One of the Israeli experts observed:

> We have no professional advantage over Europeans in producing drugs. But we are used to a small market, to problems of competitive imports from countries with longer traditions in drug production, to lack of faith in a domestically-manufactured drug, to labelling small packages in more than one language, and to translating medical terms into a new language.[9]

FUTURE PLANS

Israel expects to continue to introduce clinics or hospital departments in specialities such as pediatrics and ophthalmology. But the officials in charge of the medical assistance program realize that what Africa needs most are general practitioners in the outlying rural areas. A team of two such doctors and a nurse can do wonders in a regional clinic, provided they are familiar with the necessary fields of medicine and public health, and are able to perform simple operations. In Israel, as in Europe, the trend in medicine is toward specialization and away from general practice. But in view of the surplus of doctors in Israel, it has been proposed that young physicians be selected to receive all-around training in the various departments of a general hospital. Subsequently they could staff clinics in African towns on a rotation basis, until local personnel was available to replace them.

---

9. They introduced Burmese labelling on the packages.

PART *IV*

PART *IV* PROBLEMS AND ACHIEVEMENTS

Parts II and III of this study were devoted to the content of Israel's technical-aid program. Individual topics were treated separately and the various segments of the program were discussed with special emphasis on their points of weakness and strength.

It is too early to attempt a conclusive over-all assessment of a program which has been in existence for less than a decade. An "incubation period" of several years must elapse before the full impact of technical-assistance projects can be felt and appreciated. Even in the case of short courses, the final verdict must await the performance of returning students in old or new tasks to which they are assigned in their own countries.

Nevertheless, a useful purpose can be served by evaluating the courses and the services of experts on their merits. After three to four years in an "infancy stage", Israel's program is now at a turning point. With a firmly entrenched position in Africa, Israel can exercise more control over the future direction of her technical cooperation with underdeveloped countries.

It is for this reason that I have made special efforts in this study to identify problems and suggest modifications in the execution of certain projects. Yet, despite the need for continuous reappraisal that I have stressed, I have formed an emphatically positive view about the effectiveness of the Israeli program and its contribution to the raising of the level of technology in newly emerging nations. The teaching and advice Israel offers to the Afro-Asian world is usually executed with vigor and imagination. As a general rule the Israelis concerned with the program are competent and strongly motivated. Many of them compare favorably with experts and instructors from other countries in competence and efficiency, and are worthy of the wide acclaim which they receive in Africa and elsewhere. Furthermore, the conditions in Israel under which they obtained their own training and experience often add to their qualifications for serving in Afro-Asian countries. Agriculture is one area in which such favorable circumstances exist.

But Israel's strength in extending aid lies not only in efficient execution of technical projects. Added to it are some of her own social organizations whose like can rarely be found elsewhere in the Western world, and which are capable of wide adaptation in the new nations. Thus, her youth organizations may offer a ray of hope for solving one of the most depressing problems in Africa. The cooperatives and regional planning in agriculture and the joint enterprises in the construction and other fields are efficient devices for attaining rapid economic progress. And, finally, the structure of her trade union movement contains features that may beneficially be a-dopted elsewhere. In general, the social values embodied in the program are at least as important as its purely technical aspects, and hold considerable promise for adaptation in Africa. Some of these points were underscored in a recent editorial:

> The Israelis, unlike former white "colonists" or administrators and specialists, went to Africa to work with the Africans, to experiment together in new forms of economic, social and political development. It was in many ways a joint enterprise in trial and error..... And, despite the sceptics in Africa and Israel, and despite the cynics in the western world, the enterprise is flourishing and deepening, even though there must be occasional setbacks.....

> It was Africa—Ghana, Nigeria, Liberia, Ethiopia, Kenya, and the countries of the former French African Community—who..... demonstrated to the Israelis that their social and economic ideas were not necessarily confined to the narrow geographical limits of Israel, that they could fructify with striking results in African soil as well.[1]

Ranked by sheer size and measured in terms of the number of experts and trainees, Israel's program is very small. Moreover, if it is to maintain its efficiency and sense of purpose, it cannot be expanded too quickly. But what extends Israel's contribution to African advancement beyond the limitations of her own manpower and resources are the social values embodied in many of her projects. In most cases it is not merely methods of production that Israel is exporting, but techniques plus new attitudes and/or social patterns. These additional ingredients, which have been emphasized throughout this study have a primary attraction for the Afro-Asian leaders.

To the outside observer, it is indeed gratifying to see a small nation, herself facing grave problems, ready to contribute from her meager resources and share her technological know-how with others who are in dire need of them.

However, as may be clear from the previous chapters, this positive judgment does not ignore the considerable variation in effectiveness of

---

1. "What Africa Has Done for Israel," Jewish Observer and Middle East Review, October 19, 1962.

certain segments of the program. In discussing individual subjects, special pains were taken to point out deficiencies and to suggest means of rectifying them. But in addition to these difficulties, there are shortcomings common to experts and trainees in all fields which prevent Israel's program from realizing its full potential. It is now appropriate to focus attention on these problems, and to raise some issue of significance to the entire program.

CHAPTER **12** RECURRENT PROBLEMS

SOCIAL ENCOUNTERS IN ISRAEL

Recognizing that performance in the courses presented for foreigners can be greatly enhanced by social satisfaction, the Israeli government employs a staff of "social instructors" of whom at least one is assigned to each course. Working alongside the professional director, the social instructor attends to the social and personal needs of the trainees, and discharges his responsibility by organizing social events during free hours, arranging for student participation in national events such as the Independence Day celebrations, and establishing contacts between the trainees and Israeli families or social groups. In most internal social activities, those designed in part to increase the social cohesion of each group, he is aided by the African "leaders" in the course. (There is a "leader" for each national contingent of trainees.) The institutes of higher learning also attempt to provide social guidance to their foreign students.[1]

Although the social instructors play an important role in making the trainees feel at home in Israel, not all problems can be resolved through their efforts. In one course, for example, there was considerable friction between the Nigerian and Ghanaian groups and all that could be done was to minimize its disruptive effects.[2] Likewise, quite often there is hardly any contact between the English- and French-speaking trainees in the same

---

1. There appears to be a need, however, to coordinate these activities among the three or four independent institutions. For example, I found one "social director" preparing to receive a post-graduate research fellow from Thailand. His main purpose was "to make the student feel as much at home as possible," yet he did not know of the presence of three Thai doctors at the Hebrew University Medical School who could have made his task considerably easier.

2. The Nigerians, representing the largest country, refused to yield pre-eminence to the Ghanaians, whose claim was the earlier date of their country's independence.

course. Their only common language is the few Hebrew words they learn while in Israel. This last point was brought to the fore in one course where the English-speaking contingent was strongly opposed to a selection procedure introduced by the course management. For months this issue was a subject of intense anxiety to all of them. By contrast, not only did the French-speaking group not share these feelings -- they were totally unaware of what was the main subject of conversation among their course-mates. A further problem is sometimes created by the difficulties of satisfying the religious needs of trainees in a country where the Jewish religion is predominant. Thus students may complain about the inadequacy of church visits and the necessity for working on Sundays. (The Seventh-Day Adventists, whose Sabbath is Saturday, fare better than the others.) There are other thorny issues within many of the courses which are not always easy to cope with. But where the social instructor is almost completely helpless is in dealing with the problems some Africans encounter away from the school grounds.

Trainees in Israel gather a variety of impressions of the country and its people. Their daily contacts with residents outside the confines of the course influence their attitude toward Israel almost as much as the learning experience itself. Moreover, the two factors tend to interact. Congenial social surroundings invariably increase the benefits they derive from their training.

Indeed, the absence of a color line considerably enhances the attractiveness of training opportunities in Israel for Africans. Many of the students interviewed reported a very pleasant stay in the country, a friendly atmosphere in both city and village, and absence of any discriminatory or embarrassing incidents. A Nigerian visitor had this to say:

> I found out that there is no discrimination here in any form. Everybody moves freely irrespective of colour or race. I came to this conclusion throughout our tours of the country from North to the South — there was no place where we were discriminated against. At first I thought that this happened because we were guided in our tours by a well-informed Jew, who might have sent information before us that the people should tolerate us. Then I decided to go out on my own. I hired a jeep for two days and travelled with it to various places, and in each place I went I met with the same hospitality.

Another West African student said frankly: "Israelis are always willing to make friends, and my experience of visits to families through their invitations have proved this. Their doors are wide open." And an Indian trainee reported: "I happened to walk and travel alone in the country and met strangers who often asked me whether I needed their help. Wherever I went I was warmly received and treated as if I had been an Israeli Sabra.

I have been to many restaurants and hotels and was welcomed with brotherly spirit and affection. I have never experienced any slight amount of discrimination or segregation in Israel."

Such pronouncements are by no means rare; they characterize the experience of many trainees. Nevertheless, there is a sizeable minority of students who have voiced complaints about their social encounters in the country, and it is to these trainees that attention will be turned now. While definitely in the minority, unpleasant incidents spread by word of mouth and tend to color the feelings of many a visitor. They consequently warrant exploration, with a view to limiting them in the future — or at least minimizing their effects.

By far the most widespread complaint of Africans in Israel is being called Kushi by children, and sometimes by adults. There is nothing literally degrading about the word Kushi. It has its origin in the Old Testament — Kush was a son of Noah — and is commonly used to denote Africans.[3] But just as the east European Jew did not appreciate being called Zhid (literally, Jew) by his gentile neighbors, so the circumstances and contex in which the word Kushi is used can evoke a feeling of inferiority and hostility. The fact that Israeli children call their black dogs Kushi, and that they are reproached by their parents for applying the word to Africans, gives the word a derogatory connotation. Regardless of any advance explanation by Israeli officials, Africans invariably resent it. Compounding the problem are embarrassing situations in which trainees sometimes find themselves — with people either staring at them or shunning them. The explanation that a white visitor to their village would also be an object of curiosity may satisfy them intellectually, but emotionally they remain uncomfortable.

Other problems which are fairly common are feelings of loneliness and difficulties in finding members of the opposite sex who are willing to date them. On weekends, many trainees find themselves aimlessly roaming the streets of Tel-Aviv, or congregating around theaters. The language barrier tends to compound the feeling of loneliness. This experience is worse for single students than for those who are part of organized courses, since they are usually left completely without guidance on weekends and after duty hours.

Not only is it difficult for Africans to find girls to date, but those who do find dates are stared at curiously in the city streets, and may hear such remarks as: "Look! Kushi with white," or (to the girl) "Can't you go out with Jewish men?" Some Africans regard the Jewish law prohibiting inter-faith marriages as discriminatory.

A final fairly common problem is the feeling of being looked down on by the Israelis. Several students, for example, complained of being asked

---

3. Genesis 10,6.

for the time by passers-by who were wearing watches, as if to determine whether the Africans were able to use a watch. And one trainee said, "Even people who are narrow and who have hardly traveled outside this country look down on us. They treat us as backward individuals, instead of trying to learn about our countries and experiences."

Isolated more serious incidents have also occurred, but they are rare enough so that they have no impact on the program, and need not be recounted here. On the other hand, it should be noted that even those who are directly involved in the program sometimes make thoughtless errors, like the teacher who used the words "black" and "white" to denote "bad" and "good."

All these problems are compounded by the sensitivity of the Africans. To illustrate: In a Hebrew class, the teacher demonstrated the word "to eat" by putting her hand to her mouth. The students felt that she was implying that Africans did not know about table utensils, were offended, and refused to continue the class. And often trainees complain of discrimination when there was none at all: "The bus of the other group is better," "The food served to the other contingent is superior." Whether the complaints are based on reality or not, the training staff must try hard to soothe such feelings.

While generalizations are usually dangerous, two general statements may be reasonably offered in this context. First, Africans feel better accepted in agricultural settlements than in the city. The closer they are to the big urban centers, the more frequent and varied are their complaints about discrimination and insults. The Afro-Asian Labor Institute, situated at the heart of Tel-Aviv, suffers most from such complaints, while the Youth Organization Courses, with limited access to the towns, are almost completely free of them. Second, while Africans may be given a cold shoulder on the streets, they are warmly welcomed in Israeli homes. The few trainees interviewed who lived with Israeli families felt secure enough to ignore all the street incidents even though they resided in the middle of a big city.

Overcoming these problems requires a long-range educational process. The government has already inaugurated a school program designed to teach children about Africa. It also brings Africans to the schools to tell the pupils about their countries. If, as a result, the children learn to refer to them as Nigerians or Kenyans instead of Kushim, this will be an important achievement. Likewise, a small program has been begun under which trainees are attached to individual families. It should be expanded to include all families in the coastal area who are willing and able to "adopt" students for the duration of their stay. That is, each trainee should be "attached" to a home which he could feel free to visit in his spare time.

Other steps could be taken which might have more immediate results. Many trainees complain that when they visit the city on weekends they have no place to talk or be entertained in a congenial atmosphere. A small foreign students' club in each of the major cities (beginning perhaps with Tel-Aviv), with organized programs and visits by Israeli youth groups, would go a long way toward accommodating this need. Secondly, ways must be found to give the average Israeli a realistic picture of Africa. Since Israelis are movie-goers, one method of advancing this cause would be the presentation of short travelogues on Africa.

Efforts must be made to standardize the services offered to trainees in all courses -- pocket money, trips in the country, laundry facilities, free mailing of personal letters, telephone calls, newspapers, gifts, discipline in the course and measures to enforce it, living conditions (room and board), social events, movies and other extra-curricular activities, contact with private Israeli families, modes of transportation, and the like. As much as possible the same "extras" ought to be provided to individual trainees. As it is, they often complain of being deprived of the sightseeing tours which their friends in the organized courses enjoy. Indeed, it could serve to increase mutual understanding if small groups of Africans could be attached to Israeli travellers while on such tours.

SOCIAL RELATIONS ABROAD

In a sense, the social problems in Israel are the counterpart of relations between Israeli advisors and the local population in Africa. Here again the majority of the Israelis are modest, informal, hard working, and well liked. In the words of one Congolese official: "Their patience, to which they added a note of unassuming simplicity, earned them the reputation of being extraordinary persons." Nevertheless, there is a sizeable minority which presents difficulties on this score, and it is with these individuals that the following pages are concerned. The problems discussed are more common among employees of the joint companies than among experts dispatched by the Israeli government. The latter are usually professional people, selected carefully, and on an individual basis. By contrast, in recruiting (almost en masse) foremen for the construction and water development companies, very little attention is paid to personality characteristics which in large measure determine social relations.

In addition to rare but serious incidents, there are two common problems susceptible to corrective measures. The first is a tendency of the Israelis in a town to reside in one neighborhood. To be sure, there are certain objective reasons for this phenomenon. Often the wives do not speak English or French, and since their husbands' work may take them out of town for long stretches of time, convenience dictates the geographical proximity of residence. Likewise, concentration makes it easier to educate the children. In the absence of a "boarding school tradition" in Israel, it is almost impossible for parents going to Africa to leave their children behind. Consequently, wherever there is a large enough contingent of Israelis, they operate a Hebrew school (supported in part by the companies); several qualified wives serve as teachers, and at times the school is supervised and certified by Israel's Ministry of Education. The Israelis in Africa gravitate toward the big cities where such schools exist, even when the husbands' jobs are in the outlying rural districts. This arrangement calls for continuous commuting, and often means the complete absence of the husband from home during the week. The wives, therefore, find it convenient to reside in the same neighborhood with other Israeli families.

There would be little wrong with geographical concentration if it did not accomodate a natural Israeli instinct for social segregation. "Israelis like to keep to themselves," said an African minister. And what results is a closed-in community, having little social intercourse with the local population. One British Jewish periodical wrote: "There is already a tendency among Israelis and their families to reconstruct the former British pattern of living apart from the local people in their closed-in communities, with their children attending their own special schools."[4] The tendency to avoid social contact with Africans is reinforced by the severe pressure of work and the frequent lack of fluency in English or French. It is generally resented by Africans — even by those who otherwise like the Israelis very much.

A second common problem is caused by the Israeli wives. Because of the availability of cheap domestic help, they have very little to do — and idleness often breeds discontent. They spend their time drinking tea, gossiping, and complaining. Their internal social contacts tend to be stratified according to their husbands' positions, which results in jealousy and unsatisfactory relations among themselves. They sometimes exhibit considerable conspicuous consumption, and their social conversations often revolve around shopping and the quality of domestic help. Needless to say, their contact with African women is virtually nil. One Israeli expert in an Asian country, whose entire life in Israel has been spent on a <u>Kibbutz</u>, was really shocked to encounter such a materialistic outlook among his own countrymen. He observed: "You could not spend one evening with them without discussing money, purchases in Hong Kong, and the like."

One visible result is the unwillingness of Israelis to work in rural areas. In one case, a few childless couples, teaching in a regional town school, asked to be transferred to the capital city. It is uncommon to find Israelis residing outside the big cities, and this tends to limit their effectiveness in

---

4. <u>Jewish Observer and Middle East Review</u>, November 25, 1960.

providing agricultural and other advice. [5]

To be sure, the situation is not as grim as the above illustrations might seem to imply. There are many Israelis who approach a foreign assignment with total dedication, who do not balk at serving in remote areas, who mix readily with the local population, and exhibit no conspicuous consumption or spirit of aloofness. The team which served in Namsang, Burma, is one case in point; and the Israeli doctor in Africa who was a victim of highway robbery and did not even complain, but just continued his work, is another.

First, more Israelis should be found who are willing to go to rural areas. Current plans in the area of agriculture call for teams of four to six experts to staff instruction and demonstration centers; the work of joint companies may also require such teams in the outlying districts. In solving the problems common to such situations, it would be well for Israel to draw on experience accumulated in the past. The five families in Namsang, for example, had ten children representing six different school grades. One of the wives, a school teacher, was able to instruct them (at times on a tutorial basis), so that upon their return home they were able to rejoin their respective classes. Comparable cases happened elsewhere. The Ministry of Education should prepare an instruction manual to govern all such cases which would draw on past experience. Of equal importance is the continuous cooperation of that ministry with the teams scattered around two continents. Aid in supplying teaching material and answering questions is imperative, but has not always been forthcoming in the past. [6]

What is needed for education is equally necessary for other social and technical matters. Manuals should be compiled, discussing problems experienced by experts overseas, and the solutions applied. Failures as well as

---

5. In view of this, it would be advisable to require at least a certain degree of modesty from the Israelis serving abroad. Their frequent conceit concerning their contribution relative to that of other foreign experts is not only in bad taste; it tends to antagonize Africans and Europeans alike. One Israeli agronomist was made aware of this problem during a survey of several west African countries. Prior to his departure for Africa he had heard many disparaging comments about the European advisors who engage only in research, the results of which never penetrate down to the village level. Consequently, he "was surprised to find in one remote area a group of French college graduates working in the most backward village in the region. They introduced permanent cultivation, crop rotation and fertilizers, thereby increasing yields substantially. Other villages have observed the improvement and asked to join in."

6. A report in The Jerusalem Post Weekly for October 19, 1962 indicates that the Israeli authorities plan to embark on another, equally effective, course of action: that of opening boarding schools in major African cities for the children of Israeli experts scattered in the respective countries.

successes must be recorded. And the material should be placed at the disposal of those preparing for foreign assignments.

In selecting foreign advisors, attention must be paid to the personal characteristics and social attributes of both the man and his wife, and each should be given preparatory training prior to departure.[7] In Africa continuous leadership must be exercised in the field of social behavior, either by the diplomatic representatives or — where there is a large concentration of Israelis— by individuals specially assigned to this task. To prevent undue conspicuous consumption, it might be desirable for the joint companies to pay part of the employee's salary into an Israeli bank, where it would be available to the employee (in any currency) at the end of his tour of duty.

Finally, the presently wasted energy of the Israeli wives could be channeled into some constructive cause, such as volunteer public service in the community. Some efforts in that direction have already been made. In Accra and Rangoon Israeli women were doing social work and staffing hospitals, nurseries, and mother and infant stations. Where permitted by local law, such volunteer services should be expanded to encompass more women in additional cities.

RELATIONS WITH OTHER AID-GIVING NATIONS

Although the needs for technical aid in Africa are vast, there is considerable political rivalry in the field. Any "newcomer" must cope with problems created by other aid-giving countries, and Israel has certainly had her share of them. Needless to say, representatives of the Arab bloc did everything within their power to halt the employment of Israeli technicians in Africa, in which they had the full support of Soviet propaganda, which attempted to brand Israel as a tool of Western imperialism.[8] In actual field work, Israel sometimes encounters competition from Yugoslavia, which may bid on the same projects. Although ten times larger than Israel, Yugoslavia has some of the attributes mentioned in the first chapter with regard to Israel. It is relatively small, engages in intensive development efforts, has

---

7. One Israeli official suggested the following additional criteria for composing a foreign advisory team: team members should be experienced in working with primitive people; they should get along with each other; they should be competent in their subject and the language spoken in the country; and, last but not least, they should be attracted to the mission by the challenge and interest it offers and not merely by financial inducement.

8. The Soviet monthly Asia and Africa Today, for example, recently published a sharp attack on the introduction of Moshav-type settlements to Africa. (Reported in the Jewish Observer and Middle East Review, February 8, 1963.)

been able to preserve a certain (though small) measure of neutrality, and possesses social institutions which many African nations consider valuable in their attempt to shift from tribal to modern society. Yugoslav technicians, engaged mainly in industry and shipping, are active in the UAR, India, Burma, Ceylon, Indonesia, Ethiopia, Ghana, Guinea, and Mali.

Opposition to Israel's "penetration" into Africa is sometimes presented by officials of the former colonial powers who are still in the service of their respective African governments. Such interference is felt most strongly by the construction companies, which might take business away from expatriate European firms, and by institutes with a military potential, such as a flying school or a nautical college. But the opposition is notable in other fields as well. In one case, an obstructive British official did not process the applications of five Africans who wanted to participate in an Israeli poultry-rearing course; in another, British expatriate officials refused cooperation with Israeli fishing instructors where their help was essential. Cases can be cited to illustrate similar attitudes on the part of French officials. However, such obstacles are not universal. Expatriate officials in East Africa, for example, often welcomed the Israeli technicians. At times the African ministers, acting tactfully, have secured the cooperation of their expatriate officials for the Israeli missions. In one French-speaking country, the agricultural minister stressed to his expatriate officials that several visiting Israeli experts had been educated in the French tradition, and thereby secured considerable goodwill for them. In general, as Israel's position in Africa becomes more entrenched, the measure of interference will undoubtedly diminish.

Israel maintains reasonably close contact with the specialized agencies of the United Nations and other multilateral organizations active in the technical assistance field. To be sure, a few FAO officials occasionally complain of Israel's aggressive attitude, and of her use of United Nations financing for bilateral programs. One of them described a couple of cases in which African countries were induced to request Israeli technicians through the FAO, and said, "We supply technical advice by field and not by nationality." However, the prevailing attitude among United Nations officials is that of praise for the competence of Israeli experts and for their cooperation with United Nations advisors. Indeed, several national representatives of the U. N. specialized agencies have intimated their desire to visit Israel and to be appraised of her activities in the field in order to secure a higher degree of coordination.

THE QUESTION OF PLANNING

The proliferation of aid-giving countries and agencies in the technical assistance field makes it difficult for both the aid-giving and aid-receiving countries to set up a well-planned operational framework. On the international level, the United Nations and its eight specialized agencies extend technical assistance to the entire underdeveloped world. On the regional level, organizations such as the Colombo plan in Asia and the Foundation for Technical Cooperation in Africa South of the Sahara in Africa are active in the same field. And, finally, a multitude of nations conduct bilateral programs of their own. There is nowhere a compilation of all the technical assistance projects, although such a list (accompanied by a short description of each project) would be very useful in coordinating the work of all concerned. The United Nations Technical Assistance Board could collect and publish such data on an annual or biennial basis, with information obtained from both giver and recipient.

As it is, the agencies working in the field know comparatively little about each other's activities in any one country. The only source of technical advice in comprehensive economic planning is the International Bank Missions. The Missions' reports exist now for several countries, but their main focus is investment opportunities rather than technical assistance needs.[9] The same thing can be said about the economic planning missions financed by UN Regional Economic Commissions and by such private agencies as the Ford Foundation. They are indispensable to the planning of technical assistance, but do not address themselves specifically to that problem.

Planning and coordination of technical assistance by United Nations agencies, regional organizations, and bilateral programs are thus left to the recipient country. The coordination is usually judged to be uncomprehensive and unsystematic, and all too often technical assistance projects are not an integral part of the country's development plan. The FAMA states:

> The Foundation considers it desirable that each State should possess the appropriate machinery enabling it to remain continuously informed of all proposals of assistance in which it is interested. It is also important that donors should be informed of long-term developments of such needs in order that they may take these into account in the planning of their offers, where applicable. Such information can be based only on the development plan of each individual country in Africa, since assistance must be integrated in the over-all national development decided upon by governments.[10]

What, under these circumstances, can be expected of a small aid-giving

---

9. For a concise review of these reports see F. T. Moore, "The World Bank and Its Economic Missions," Review of Economics and Statistics (February 1960), pp. 81–93.

10. FAMA, Third Annual Report (Lagos, 1961), pp. 33–34.

nation like Israel? Israel does not have trained manpower to advise on overall development planning. In the opinion of one high-ranking official in Jerusalem, "Israel lacks a generation of social and management scientists — namely, individuals with modern education and, say, 15 years of experience. She either has experienced people educated 35 years ago, or young scientists with five years' experience. The generation aged 40 to 50 is missing." Since it is this "generation" on which one must draw for overall planning, Israel should refrain from offering advice in this field.

On the other hand, the specific operational projects Israel undertakes, particularly those involving sizable expenditures, ought to be well integrated into the economy of the recipient country. In proposing and executing such projects, their total impact on the economy must be appraised, along with their independent merits. Indeed, the success of the USOM efforts in Israel is often attributed to careful planning. In the words of one past USOM director in Tel-Aviv, "One reason for the great success of the Technical Assistance programme in Israel was that the Israelis knew what sort of advice they wanted and how to use it when it was given. (It is sometimes as hard to take advice as to give it.) Planning was both long-range and short term, and every project was worked out by the Government and USOM with great care."[11] And H. Cleveland of the U.S. State Department writes in the same context:

> We have learned how small are the benefits of isolated projects not related to some concept or plan for economic development. A few miles of road in the wilderness, a lonely health centre, a few country school houses, a clean-up campaign in one village — all of these are good as far as they go, but they don't go far enough or fast enough by themselves. Because of the scarcity of resources available for development, all projects and programmes paid for with public funds must grow out of comprehensive plans for economic and social development.[12]

That some Israelis, connected with the technical assistance program, are fully cognizant of this fact is evidenced by the following statement by one highly placed official:

> One must get used to examining a development plan as a whole, and to assess the results of each action or branch not on their merit, but also on how they are integrated into the general development plan. It is a mistake to dispatch experts when they are not integrated into the overall development plan, and also a mistake to copy Israeli economic and social institutions without adapting

11. The Jerusalem Post Supplement [Mission Accomplished] , July 4, 1962.

12. Ibid.

them to local conditions. We cannot hide behind the contention
that we had been asked to prepare an irrigation network, and the
economic results are really none of our business.[13]

Unfortunately, not all of those occupying positions of responsibility share
this view. In the foreign office, which is aware of the sensitivity of African nations, it is not uncommon to find an attitude that it is hardly possible
to advise. Africans what is good for them without giving offense. And an
Israeli envoy to a country in which his compatriots are setting up centrally
managed farms said, "I do not know what will eventually become of the
farms -- and I don't care. It is not for us to worry about how the products
will be marketed. In general, it is not our concern whether our program is
well-integrated into the development plan. We simply execute concrete
workable projects."

A change in the attitude embodied in the latter statement is absolutely
essential.[14] Wherever development plans exist, it is incumbent upon Israel
(and other aid-giving nations,) to work within the general guide lines set
by the plan. An interesting proposal was advanced by one Israeli official
who was concerned with the problem. When asked for his opinion on mixed-
nationality technical assistance teams (as is common in internationally
sponsored missions), he said he was against them, claiming that the team
members would have too little in common by way of background and approach. Instead he proposed that an international agency draw up for each
country development plans which would also specify the technical assistance requirements. Individual projects within the general plan would
then be assigned to small aid-giving nations. The advantages claimed for
such a scheme are overall coordination, enlistment of more of the small
developed countries into the aid-giving enterprise, and perhaps the injection
of salutory international competition into the technical assistance field.

Apart from integrating her work into the development programs of the
recipient countries, Israel should improve the overall planning of her own
activities. Currently the inclination of the foreign ministry is against planning: "Technical cooperation is an integral part of our relations with other
nations. We respond to requests for aid as they come, the same way we
respond to other diplomatic inquiries," said one official. While this approach may have been satisfactory when the program was in its infancy, it
is likely to impair the effectiveness of a full-blown operation. At present,
the only segment subject to advance planning is the instruction offered in

---

13. W. R. Witz, Molad (June–July, 1960), pp. 257–9.

14. In October, 1962, Israel undertook to supply skilled manpower for a
number of projects included in Nigeria's six-year national development plan.
(The Jerusalem Post Weekly, October 19, 1962).

Israel. Courses are announced about a year ahead in order to solicit student response. No such thinking is devoted to the dispatch of experts abroad, or to the integration of instruction and advice.

In the first place, it would be well for the officials in charge of the program to delineate, at least for themselves, the fields in which Israel should work, with as detailed a system of priorities as possible. One piece of essential preliminary information is the availability of professional and vocational personnel for overseas assignments. An Israeli man-power survey, especially in the fields of agriculture, cooperation, medicine, and construction, should be undertaken and should include both language and professional qualifications.

Several types of errors could thus be avoided. Recruiting difficulties in specific fields would be known ahead of time, rather than after a search for people had begun. Likewise, the impact that freeing experts in various fields would have on Israel's economy could be determined in advance, and thus be a factor in the decision-making process. In the past, survey experts abroad have proposed a massive infusion of Israeli advisors to a certain country, whereas officials familiar with manpower available in the field have suggested that very few people could be spared for the assignment. On other occasions Israel has undertaken to conduct surveys in French-speaking African countries, only to find that there was insufficient personnel with the necessary combination of expertise and language ability. Since the responsibility had been assumed, missions had to be made up of individuals who were not fluent in French (and many of them had no knowledge of the language), which hampered subsequent activities.

Israel should also have a clearer idea of the adaptability of her own social institutions to Africa. As one FAO official says, "There is a danger in visiting delegations to Israel who get very enthusiastic and want to copy everything." True, the Israelis are usually careful to point out that not everything seen in their country can be applied elsewhere, but such general warnings are usually not effective. What are needed are specific indications of the pitfalls inherent in too-casual attempts to transfer social patterns across cultural boundaries. One way of providing Israel with a deeper insight into this problem would be a month-long conference to be attended by outstanding African anthropologists. It could be patterned after the "Rehovot Conference on Science in Developing Societies" (see Chapter 8) and have as its focus the applicability to Africa of Israeli social and economic institutions.

Once the scope of a program is determined, more thought should be devoted to its general composition. Most Israeli officials prefer to train Africans in Israel rather than to dispatch experts abroad: "Here we have more control over the activities, and that almost doubles the chances of success," says one of them On the other hand, we have already noted the problems trainees have in adjusting to conditions at home after they have been trained elsewhere.

Ideally, the two phases of the program should be treated together, not separately. Once the technical-aid program is a "going concern" (as it is now), training in Israel should be a supportive element to, and an integral part of, the advice given abroad. Courses must not be planned without regard to Israel's advice given in Africa and Asia. Likewise, there is no reason to dissipate the knowledge and experience of the experts returned from overseas missions. That this knowledge is often lost in the field of agriculture has already been alluded to, but similar situations exist in other fields. One cooperatives expert has said: "I am sorry to say that since my return home no one from the foreign office or the Histadrut has invited me to participate in the local training program." As much as possible, course-graduates should be used as counterparts of advisors working abroad, and returning experts should be enlisted in the instruction program in Israel. Finally, experts who have served in responsible technical positions sometimes complain that they are not consulted in the choice of the man who is to replace them when they leave. Such consultation in one case, for example, could have prevented the dispatch of an incompetent nurse overseas.[15] A shift of emphasis to "integrated projects," and (whenever appropriate) to "institutional adoption," can go a long way toward meeting these objectives.

Along with the over-all planning, more consideration should be given to specific details. Before going overseas, experts should be given extensive instructions and preparation. Any such orientation program should include the fruits of their predecessors' experience - made available either orally or in a printed manual. "Home support" for advisors fulfilling foreign assignments, in both professional and adminstrative matters, must be continuous and intensive. At present, says a responsible foreign ministry official, "We do not have the time to provide adequate home support and fulfill their professional and social needs. We can't read all their reports or derive inferences for improving the program." Indeed, several experts complained that they felt "abandoned" by the agency which had sent them whenever they had professional problems, or needed to iron out administrative

---

15. While matters of administrative organization are beyond the scope of this study, a suggestion may not be inappropriate. The Department of International Cooperation in the foreign ministry appears to be too over-burdened with routine affairs to engage in long-range and intermediate planning. Therefore, a small but highly-qualified staff could be placed in the office of the Deputy Director General in charge of that department, to engage in planning and coordination.

details with the host government.

To prevent misunderstanding, it is useful to clarify in advance with the host country the experts' rights and responsibilities, and the nature of their assignments. Whenever possible, it is a good idea for the Israeli team to work on well-delineated projects, with independent organization and control over their budgets. That would eliminate the red tape in securing funds and counterpart personnel which sometimes hinders progress. Instances like that in which a $30,000 Roentgen machine was inoperable for two years because a $15 screen was missing should not recur.

Although courses are planned and announced in advance, much can still be done to improve their execution. Of utmost importance is the selection of students. Perhaps the worst failure in the training program was that of four trainees with inadequate backgrounds, deficient motivation, and insufficient interest in the field. Their instructor summed up the difficulty succinctly: "The only thing they knew was that they wanted to assume office jobs now occupied by Europeans. They absolutely refused to work, claiming that in the future they would be supervisors, not workers." Proper selection methods which defeated the claims of nepotism and favoritism and made it possible to choose trainees according to qualifications would prevent such fiascos. All candidates should be experienced in their respective fields, since refresher courses are of little use to novices. Furthermore, students in the same course should have homogeneous backgrounds. If heterogeneity is desired for social reasons, it can be attained through occasional mixing of the students from different courses.

Examinations and terminal written compositions (the latter stressing the applicability of the course material to home conditions) should be introduced into all courses from which they are now absent. And the final certificate should show the degree of the student's success. If it does not indicate the level of achievement, the Israeli diploma will in time be regarded as a meaningless piece of paper. By contrast, the stiffening of standards will raise the respect for Israeli training. In order to keep herself and others appraised of the value of the instruction program, Israel could conduct follow-up studies of the graduates of her courses. Their subsequent contribution to the development of their countries can serve as a guide for continuous evaluation of the program.

13 ECONOMIC AND POLITICAL CONSEQUENCES

ECONOMIC EFFECTS

Although the economic effects of technical assistance do not constitute a proper criterion by which to evaluate its impact on international relations, and while they do not readily lend themselves to short-run measurements, they should not be overlooked. In the more distant future trade relations may come to play an increasingly important role as compared to technical cooperation. In the words of Ghana's ambassador to Israel:

> Our independence in Africa will be meaningless, if we must perpetually depend upon foreign experts. Ghana, in another decade, will no longer depend on foreign experts. Anyone who believes that sending experts to Africa is the only basis of establishing friendly relations, operates under a grave illusion. When the experts leave, there must be other avenues of promoting friendly relations. One of the most important ties between nations surely is increased trade.

Originally, Israel's trade with Africa was rather one-sided, being confined to Israel's purchases of cocoa, coffee, oil-seeds, diamonds, tropical wood, hides, and the like. In 1957, prompted by a desire to develop a flow of trade in the opposite direction in order to provide cargoes for the ships headed for West Africa, Israel's Zim Lines initiated the establishment of the Dizengoff West Africa Co. The main function of the new enterprise was to penetrate and expand the remote markets of West Africa – an undertaking clearly beyond the reach of individual Israeli manufacturers. A semi-public company, Dizengoff operates fourteen branches and warehouses in large cities in Nigeria, Ghana, and Sierra Leone. Similar companies have been set up more recently for export to the Far East (Asian Trading Co.) and East Africa (Amiran), which can use Israel's outlet to the Red Sea at the southern port of Eilat.[1] Most of Israel's export to the Afro-Asian countries

---

1. That port was opened to Israeli navigation by the Sinai campaign of 1956.

is conducted through these companies.

Export to Africa increased steadily from $2 million in 1956 to $10.5 million in 1960, making up about six per cent of total Israeli exports and twelve per cent of her industrial exports.[2] Three main groups of commodities constitute the bulk of this trade. The first consists of building materials, notably cement, but also plywood, panels, tiles, sheet glass, paints, locks, and screws. While the demand for these products is doubtless spearheaded by the activity of the Israeli building contractors (see Chapter 10), their high quality is likely to establish a demand for them in other quarters as well. Orders by agricultural advisors and water development companies play an important role in the second category, which is made up of irrigation pipes and agricultural equipment. The third group includes durable consumer goods such as refrigerators, air conditioners, etc., as well as motor vehicles and parts, textiles and knitted articles, shoes, canned food, detergents, stationery, pharmaceuticals, and even jewelry and pictures. In marketing these commodities, Israeli producers face stiff international competition in untried markets. But even products in the first two categories are not usually ordered from Israel unless they are of the same general quality and price as the competing brands. Other things being equal, and when prompt delivery can be assured, Israeli goods are preferred by the Israeli experts who are already familiar with their features and usage. Officials of the Dizengoff West Africa Co. estimate that about fifteen per cent of Israel's export to Africa can be traced to the activities of the joint companies, and another ten per cent to orders by individual advisors.

Apart from the expansion of export markets, Israel's technical assistance program has other economic implications. The joint commercial enterprises and their Israeli employees bring in foreign exchange earnings estimated at $2 million per year. Israel has obtained direct access to such materials as diamonds, tin, rubber, and wood, and is no longer dependent on London syndicates for their acquisition. And, finally, American and European manufacturers of agricultural machinery decided recently to set up production facilities in Israel, perhaps in partnership with local interests, despite the risk of an Arab boycott of their products.[3] One reason for their decision was that Israel has "become something like a show-window for farm machinery for developing countries, and also a convenient place for the supply of these rapidly growing markets, which get ready instruction and easy procurement terms in Israel. The firms.....have chosen Israel to do business with, not for her own sake, but because they consider close

---

2. Export to Asia reached $900,000 in 1960.

3. These are the New Holland Machines Company and John Deere Intercontinental (both of the U.S.), and the Hako Company (German).

cooperation with Israeli industries and export houses the best way to assure them a share in wide markets to which they do not have access directly." [4]

POLITICAL EFFECTS

In assessing the political impact of Israel's aid program, one must compare what is with what might have been in the absence of technical cooperation. There is only indirect evidence concerning the hypothetical "might have been," but it looks pretty bleak for Israel. Israel's religion and cultural heritage are far removed from those of the Afro-Asian countries, and outside of the biblical stories very few people in the two continents knew anything about the Jews or Israel. For example, one African premier who was educated in a Methodist College said he had read about Israel in the Bible from his early childhood, "but only much later did it dawn upon me that Israel was a real country."

These nations would have been easy converts for the intensive Arab propaganda to which they are continuously subjected.[5] The first Burmese delegation, whose 1950 visit to Israel sowed the first seeds of cooperation, spoke of their exposure to propaganda which gave Israel a sinister character. And the following statement by a visiting Nigerian personality is typical of many delegates and trainees: "Had I not come here to see things for myself, I would still be in the belief that the Jews are enemies of Africans, aggressors and exploiters, as they were said to be by the enemies of the Jewish nation." Likewise, some of the first group of Guinean students in cooperation were Moslems who arrived with strong prejudices against Israel. Their stay in the country changed their attitude radically.

By comparison, the very acceptance of Israeli assistance by Afro-Asian countries constitutes a break from political isolationism and creates an atmosphere in the emerging continent which is generally favorable to Israel. Secondly and more tangibly, all newly independent African countries outside of Somalia and Mauritania which are under close Egyptian and Moroccan influence, respectively, have established diplomatic relations with Israel.[6] (Ethiopia accorded full diplomatic recognition to Israel in October, 1961, after

---

4. The Jerusalem Post Weekly, August 3, 1962.

5. The Arabs can and do take advantage of the fact that certain African countries are predominantly Moslem. About half of the 5,000 African students in Egypt, for example, are enrolled in the religious university Al-Azhar.

6. In Asia, Indonesia and Pakistan are openly hostile to Israel. But one distinguished visitor from Indonesia, who had arrived in Israel feeling strongly that "Israel was attacking poor Egypt and serving as a tool of British Imperialism," came away with a completely different attitude, and stated that he had been "a victim of destructive Egyptian propaganda."

having withheld it for many years under Arab pressure.) Certain predominantly Moslem territories like Northern Nigeria refuse assistance from Israel.[7] Others like Niger, Senegal, and Iran, do not hesitate to cooperate.[8] In fact, Sierra Leone's Moslem religious leader, the Chief Imam, has asked Israel to train Arabic teachers for his school system. The embassy of the four Conseil de l'entente countries (Ivory Coast, Niger, Upper Volta, and Dahomey) was set up in Jerusalem rather than in Tel-Aviv, thus being one of the first recognitions of that city as the capital of Israel.

Thirdly, Israel has received overt indications of friendship and support from many African countries. Many heads of state have affirmed friendship by visiting Israel and acknowledging its contributions, as did leaders of East African countries when they sought cooperation even prior to their independence. Friendship was shown in the courageous stand of Prime Minister U Nu of Burma when he successfully opposed an Arab-sponsored motion at the Belgrade Neutralist conference to censure Israel as a bridgehead of imperialism in the Middle East.[9] It was again shown in the repudiation of the anti-Israel Casablanca Declaration (see below) as a political maneuver by such statesmen as President Yameogo of the Upper Volta and Premier Okpara of Nigeria's eastern region: Premier Okpara stated that both Israel and Nigeria attained their independence after a long fight against imperialism, and President Yameogo went further in declaring that he was aware of the complexities of Israel's political circumstances, and that his nation was prepared, without hesitation, to stand at Israel's side in her quest for peace. Similar statements were issued by many leaders in both East and West Africa.

Finally, and most emphatically, support was exhibited by a resolution introduced at the United Nations in December, 1961, by the twelve-nations

---

7. The refusal of the region's premier to accept aid from Israel has, on occasion, been strongly criticized by the press in the two southern regions of the country. And Premier Okpara of the eastern region is reported to have said in reaction to the attitude of the northern premier: "I myself am almost an Israelite. I love and admire Israel. It's not big but I have seen what they can do, and I think it is praise-worthy" (The Jerusalem Post Weekly, October 26, 1962).

8. Israel's technical aid to Iran covers the fields of agriculture, construction, and water resource development. In addition there are expanding commercial relations between the two countries (see F. Schul, "Israeli Mission in Teheran," The Jerusalem Post Weekly, October 19, 1962).

9. Burma's Undersecretary for Foreign Affairs, while on a visit to Israel in January, 1961, stated: "Burma's attitude to Israel is one of everlasting friendship which is so genuine and so deep that I am quite sure it cannot be disturbed by anybody or anything."

Brazzaville group, appealing for direct Arab-Israeli peace talks. At that time the President of Congo (Brazzaville) declared: "Israel can always rely on the Brazzaville States, especially in the discussions in the U.N." And the President of the Ivory Coast, signing a friendship treaty with Israel, remarked that with the solution of the Algerian problem which had hitherto stood in the way of closer contact between the Ivory Coast and the Casablanca group of African states, it would be possible for his government to raise the question of the Middle East dispute directly with the Arab states. In reply to an Arab U.N. delegate who blamed the Africans for "selling out" to Israel, the Ivory Coast representative retorted pointedly: "The representative of Saudi-Arabia may be used to buying Negroes, but he can never buy us."[10]

This is not to say that Israel has suffered no political setbacks. Perhaps the worst reversal was the evolution of her relations with the Casablanca group (Ghana, Guinea, Mali, Egypt, and Morocco).[11] As early as mid-1958 there were signs of Egyptian influence on Ghana. A joint declaration of the two countries in Cairo said that they were both interested in a "just solution" to the Palestine problem, and contained sentiments unfavorable to Israel. A year later, Israel was the only country omitted from the "African Day" celebration at the United Nations, when Ghana and Guinea, along with five north African nations, played hosts. Again, at the end of 1959, Israel was the only United Nations member excluded from a reception honoring President Sekou Touré of Guinea. This succession of events was culminated by the Casablanca Declaration of January, 1961. There the presidents of Egypt, Ghana, Guinea, and Mali branded Israel as "an instrument of imperialism and neocolonialism." Israel's expressions of regret and dismay, directed to the African participants after the conference, were rejected. On a subsequent occasion, Presidents Nasser of the United Arab Republic and Keita of Mali denounced Israel as a country "which forms a bridgehead for imperialism and poses a serious threat to the security of the Middle East, Africa, and Asia". And, finally, a six-nation

---

10. Reported in Newsweek, August 20, 1962. Further evidence of friendship and confidence was supplied in mid-1963, when the Congo requested Israeli participation in a six-nation military mission to train the Congolese army. Despite Arab pressure, Premier Adoula remained firm in his insistence on Israeli aid.

Also in May of that year, the African summit conference in Addis Ababa rejected Egypt's attempts to introduce anti-Israel resolutions. The Foreign Minister of Sierra Leone "put it straight to the Arab leaders that they would have to choose between 'Pan-Arabism' and Africanism". (The Jerusalem Post Weekly, September 18, 1963).

11. Now Algeria may be added to it.

conference in June, 1962, attended by Mr. Ben-Khedda of the Algerian National Government, Presidents Sekou Touré of Guinea, Modibo Keita of Mali and Nasser of Egypt, King Hassan of Morocco, and Foreign Minister Ako Adje of Ghana, launched an unusually strong attack on Israel. As it was reported in the press,

> The Heads of Government warn against the attempt by Israel, which was created by imperialists by settling a group of Zionists in the heart of the Arab world so as to undermine Arab security and to further imperialist aims, to act as an imperialist instrument in the penetration into the African countries and in the domination of their economies behind a screen of economic and technical aid. The Heads of Government call on all countries of Africa and Asia to resist this imperialist-inspired policy.[12]

Despite denunciations of these statements by other African leaders, the immediate reaction to them in the Israeli press and among the public was quite violent. There was even talk of failure of the program to win friends, and of withdrawal from the field of technical assistance. The bitterness of the attack on Israel and the alliance of Ghana with Egypt are perhaps sufficient explanations of this reaction, but other factors were responsible for the intensely emotional response evoked by the declaration.

One such factor is the usual manner in which the technical assistance program is reported in the Israeli press. Any reader of the newspapers and magazines in Israel is likely to get the impression that Africa depends solely on Israel, and that the continent would topple if Israel's aid were withdrawn. When an African ministerial delegation includes Israel in a tour of seven nations, the impression given to the Israeli public is that the visit was confined to Israel. The lack of proper perspective in press reports embarrasses Israeli diplomats and annoys their African counterparts. Two statements by Ghanaian representatives in Israel illustrate the point: "Do not allow your press to remind us too often of the benefits we receive as a result of your aid, because we know it, because this is not the custom in Black Africa, and because it is embarrassing." "The belief that Israel experts have virtually 'invaded' Ghana is entirely erroneous. A comparison of their number with those lent by other governments and agencies will prove the contrary."[13]

But more serious than diplomatic irritation is the effect of such reporting on the Israeli public. Readers are simply not given to understand

---

12. Jewish Observer and Middle East Review, June 22, 1962.

13. A technical assistance manual, issued by the Nigerian Ministry of Economic Development, lists sixteen aid-giving countries and agencies. Ranked sheerly by size of assistance, Israel is almost the smallest of them all.

that her size alone places a severe limitation on Israel's ability to aid Africa, and that although it is important and welcome, her technical assistance program cannot play an overwhelming role in transforming the continent into a modern society. Furthermore, the Israeli public fails to appreciate that, just as Israel has interests outside Africa, so do African nations have interests outside of their policy toward Israel.

Indeed, the policies pursued by Israel are sometimes in sharp conflict with the interests of certain African nations. Her close relations with France were disturbing to those concerned about the Algerian issue and the French atomic tests in the Sahara, while the Sinai campaign was regarded by many as an aggressive act. For a long time Israel abstained from voting on the anti-colonial declarations in the United Nations, and did not vote against South Africa on the racial question. And to top it all, Israeli submachine guns sold in Europe were alleged to have armed Portugese troops in Angola.

By the same token, the African countries have interests which may place them in a camp hostile to Israel. They may, for example, consider Arab support for African independence a crucial enough factor to push any concern for friendship with Israel far down the list of priorities.[14] The Casablanca nations gradually polarized around the neutralist group of states — a political line which brought them into tactical alliance with the United Arab Republic for at least the time being. Thus they became subject to the Arab and eastern bloc propaganda campaign which insists that Western strings are attached to Israel's technical aid.[15] Israel's change in over-all policy to accommodate African views (she now actively supports anti-colonial resolutions at the United Nations, sharply attacked the colonial policies of Portugal, voted against South African racial policies, and abstained on whether or not to seat the Kasabubu delegation from the Congo) did not change the Casablanca group's stand.[16]

In spite of the compelling reasons behind the signs of hostility to Israel, and despite the mitigating effect of the continuing diplomatic and

---

14. A Ghanaian diplomat suggested the possibility that ten years hence, after all of Africa is independent, we may witness another conflict — tropical versus north Africa struggling for the hegemony of the continent. That might drive Ghana into an alliance with Israel.

15. Although Africans often see overt competition between Israel and Western countries, as in the case of Ghana's flying school, some states are not convinced by it.

16. In drifting somewhat from an active pro-Western stand, Israel has been aided by the flexibility in Western policy which no longer regards honest neutralism as anti-Western.

technical relations with the same African countries,[17] the strong declarations of hostility cannot but be regarded as a diplomatic reversal for Israel.   An equal setback is the continuing absence of diplomatic relations with India. The long-standing techincal cooperation between the two countries through United Nations agencies and the aid extended to private Indian groups brought considerable internal pressure on the Indian government to recognize Israel. The editor of the Indian Express, for example, is reported to have said that "it is improper for countries like India not to recognize small countries like Israel which are trying their best to develop politically and economically."[18] Yet the Nehru government has so far been steadfast in its refusal to grant recognition.

But these setbacks are clearly outweighed by the friendly attitude and staunch support for Israel by almost all the African nations. Remarked a Liberian diplomat: "Technical cooperation does have indirect political implications. By working with Israelis we get to know them, understand their problems, and get more sympathetic to their aspirations. For that reason Liberia was the second country to have signed a friendship treaty with Israel." And a Congolese official, referring to the friendship between his country and Israel, said: "This friendship is consolidated day by day, thanks to the unparalleled welcome that young Congolese receive in Israel. All of them, upon return to the Congo, made themselves bearers of pro-Israel propaganda. They talk to the Congolese masses on the courage which raises mountains and the perseverance which makes cabbages grow on rocks."

Moreover, Israel's image as a storehouse of technical skills and useful social values has extended beyond the reaches of the underdeveloped world. The French Professor DeRousche proposed that the Common Market cooperate with Israel in the training of agricultural planners for Africa. And in the 1962 exchange of visits between the premiers of Israel and three Scandinavian countries, it was suggested that the four nations embark on joint technical assistance projects. This idea opens up a wide range of interesting possibilities. All the countries involved are relatively small and technically efficient. They are not suspected of strong attachment to either political bloc, and would be considered a relatively neutral source of assistance. They could make wide use of commercial partnerships with African public and private interests as a vehicle for transferring industrial knowhow along the lines suggested in Chapter 10, and at the same time contribute to rural progress through the promotion of cooperatives (with which they

17. For example, as late as mid-1961 President Nkruma headed a special committee for Ghana-Israel technical cooperation.

18. The Jerusalem Post, October 1961.

have all had experience) and other methods.[19] These avenues of technical assistance deserve further exploration in the interest of human betterment.

19. An indication of the possibilities of such ventures is given by the founding in 1961 of the Liberian National Shipping Lines, Ltd., as a joint Liberian-Israeli-Dutch venture. The Liberian Government has a half-interest in the Company; Aaron Rosenfeld, Ltd., of Haifa, a quarter-interest; and the Verolme concern of Rotterdam, a quarter-interest. Reported in The Jerusalem Post Weekly, September 22, 1962.

APPENDIXES

APPENDIX I

METHODOLOGY

The materials on which this study is based are drawn mainly from several hundred interviews of individuals from Israel and Afro-Asian countries involved in the technical assistance program. In addition, extensive use was made of numerous reports written by trainees, experts, instructors, and other officials. The average length of an interview was between one and two hours. Most of the field work was conducted between July, 1961 and March, 1962, in Israel and several West African cities.

The nature of the study dictated open-ended interviews, with each respondent discussing the salient features of his experience. The questionnaires must therefore be regarded merely as a convenient means of soliciting information and guiding discussion. Because of the variety of capacities in which the respondents served, questionnaire guides were developed for the following:

a) officials and dignitaries of the aid-receiving nations, and of U.N., regional, and bilateral aid agencies

b) Israeli officials.

c) Israeli advisors serving (or having served) overseas.

d) Israeli survey experts.

e) Israeli instructors and others involved in the foreign training program.

f) Afro-Asian trainees in Israel.

g) the superiors of the trainees in their respective countries.

h) officials of the joint commercial enterprises.

i) employees of the joint commercial enterprises.

j) Israeli organizations providing practical training to Afro-Asian students.

Three of these questionnaires are reproduced below.

I. Questions asked of Officials and Dignitaries of Afro-Asian Countries, and (with appropriate modifications) of United Nations Officials:

A. INTRODUCTION

1. For what political and technical reasons does your country solicit or accept technical aid from Israel? Does Israel have anything unique to offer compared to nations with a longer tradition in technical cooperation? Please document if possible.

2. What is the history of your country's relations with Israel in the

field of technical cooperation?

3. In what fields does your country receive technical assistance from Israel?

4. Is your country in need of advice in such fields as agricultural cooperation, in which Israel has gathered wide experience? To what extent can Israel's experience help solve some of your social and economic problems?

B. ISRAELI ADVICE IN YOUR COUNTRY

5. Can you evaluate the degree of success of the projects run by Israelis in your country? How well equipped (both professionally and socially) are the Israeli advisors? What problems are involved in their operations?

6. Are you familiar with cases of success or failure in Israel's aid program? Please elaborate on the reasons for these results.

7. How does Israel's work compare, qualitatively and quantitatively, with technical aid received from other countries?

C. TRAINING OPPORTUNITIES IN ISRAEL

8. What is your evaluation of the educational opportunities offered to your nationals in Israel? How are the students selected? How well did they do upon return from a study tour in Israel?

9. What social and professional problems arise from educating your nationals in Israel?

10. How do you feel about the short courses in specialized subjects offered by Israel to your nationals? What are the pros and cons for offering them in Israel? In another foreign country? In your own country?

D. COMMERCIAL VENTURES (when applicable)

11. What is the value to your country of the joint enterprises with Israeli firms? Are they superior to technical aid, per se?

12. What aspects of training and technical cooperation do they embody? How do they compare, on that score, with enterprises of other foreign nations?

13. Do you have any criticism or praise for their Israeli employees in your country? How do they compare with employees of other foreign companies?

E. SUMMARY

14. In what fields should Israel specialize in extending technical aid? To what extent should "Israeli projects" be a part of larger inter-

national programs?

15. How well does Israel's aid fit into your country's priorities for economic development?

16. What is the effect of technical cooperation on the political and economic relations between your country and Israel?

II. Questions asked of Israeli experts serving or having served overseas:

1. What was the nature of your assignment?

2. How were you recruited? Who did you work with? Who financed your mission?

3. What preparation did you receive for the overseas assignment? Were you hampered by deficient background information?

4. What is the nature of your work in Israel? How were you released from your position? What considerations led to your decision to undertake the overseas mission?

5. What were your relations with African and expatriate (i.e. European) officials abroad?

6. To what extent was your work a part of a larger program? Was it integrated into the country's development plan?

7. Can you say something about successes and failures in your mission (with documentation)?

8. Did you have a proper counterpart? Was the project "self-liquidating"? Where you replaced by an African or another foreign advisor upon the completion of your duty?

9. Did you enjoy adequate administrative and professional support from the host country? From Israel?

10. Did you send trainees abroad? (to Israel?)

11. Can you point to any visible results of your work? Was your work subject to any criticism? If so, by whom? What was the nature of the criticism?

12. Were you satisfied with your assignment? Would you be willing to go again?

13. Upon return home, were you involved at all in the instruction of foreign trainees or other aspects of the technical assistance program?

14. Can you tell me something about your social life in Africa? About the social life of the other Israelis who served in the same town?

15. Do you have any comments about Israel's competence in supplying technical aid in your profession? About the availability of competent personnel in the country you worked in?

16. General observations on the technical assistance program not touched upon earlier.

III. Questions asked of Afro-Asian Trainees in Israel:

1. Could you briefly describe the content of the course (or training?)

2. Were there any phenomena (inside or outside the course) which left a particular favorable or unfavorable impression on you?

3. Of all you have seen and learned here, what may be applicable to your own country? What problems may be involved in introducing such subjects or methods there?

4. In what ways will the training affect your future work? Do you anticipate objections from your superiors when you try to introduce new methods acquired in the course?

5. Was the course well planned? Was there good coordination between lecturers? Between lectures and practical work? Was the time distribution satisfactory?

6. Was the level of the course appropriate? Were the students' backgrounds adequate? Were they uniform? If not, how did the diversity affect the course?

7. Was there sufficient written material to accompany the class instruction?

8. Were there any problems during the periods of practical observation (work)?

9. Were the lecturers effective as teachers? Did they know much about conditions prevailing in Africa? If not, did this diminish the usefulness of the course?

10. Is Israel a good place to study this subject? Why?

11. Do you have any other observations on, or criticisms of, the course? Do you have any suggestions for improving the course?

12. Do you have any comments to make about the laundry and other services in the course and the social life arranged for the trainees?

13. What about your stay in the country? Was it all pleasant? Did you encounter any embarrassing incidents? Were you particularly friendly with any Israeli families?

14. Before coming to Israel, did you meet any Israelis in your country? What were your impressions of their behavior?

APPENDIX II

ASSISTANCE IN NON-AGRICULTURAL COOPERATION

Although Africa's most urgent needs are rural, Israel's aid in cooperation is not confined to this area. Two Israelis hold key executive positions
in the Nigerian cooperative supply association; the courses offered in Israel cover industrial and service societies as well as farm cooperatives,
and many trainees choose to do specialized work in such societies. This
"specialization", however, is usually quite superficial. A two-day tour
of the national supply, marketing, or transport cooperatives can give only
a very cursory view of their structure and activities. Only on rare occasions do these organizations receive a serious student who spends a month
in a specific department and becomes conversant with its operation. Those
cases require considerable efforts on the part of the host institutions,
since forms and memoranda must be translated from Hebrew to English or
French.

Three cooperative surveys which were made by Israelis in Ghana and
Eastern Nigeria dealt with a wide range of problems. In both countries the
experts recommended the setting up of fishing societies, beginning perhaps
with a model cooperative fishermen's village. Fishing is essentially a cooperative venture. With government assistance, the societies can purchase
and maintain motor boats, erect storage and processing plants, and establish marketing and purchasing facilities. One advisor, however, objected
to the introduction of cooperative marketing, since it would interfere with
the traditional division of labor in which women perform the trading functions.

The Nigerian survey was the most comprehensive of the three. It recommended a reorganization of the government's cooperative division involving
a shift from regional to functional administration, and the setting up of a
separate division for cooperative development.[1] It also called for the establishment of a cooperative supply and consumer association which would
consist of a wholesale and import agency, and a whole network of cooperative stores to serve the consumer in cities and villages.

The wholesale and import organization is needed in order to introduce
an indigenous firm into an area run almost exclusively by expatriates, and to
enhance competition in what is currently a semi-monopolistic field. This
recommendation was accepted by the government.

On the other hand, the idea of consumer cooperatives touched off a
heated debate. In its support, the surveyor claimed that there is a need

---

1. A Senior Assistant Registrar should be put in charge of each of the
following types of societies: agricultural producers, marketing, supply and
consumer, credit, crafts industries and housing and fishery.

for wider distribution of a larger variety of goods and under more hygienic conditions than the present distribution system makes possible. On the other hand, competent local observers pointed out that the city department store and the local market perform these functions adequately. "The petty trader performs a very useful economic service at low mark-up. You can get anything in the local market --- and in satisfactory condition," stated the registrar of cooperative societies. G. Kimble's account of the African market strongly supports this view:

> The oldest and most widespread of tropical Africa's shopping centers is the market. It is also the most liked, for it is a place of companionship, color and, frequently, gaiety, where a man may dawdle, drink, gossip or haggle as his fancy takes him. When it comes to doing business, there are few better places than a market. Its running costs are low compared with those of a shop. Its wide range of offerings, all in view, provides opportunities for examination and comparison equaled only by the large city store.
>
> The Aba market usually has between 7,000 and 8,000 sellers, the Kumasi market up to twice as many. In some parts of Nigeria there are so many markets, large and small, that no village is more than a short ride by "mammy lorry" from one or more of them.
>
> In most west African markets, and increasingly elsewhere, the merchandise is well organized. It is common practice for the sellers to group themselves according to the class of goods in which they specialize, and the tendency to specialize has increased noticeably in recent years.[2]

Add to this the fact that women who run the African markets (the "market mammies") would have to give up their traditional role, and it indeed becomes highly questionable whether government investment in cooperative stores would be warranted.

---

2. G. Kimble, Tropical Africa, New York: The Twentieth Century Fund, 1960, Vol. I, p. 556.

APPENDIX III

PROGRAMS OF SELECTED AGRICULTURAL COURSES

A. Irrigation Techniques

The four-month course, in the summer of 1961 (for obvious technical reasons the course can be offered only in the dry season), consisted of four phases:

a) Two weeks of introductory lectures at the Ruppin Institute, on the following subjects:

Subject	Hours
Introduction to agriculture	14
Soil-water relationships	15
Plant-water relationships	15
Soil and water conservation	19
Forms of settlements and tour	11
	74

b) Six weeks of practical work on settlements
c) Three weeks of lectures on following subjects:

Surface irrigation methods	20
Sprinkler irrigation	16
Engineering phase of irrigation	20
Agricultural and economical considerations	22
	78

d) Five weeks of practical work, partly in specialized subjects

B. Course for Agricultural Instruction Trainees from East Africa

The four-month course, in the spring of 1961, consisted of six parts:

a) Three-week introductory session: Lectures at Ruppin Institute and tours throughout the country.
b) Five weeks of practical work on a Moshav (2), a Kibbutz (2), and a Moshav Shitufi (1). During this phase trainees worked in the morning and spent the afternoons studying the settlement's organizational structure and its agricultural branches.
c) Two weeks of theoretical study at Ruppin Institute, including such subjects as irrigation, cattle husbandry, field crops, and training methods.
d) Two weeks of study in extension methods. Students accompanied Israeli field assistants in their daily work, and observed the extension system at first hand.
e) Ten days of study of farm planning, regional settlement, and fertilizers.
f) Two weeks of summing up and reading of student reports at Ruppin.

Selected students remained for two additional months of specialized training in chosen fields.

C. Course in Poultry Rearing

   a) Two weeks of introductory lectures at Ruppin, covering Israel, her economy and her poultry industry.

   b) Five weeks of work on the settlements, alternating between Kibbutz and Moshav.

   c) Two weeks of theoretical study at Ruppin.

   d) Three weeks of practical work on settlements.

   e) Two weeks of theoretical study at Ruppin.

   f) Two months of individual specialization in selected areas such as extension methods, nutrition, farm management, incubation, and the like.

APPENDIX IV

FOUR-YEAR STUDY PROGRAM IN AGRICULTURAL ENGINEERING FOR STUDENTS FROM ASIA AND AFRICA

The first two years of the course—three trimesters per year—are planned to give the student a thorough grounding in the basic sciences: mathematics, physics, chemistry, and biology, and in such applied sciences as descriptive geometry, engineering mechanics, and technical drafting.

Students who choose the Water, Soil and Farm Structures Option will study surveying and aerial photogrammetry, building materials, and construction techniques, while those who have elected the Option of Farm Power and Machinery will concentrate on thermodynamics, machine tools, and metallurgy.

In the third and fourth years—comprising two semesters each—subjects common to both options are elementary farm machinery, hydraulics, agronomy, and agricultural economics.

Students of the Soil, Water and Farm Structures Option specialize in soil and water conservation, irrigation and drainage, rural water supply planning of rural settlements, and design of agricultural structures, while their fellow students specialize in agricultural machinery and power.

Students of the Special (English-speaking) Course will also be assisted in their studies by a member of the academic staff, whose special assignment is to help the students feel at home, find friends among Israeli students and families, and tour the country.

Spoken Hebrew will be taught to enable the students to come into contact with all strata of the local population.

APPENDIX V

REQUEST BY UPPER VOLTA FOR SUPPORT BY THE SPECIAL FUND FOR AN AGRICULTURAL DEMONSTRATION AND TRAINING CENTER IN BOBO – DIOULASSO

Purpose

As part of its programmes for development, the Government of Upper Volta requests the Special Fund to assist in establishing a multi-purpose agricultural demonstration center which, through training programmes, demonstration schemes and the introduction of better seed and stock and training in improved husbandry practices may assist in increasing agricultural productivity in the area.

Description of Project

The proposed centre will <u>train the first nucleus of trained agriculturists</u> who would assist farmers to increase their productivity and improve their farming practices. This will involve working with farmers at their own existing level of techniques within existing social and economic patterns which, for the most part, are family centered. The project will also serve as a model farm to demonstrate how best farming can be carried out under local soil and climatic conditions. It will at the same time serve as a pilot project for the purpose of introducing new methods designed to improve farming practices. In due course, the Government proposes to set up similar centres based on the one which would be supported by the Special Fund. The Centre could also be of assistance to other countries in the region through showing how to tackle the extremely complex problem both of developing African agriculture and assisting the African farmer.

The Centre is to be established at Farako-Ba, seven kilometres outside Bodo-Dioulasso, the main town of the area. It will comprise 1,100 hectares, of which 500 hectares will be permanently part of the Centre, the remaining 600 Hectares being available to it on a temporary basis. (The Government envisages the establishment, eventually, of a model village run on cooperative lines to serve as a demonstration centre or possibly of a cooperative citrus plantation to be run in association with the Centre).

Water will be pumped from a neighboring tributary of the Black Volta as well as from wells on the land of the Centre. From current information available there appears to be abundant ground water in the area at a depth readily accessible.

The Centre will be composed principally of a mixed farming demonstration and experimental scheme, a sheep, cattle, and poultry breeding station, a nursery with experimental plots for seed selection, an agricultural vocational training school and an agricultural machinery pool.

Taking into account the climatic conditions, the nature of the soil and the traditional patterns of cultivation both for subsistence and plantation crops, the Centre will attempt to introduce and demonstrate improved husbandry methods. As the size of herds in Upper Volta will be determined by the availability of fodder, emphasis will be placed on experimenting with the production of fodder crops. Depending upon the availability of water, an attempt will also be made to provide training in irrigation techniques principally for plantation and fodder crops.

The introduction of improved breeds of dairy cattle, beef cattle and draught animals will be pursued at the cattle breeding station. To encourage the spread of improved breeds of poultry, local poultry strains will be improved through the introduction of superior breeds and a chicken farm will be established for meat and egg production.

It will be the aim of the Centre to assist small farmers in the area to increase productivity through the introduction of improved seeds. The nursery and experimental seed beds, it is planned, will help determine what seeds are most suitable for planting in the area.

The agricultural vocational school will offer various types of training. Two year courses will be provided for farm instructors. Short courses will also be made available for the better farmers in the district. The school will also form the hub for agricultural extension workers, who, after receiving training at the school will work from the Centre amongst local farmers.

An agricultural machinery pool will also be a feature of the Centre. It will be used particularly for pest control and will be made available to local farmers in the form of a central agricultural machinery service possibly organized on a cooperative basis.

In the initial phase of the project, a series of studies, including topographic, soil and water surveys, will be undertaken on the basis of which it would be possible to determine more exactly what outlay will be involved in establishing the Centre. This will be followed by land clearance and the building of the Centre. The programmes of training, demonstration and experimentation which will follow will in turn develop into programmes of direct assistance to farmers in the area providing them with better seeds, cattle and poultry, agricultural machinery and technical advice.

Financing

Total cost of the project for the first 5 years is estimated at $1,751,200. Of this, the government of Upper Volta expects to contribute $851,200; most of which will be spent on fixed investments. The Special Fund is requested to grant $900,000 for foreign experts, fellowships, and the acquisition of machinery, equipment, breeding stock and citrus trees. It is expected that eventually the center will become self-supporting. Namely that the sale of crops and cattle will cover the current expense of running the center.

APPENDIX VI

PROGRAM OF YOUTH LEADERSHIP COURSE

The following are the topics covered in the youth leadership course, taught in English and French (numbers in parenthesis indicate number of hours devoted to the topic):

A. Field Activities (160)

   1. Camping (45): camp installations, field games, organization of youth camps

   2. First aid (15)

   3. Topography, Geography and Tours (100): map reading, geography, tours

B. Sports and Physical Training (95)

   4. Physical fitness (30): elements of physical education, gymnastics, sports, light athletics

   5. Obstacle course (15)

   6. Judo (Ju-Jitsu) (15)

   7. Organizing of sports activity (35): games, organization, public performances, ability tests

   8. Singing and dancing (20)

   9. Communal games (15): indoor games, amusements, quizzes

  10. Handicrafts (30): decoration, manual activity

  11. Organization of Social Gatherings (15): stage performance, organization, mock trials

C. Principles of Education (68)

  12. Youth club activities (25): elements of education, self-government, organizing activities, group instruction

  13. Problems of adolescence (10)

  14. Civil, political and movement studies (15): citizenship, political information, movement ideology

  15. Methodology (18)

D. Adminstration and Organization of Youth Movements (57)

  16. Personnel training (10): group leaders, youth leaders, regional supervisors, heads of movements

  17. Staff organization (10): elements, staff work

  18. Work procedures (15): definitions, procedures of the branch of

organization, quartermaster branch, education branch

19. <u>Program of instruction (22)</u>: framework of activities, program of activities, tools of instruction, central displays, organization of specific clubs, specialization

E. <u>Miscellaneous (60)</u>

20. <u>Food drill (15)</u>

21. <u>Marksmanship (15)</u>

22. <u>Reserve (30)</u>

APPENDIX VII

PLANNED OUTLINE OF COURSE FOR
RURAL COMMUNITY DEVELOPMENT

I.   ORIENTATION - 2 weeks:

An Introduction to Israel and its Institutions - Lectures and Study
Tours.

This section will embrace talks and discussions on services such
as Health, Welfare, Education, Agriculture, Local Government,
Women's Organizations, etc.; tours to the Institutions of these
Services; tours of general interest.

II. PRACTICAL WORK - 1 week:

(a) Survey of community problems and projects of participants'
    countries.

(b) Planning of practical work programs for period of course.
This section will include talks by participants on projects they
have undertaken or intend to undertake in their countries; planning of work programs in study groups with tutor.

III. TRAINING IN SKILLS - 4 weeks:

This section will include refresher training in skills required for
the execution of community projects, e.g., Nutrition and Foods,
Agriculture, Health Education, Literacy, Handiwork - how to teach
these skills.

IV. METHODS - 4 weeks:

This section will include lectures, discussions, and demonstrations
on all aspects of working with the family and the community.

V.   FIELD WORK - 4 weeks:

Practical work with Extension Services in rural communities, e.g.,
Health, Education, Welfare, Youth, etc.

VI. SUMMARY - 2 weeks:

Summarizing material covered and preparing working plans for use
in own countries.

APPENDIX VIII

AD HOC VOCATIONAL COURSES

a) Automechanics: Fifteen primary school graduates from Cyprus have undergone a two-year course in automechanics in a Jerusalem ORT school, designed to train them to handle any internal combustion or diesel engine or vehicle. Their program consisted of 14 hours of theory and 32 hours of practical work per week. b) Telecommunication: Ten Nigerian government technicians (with considerable practical experience) underwent a six-month course in telecommunication, including two months of theory and four months of practical work in the Israeli telephone and telegraph service. c) Broadcasting: Israel's broadcasting service trained one person from Sierra Leone and two from the Congo and has subsequently organized a course in radio techniques. d) Nepal Group: Ten Nepalese high-school graduates were sent by USOM for 15 months of training in: electricity (2), woodwork (2), mechanics (3), automechanics (1), and building construction (2). They were attached to various vocational schools in the Tel-Aviv area for instruction on an individual basis, designed to prepare them to be instructors in their respective subjects. e) Linotype and Printing:[1] A Jerusalem vocational school undertook to train two individuals from a Liberian newspaper — one in linotype and the other in printing. f) Education for the Blind: An Israeli expert, upon surveying this field in Ethiopia, found an acute shortage of qualified teachers, and in particular those with vocational backgrounds. "There seems to be a complete lack of practical education .... and preparation for independent life," he states.[2] His recommendation called for the training in Israel of six qualified teachers in problems of education, and pre-vocational and vocational training of the blind. Upon completion they would return to Ethiopia, accompanied by an Israeli instructor, to instruct other teachers from the rural and more remote regions. g) Physical Education: Twenty-three teachers from two Asian and five African English-speaking countries studied physical education in a special one-year course organized by Israel's physical education teachers' college. Some of the participating countries had no qualified teachers in the field prior to the course, and planned to introduce the subject into their school system. Other

---

1. An Israeli printing expert was sent to Nigeria to help set up a printing press in Ibadan. Another advisor went to Tanganyika and would in turn send a few trainees to Israel.

2. A. Resheff, Blindness in Ethiopia — Present and Future, Jerusalem, 1961. Among other things, the report recommended the separation of blind school-age children from adults and the integration of the first group into the regular school programs.

countries, in which the field already exists, are short of instructors, and were testing the feasibility of accelerated training. h) General Education: Twenty-two school inspectors participated in 1962 in a three-month course in methods of teaching English, arithmetic, health, and hygiene. i) Foreman Training Course: Israel's Productivity Institute conducted a four-month foreman training course in building and construction. Two-thirds of the twenty-one English-speaking African trainees were sent to Israel by the joint Israeli-African companies (see Chapter 10). The course consisted of 2½ months of theory followed by 1½ months of practical work where trainees, in small groups, were attached to various construction projects and worked under supervision.[3]

---

3. The subjects taught were structure and statics, quantity surveying, building materials, cost analysis and calculations, reading of building plans, planning of execution and site layout, building methods, and supervision control.

APPENDIX IX

SELECTED PROJECTS IN THE MANAGEMENT FIELD

A. Training in Administration: 1) a four-month course in public administration offered to twenty-six government officials from four French-speaking African countries, of which sixteen were from the Belgian Congo, 2) a three-month course for municipal officials from east Africa[1], 3) a 4½-month course in police adminstration for twenty-one trainees from the Congo (Leopoldville), Dahomey, Malagasy and Niger; 4) a two-week program for twenty-two visiting African students of management at the "Instut des Hautes Etudes d' Outre Mer" (University Institute for Overseas Countries) in Paris, and 5) a one-month study program in social security for three trainees from Thailand.

B. Transport: 1) An Israeli team, consisting of two technical experts and two economists, made a transportation survey in Mali. Their assignment was to propose a route to connect Bamako with the sea, alternative to the exit through Dakar. 2) An Israeli team of two was dispatched to organize and manage intra-city and inter-city bus transportation in Ethiopia, in addition to instructing local personnel. Israel has had considerable experience with quick changes in her transport system resulting from the establishment of new settlements. But in Africa the Israelis had to become accustomed to long distances involving overnight stays on the road. 3) Transport advisors will be dispatched to Nepal.

C. Foreign Trade: 1) After surveying Togo's foreign trade, an Israeli expert suggested the creation of a government export-import company, in order to curtail the semi-monopolistic power of expatriate firms. Togo invited an Israeli to head up such a company. 2) Israelis served in Burma as advisors to the state agricultural marketing board.

D. Investments: Israeli advisors in Ghana and Nigeria are engaged in developing investment plans and writing prospectuses to attract potential foreign investors.

E. Economics: 1) Israeli economic and financial advisors operate in Ghana (budget bureau), Tanganyika, Niger, and Singapore - the latest being under U.N. T.A.B. auspices. 2) A high-level Israeli official reviewed Burma's four-year development plan.

F. Statistics: Israeli statisticians conducted a population survey in Ghana and constructed a cost-of-living index in Thailand.

G. Other Areas: 1) An Israeli expert surveyed the possibility of establishing a government lottery in Sierra Leone, 3) a soccer coach is employed in Lagos, and 3) a hotel specialist works in Togo.

---

1. The course covered the following topics: organization and administration of local government, finance, sanitation, health services, town planning and engineering, education and welfare.

APPENDIX X

LECTURE PROGRAM IN AFRO-ASIAN INSTITUTE

A. Second Session

Labor Economics	84 hours
a. Trade Unions Studies and Industrial Relations	38
b. Social Security	10
c. Economics: Basic concepts	6
d. Labor Economics	30
Economic Development	60 hours
a. Economics of Development	18
b. Industrialization	18
c. Management of Manpower in Development Countries	30
Cooperation	40 hours
a. Theoretical Introduction	6
b. Cooperative Institutions in Israel	20
c. Collective Settlements in Israel	14
Israel - Land and People	20 hours
Total	210 hours

B. Third Session

Development Problems in New Countries	50 hours
a. Economics of Development	20
b. Education, Culture, Health, Technique and Science - their role in a developing society	6
c. Management of Manpower	20
d. The Role of Women in Developing societies	4
Cooperation - From Theory to Practice	60 hours
a. Short History and Principles	10
b. Cooperative Movement in Asia and Africa	6

c. Education towards Cooperation   4

d. Cooperative Movement in Israel   24

e. Cooperative Rural Settlements in
         Israel   10

f. Cooperative Adminstration and Law   6

The Labor Movement and Its Function in
Developing Countries   50 hours

a. Basic Ideas and History   10

b. The Labor Movement in Developing countries   10

c. Labor Economics - Elementary Notions -
         Wages and Employments   10

d. Social Security   10

e. Worker's and Adult Education   10

Trade-Unionism   40 hours

a. Organization   4

b. National Trade-Unions   4

c. Labor Relations   2

d. Collective Bargaining   10

e. Labor Exchange   4

f. Work Measurement and Wages   8

g. Vocational Training   2

h. Youth Organization   2

i. Labor Legislation   2

j. Trade-Unions and the State   2

NOTE: Lectures are accompanied by frequent visits to Cooperative
       and Trade-Union Institutions

Israel - Land and People   10 hours

a. Israel - Land of the Bible

b. Short History of the Jewish People

c. The Rise of the State of Israel

d. Israel's Democracy

e. Israel's Economic Structure and Development

APPENDIX XI

PLANNED PROGRAM FOR A COURSE IN INDUSTRIAL RELATIONS
(Israel's Ministry of Labor)

1. Lectures and Discussions:

    A. Introduction: The problem of Industrial Relations; Objects and Scope of Study; Bibliographical Survey

    B. Trade Union Organization:

        a. Introductory lecture; Purpose and Functions of Trade Unions; The Principle of Freedom of Association.

        b. Bases of Trade Union Organization
           1. Structure and Government
           2. Cooperation and Amalgamation
           3. The problem of Closed Shop
           4. Trade Union Rivalries
           5. The Histadrut

        c. The Legal Position of Trade Unions
           1. The Right to Strike
           2. Picketing
           3. Breach of Contract
           4. The Position of Civil Servants

        d. Political Activities of Trade Unions
           1. Relations with the Government
           2. Relations with Political Parties

    C. Employers Organization:
       Structure and Organization

           1. Structure
           2. Objects and Policy
           3. Manufacturers Association

    D. Industrial Disputes:
           1. Dispute on Rights
           2. Legal Disputes
           3. Voluntary Conciliation and arbitration and its machinery
           4. Strikes and Lock-Outs
           5. Losses from Work Stoppages

    E. Wages:

        a. Methods of Wage Payment:
           1. Time Rates
           2. Piece Rates

3. Bonus Systems
b. Bases and Principles:
1. Capacity of Industry to pay
2. The Living Wage
3. Cost of Living Allowances
4. Wage Differences between Industries
5. Wage Differences between skilled and unskilled workers
6. Relative Wages of Men and Women
7. Wage Differences between Localities
8. Equal Pay for Equal Work

F. <u>Collective Bargaining:</u>

a. General:
1. Definition of Collective Bargaining
2. Difference between Collective Bargaining, Consultation and Cooperation at the Level of the Undertaking
3. Relative Bargaining Strength of Employers and Workers
4. Conditions Essential for Successful Collective Bargaining

*Freedom of Association
*Recognition of Trade Unions
*Stability of Workers Organizations
*Willingness to Give and Take
*Avoidance of Unfair Practices

b. Subject-matter of Collective Bargaining and Agreements:
1. Provisions of Agreements
2. Recruiting Employees
3. Lay off
4. Dismissal Procedure
5. Wages
6. Hours of Work
7. Fringe Benefits
8. Seniority
9. Family Allowances

c. How Collective Bargaining Works:
1. Bargaining Machinery
2. Bargaining at the Local Level and National Level
3. Industry-Wide Agreements
4. Special Agreements
5. Extension of Agreements
6. Some Legal Aspects of Collective Agreements
7. Relation between Collective Agreements and Contracts of Employment

    d. Drafting of Agreements:
  1. Implementation of Agreements and the role of the Shop Committees
  2. Interpretation of Agreements
  3. Grievances Procedure

G. State Intervention:

    a. Legislation:
  1. Factories Act
  2. Hours of Work Act
  3. Employment of Women Act
  4. Employment of Children as Young Persons
  5. Apprenticeship Act
  6. Employment Service Act
  7. Wage Protection Act
  8. Minimum Wages
  9. The Fair Wages Clause

    b. Conciliation and Arbitration:
  1. Conciliation
  2. Voluntary Arbitration
  3. Compulsory Arbitration
  4. Courts of Enquiry
  5. Labor Courts
  6. Settlement of Labor Disputes Act
  7. Collective Agreement Act

    c. Organization and Functions of the Division of Industrial Relations at the Ministry of Labor:

H. Industrial Relations:

    a. The Israeli Experience

    b. Joint Consultation at the Workplace:
  1. Purposes and Subjects of Consultation
  2. Powers of Joint Councils and Committees
  3. Representation of Management and Workers

II. Practical Work and Excursions:
  1. Participation in the settlement of a Collective Dispute
  2. Participation in mediation and arbitration in cases of Disputes on Rights
  3. Participation in the work of the Wages Protection Officer
  4. Registration of Collective Agreements Procedure, forms, etc.
  5. Visits to the Office of the Executive of TUC and some Local Unions, discussions

6. Visit and discussions at the office of the Employers Confederations.

7. Visit to Industrial and Agricultural Enterprises and meetings with Labor Committees and Managements

III. Directed Studies with the Help of Tutors:

1. Studying and drafting of Collective Agreements
2. Drafting of Arbitration awards

APPENDIX XII

MEDICAL COURSE CURRICULUM FOR AFRO-ASIAN CLASS
AT THE HEBREW UNIVERSITY (JERUSALEM)

The Medical Curriculum offered by the Medical School covers a period of six academic years and one year of internship, leading to the Degree of Doctor of Medicine (M.D.)

The first one and a half years are devoted to pre-medical studies, offered in association with the University Faculty of Science. Subjects taught during this period are: Physics, Chemistry (Inorganic, Organic, Biochemistry and Physical Chemistry), and General Biology (all of which will include lectures, exercises, and laboratory work), and Mathematics. Supplementary work in Sociology, Psychology, and History of Science and Medicine is also offered, as are courses in the Hebrew language, a knowledge of which will be necessary for future contact with patients. At the end of the pre-medical period students are required to sit for examinations in Physics, Chemistry, and General Biology.

The following two and a half years are devoted to pre-clinical subjects, which include Anatomy, Physiology, Human Biochemistry, Bacteriology, Parasitology, Pharmacology, and Pathology, with Physical Diagnosis and introductory courses in Medicine being the main subjects in the last pre-clinical semester. Courses are also given in Social Medicine. Family and community Health, Medical Psychology, and Nursing. The emphasis in the preclinical studies is on laboratory work, and only a limited period is allotted to lectures.

During the first clinical year (fifth year of the course) the students rotate in the hospital wards as clinical clerks. The teaching method provides for bedside instruction, numerous seminars, and a few lectures. The second clinical year (sixth year of the course) is spent mainly in the Outpatient Departments of the Hadassah-University Hospital and in hospitals affiliated to the Medical School, rotating among the various branches of medicine. In each of the clinical years one month of elective work is also provided.

In addition to the clinical subjects, students receive training in Preventive and Social Medicine, Family Health, and Forensic Medicine. The practical work in the last two subjects is performed respectively at the Hadassah Community Health Centers and at the Leopold Greenberg Institute of Forensic Medicine near Tel-Aviv.

At the end of the six-year course and after passing their final examinations, each student is required to do one year of internship in a hospital in his country of origin. Following this year and on presentation of a thesis, he will receive the M.D. Degree of the Hebrew University.